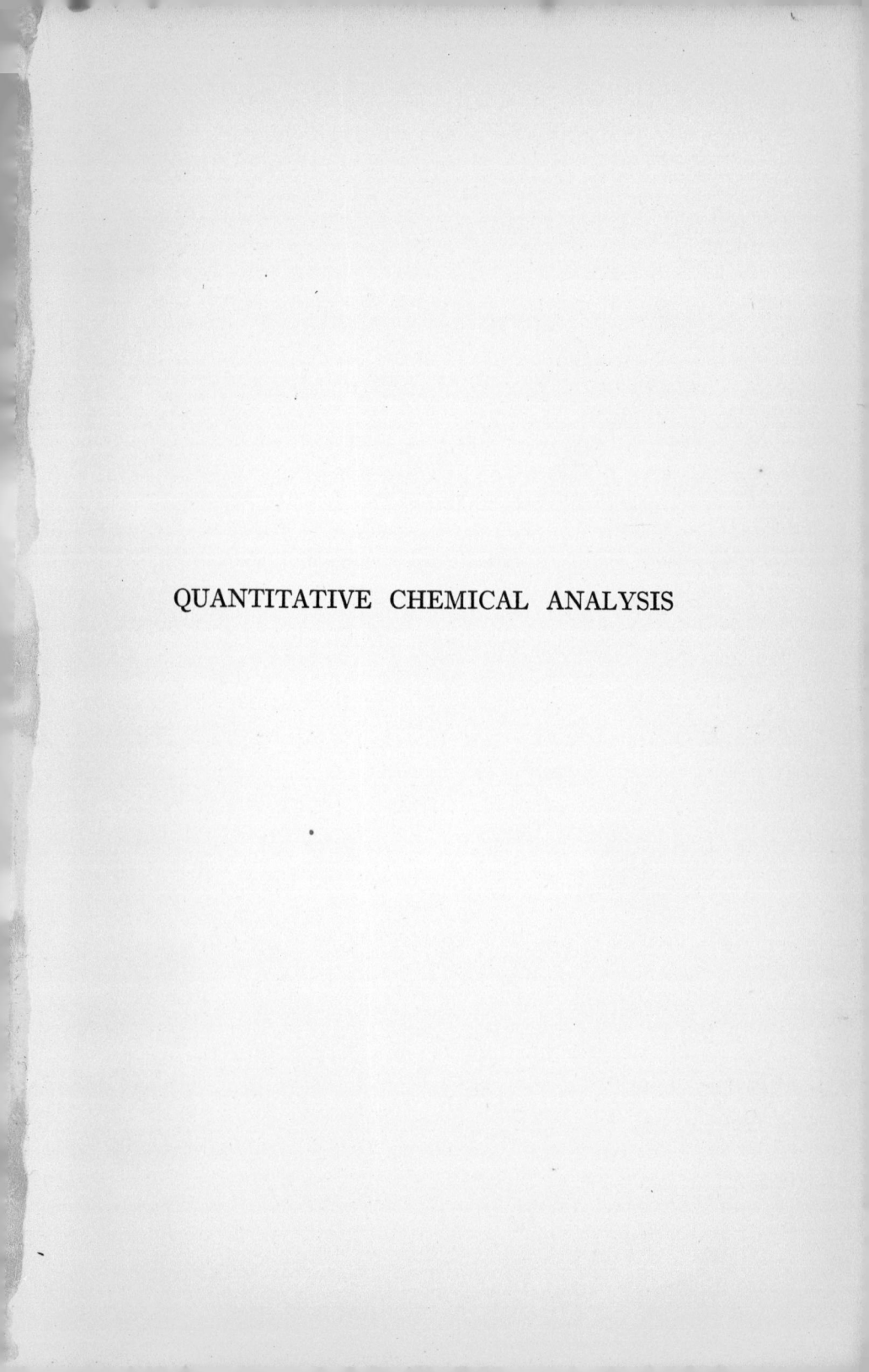

QUANTITATIVE CHEMICAL ANALYSIS

THE MACMILLAN COMPANY
NEW YORK · BOSTON · CHICAGO · DALLAS
ATLANTA · SAN FRANCISCO

MACMILLAN & CO., Limited
LONDON · BOMBAY · CALCUTTA
MELBOURNE

**THE MACMILLAN COMPANY
OF CANADA, Limited**
TORONTO

AN INTRODUCTORY COURSE

OF

QUANTITATIVE CHEMICAL ANALYSIS

WITH

EXPLANATORY NOTES

BY

HENRY P. TALBOT

LATE PROFESSOR OF INORGANIC CHEMISTRY AT THE
MASSACHUSETTS INSTITUTE OF TECHNOLOGY

SEVENTH EDITION

Revised and Rewritten by

L. F. HAMILTON

ASSOCIATE PROFESSOR OF ANALYTICAL CHEMISTRY
MASSACHUSETTS INSTITUTE OF TECHNOLOGY

and

S. G. SIMPSON

INSTRUCTOR IN CHEMISTRY
MASSACHUSETTS INSTITUTE OF TECHNOLOGY

NEW YORK
THE MACMILLAN COMPANY
1932

COPYRIGHT, 1897 AND 1908,
BY HENRY P. TALBOT.

COPYRIGHT, 1921 AND 1931,
BY THE MACMILLAN COMPANY.

All rights reserved — no part of this book may be reproduced in any form without permission in writing from the publisher, except by a reviewer who wishes to quote brief passages in connection with a review written for inclusion in magazine or newspaper.

First edition, 1897.
Sixth edition, published September, 1921. Reprinted January, 1922; January, 1923; October, 1924; December, 1925; December, 1926; May, 1928; May, 1929; Jamuary, May, 1930.
Seventh edition, May, 1931. Reprinted February; April, 1932.

SET UP AND ELECTROTYPED BY J. S. CUSHING CO.
PRINTED BY THE BERWICK & SMITH CO.

PREFACE TO THE SEVENTH EDITION

IN preparing this revision of Talbot's *Quantitative Chemical Analysis*, the arrangement of the material and the general treatment of the subject have not been materially altered, but many important changes and additions have been made.

Stoichiometric principles are discussed in detail and this phase of the subject is developed gradually and in step with the related topics in the procedures and theoretical discussions. In this connection, numerous illustrative problems are explained. About 225 problems, with answers, are available for home assignment. These problems, most of which are new, are not given as an aggregate as heretofore, but are divided into groups with each group following the corresponding discussions and illustrative examples in the text.

Of the changes in the laboratory procedures may be mentioned the inclusion of the analysis of chloride by the indirect precipitation method, the substitution of the determination of sulphur in pyrites for the determination of sulphur in barium sulphate, the expansion of the procedures for the analysis of brass to cover also the analysis of bronze, and the inclusion of a discussion of potentiometric titrations.

In addition to these, such minor changes have been made at various points in the discussions and directions as have been deemed advisable from long experience with the text as an introductory course at the Massachusetts Institute of Technology.

L. F. H.
S. G. S.

CAMBRIDGE, MASS.
April, 1931.

PREFACE TO THE SIXTH EDITION

THIS Introductory Course of Quantitative Analysis has been prepared to meet the needs of students who are just entering upon the subject, after a course of qualitative analysis. It is primarily intended to enable the student to work successfully and intelligently without the necessity for a larger measure of personal assistance and supervision than can reasonably be given to each member of a large class. To this end the directions are given in such detail that there is very little opportunity for the student to go astray; but the manual is not, the author believes, on this account less adapted for use with small classes, where the instructor, by greater personal influence, can stimulate independent thought on the part of the pupil.

The method of presentation of the subject is that suggested by Professor A. A. Noyes' excellent manual of Qualitative Analysis. For each analysis the procedure is given in considerable detail, and this is accompanied by explanatory notes, which are believed to be sufficiently expanded to enable the student to understand fully the underlying reason for each step prescribed. The use of the book should, nevertheless, be supplemented by classroom instruction, mainly of the character of recitations, and the student should be taught to consult larger works. The general directions are intended to emphasize those matters upon which the beginner in quantitative analysis must bestow special care, and to offer helpful suggestions. The student can hardly be expected to appreciate the force of all the statements contained in these directions, or, indeed, to retain them all in the memory after a single reading; but the instructor, by frequent reference to special paragraphs, as suitable occasion presents itself, can soon render them familiar to the student.

PREFACE TO THE SIXTH EDITION

The analyses selected for practice are those comprised in the first course of quantitative analysis at the Massachusetts Institute of Technology, and have been chosen, after an experience of years, as affording the best preparation for more advanced work, and as satisfactory types of gravimetric and volumetric methods. From the latter point of view, they also seem to furnish the best insight into quantitative analysis for those students who can devote but a limited time to the subject, and who may never extend their study beyond the field covered by this manual. The author has had opportunity to test the efficiency of the course for use with such students, and has found the results satisfactory.

In place of the usual custom of selecting simple salts as material for preliminary practice, it has been found advantageous to substitute, in most instances, approximately pure samples of appropriate minerals or industrial products. The difficulties are not greatly enhanced, while the student gains in practical experience.

The analytical procedures described in the following pages have been selected chiefly with reference to their usefulness in teaching the subject, and with the purpose of affording as wide a variety of processes as is practicable within an introductory course of this character. The scope of the manual precludes any extended attempt to indicate alternative procedures, except through general references to larger works on analytical chemistry. The author is indebted to the standard works for many suggestions for which it is impracticable to make specific acknowledgment; no considerable credit is claimed by him for originality of procedure.

For many years, as a matter of convenience, the classes for which this text was originally prepared were divided, one part beginning with gravimetric processes and the other with volumetric analyses. After a careful review of the experience thus gained the conclusion has been reached that volumetric analysis offers the better approach to the subject. Accordingly the arrangement of the present (the sixth) edition of this manual has been changed to introduce volumetric procedures first. Teachers who are familiar with earlier editions will, however, find that the order of presentation of the material under the various divisions is nearly the same as that previously followed, and those who may still prefer to begin the course of instruction with gravimetric processes will, it is believed, be able to follow that order without difficulty.

Procedures for the determination of sulphur in insoluble sulphates, for the determination of copper in copper ores by iodometric methods, for the determination of iron by permanganate in hydrochloric acid solutions, and for the standardization of potassium permanganate solutions using sodium oxalate as a standard, and of thiosulphate solutions using copper as a standard, have been added. The determination of silica in silicates decomposable by acids, as a separate procedure, has been omitted.

The explanatory notes have been rearranged to bring them into closer association with the procedures to which they relate. The number of problems has been considerably increased.

The author wishes to renew his expressions of appreciation of the kindly reception accorded the earlier editions of this manual. He has received helpful suggestions from so many of his colleagues within the Institute, and friends elsewhere, that his sense of obligation must be expressed to them collectively. He is under special obligations to Professor L. F. Hamilton for assistance in the preparation of the present edition.

HENRY P. TALBOT.

MASSACHUSETTS INSTITUTE OF TECHNOLOGY
September, 1921.

CONTENTS

PART I. INTRODUCTION

GENERAL CONSIDERATIONS 1
Subdivisions of Analytical Chemistry; General Directions; Accuracy and Economy of Time; Notebooks; Reagents; Wash-Bottles; Transfer of Liquids; Evaporation of Liquids

PART II. VOLUMETRIC ANALYSIS

GENERAL DISCUSSION 8
Subdivisions of Volumetric Analysis; Measuring Instruments; Analytical Balance; Weights; Experiment in Weighing; Burettes; Preparation of Burette for Use; Reading of the Burette; Calibration of Glass Measuring Devices; Calibration of Burettes, Pipettes, and Measuring Flasks

GENERAL DIRECTIONS FOR VOLUMETRIC ANALYSIS 24
Standard Solutions; Normal Solutions

PROPER RETENTION OF SIGNIFICANT FIGURES 27

I. NEUTRALIZATION METHODS

ACIDIMETRY AND ALKALIMETRY 31
General Discussion; Preparation of Standard Solutions; Comparison of Acid and Alkali Solutions

STOICHIOMETRY 37
PROBLEMS 40
STANDARDIZATION OF ACID AND ALKALI 43
Selection and Preparation of Standard; Standardization of Hydrochloric Acid; Standardization of Sodium Hydroxide

STOICHIOMETRY 46
PROBLEMS 47
DETERMINATION OF TOTAL ALKALINE STRENGTH OF SODA ASH . 50
DETERMINATION OF THE ACID STRENGTH OF OXALIC ACID . . 52
STOICHIOMETRY 53
DOUBLE INDICATOR TITRATIONS 55
PROBLEMS 57

ix

II. OXIDATION PROCESSES

	PAGE
GENERAL DISCUSSION	62
OXIDATION AND REDUCTION EQUIVALENTS	63
PROBLEMS	65
PERMANGANATE PROCESS	68
Preparation of Standard Solutions; Comparison of Solutions; Standardization of Permanganate	
STOICHIOMETRY	72
PROBLEMS	74
DETERMINATION OF IRON IN LIMONITE	76
Reduction with Zinc; Reduction with Stannous Chloride	
STOICHIOMETRY	82
DETERMINATION OF MANGANESE DIOXIDE IN PYROLUSITE	84
STOICHIOMETRY	85
PROBLEMS	87
BICHROMATE PROCESS	91
Preparation of Solutions; Indicator Solution; Comparison of Solutions; Standardization of Bichromate	
DETERMINATION OF IRON IN LIMONITE	98
STOICHIOMETRY	98
DETERMINATION OF CHROMIUM IN CHROME IRON ORE	99
STOICHIOMETRY	101
PROBLEMS	102
IODIMETRY	104
General Discussion; Preparation of Standard Solutions; Indicator Solution; Comparison of Solutions; Standardization of Solutions	
STOICHIOMETRY	110
DETERMINATION OF ANTIMONY IN STIBNITE	113
STOICHIOMETRY	114
DETERMINATION OF COPPER IN ORES	116
STOICHIOMETRY	118
PROBLEMS	120
CHLORIMETRY	123
DETERMINATION OF AVAILABLE CHLORINE IN BLEACHING POWDER	124

III. PRECIPITATION METHODS

GENERAL DISCUSSION	126
THIOCYANATE PROCESS	127
Preparation of the Solution; Standardization	

CONTENTS

	PAGE
DETERMINATION OF SILVER IN COIN	129
DETERMINATION OF CHLORINE IN CHLORIDE	130
STOICHIOMETRY	131
PROBLEMS	134

PART III. GRAVIMETRIC ANALYSIS

GENERAL DIRECTIONS 136
  Weighing; Precipitation; Funnels and Filters; Filtration and Washing of Precipitates; Desiccators; Crucibles; Preparation of Crucibles for Use; Ignition of Precipitates
STOICHIOMETRY (Chemical Factors) 145
PROBLEMS 147
DETERMINATION OF CHLORINE IN CHLORIDE 149
STOICHIOMETRY 154
PROBLEMS 156
DETERMINATION OF IRON IN FERROUS AMMONIUM SULPHATE . . 158
STOICHIOMETRY 161
PROBLEMS 163
DETERMINATION OF SULPHUR IN FERROUS AMMONIUM SULPHATE 164
DETERMINATION OF SULPHUR IN PYRITE 168
STOICHIOMETRY 170
PROBLEMS 170
DETERMINATION OF PHOSPHORIC ANHYDRIDE IN APATITE . . 173
STOICHIOMETRY 179
PROBLEMS 181
ANALYSIS OF LIMESTONE 184
  Determination of Moisture; Determination of Insoluble Matter; Determination of Combined Oxides; Determination of Calcium; Determination of Magnesium; Determination of Carbon Dioxide
STOICHIOMETRY 196
PROBLEMS 198
ANALYSIS OF BRASS AND BRONZE 201
  Electrolytic Separations; Determination of Tin; Determination of Copper and Lead; Determination of Iron; Determination of Zinc
STOICHIOMETRY 211
PROBLEMS 216
DETERMINATION OF SILICA IN SILICATES 219
STOICHIOMETRY 225

	PAGE
PROBLEMS	227

APPENDIX

POTENTIOMETRIC TITRATIONS	229
PROBLEMS	238
SAMPLE PAGES FOR LABORATORY RECORDS	240
STRENGTH OF REAGENTS	242
DENSITIES AND VOLUMES OF WATER	243
SENSITIVENESS OF INDICATORS	244
ELECTROMOTIVE SERIES	244
ATOMIC WEIGHTS	245
TABLES OF LOGARITHMS	246
INDEX	251

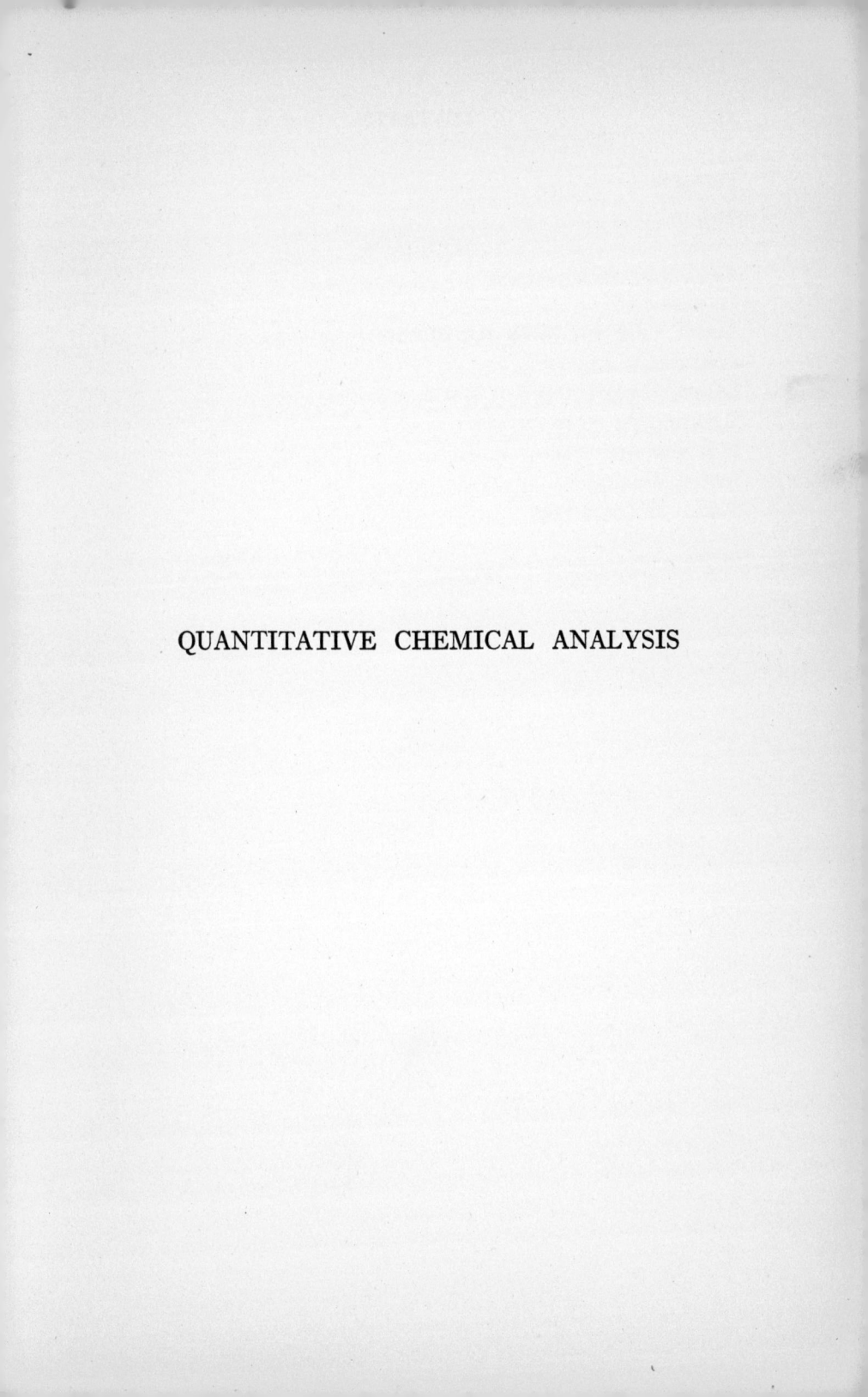

QUANTITATIVE CHEMICAL ANALYSIS

PART I

INTRODUCTION

GENERAL CONSIDERATIONS

SUBDIVISIONS OF ANALYTICAL CHEMISTRY

A COMPLETE chemical analysis of a body of unknown composition involves the recognition of its component parts by the methods of *qualitative analysis*, and the determination of the proportions in which these components are present by the processes of *quantitative analysis*. A preliminary qualitative examination is generally indispensable, if intelligent and proper provisions are to be made for the separation of the various constituents under such conditions as will insure accurate quantitative estimations.

It is assumed that the operations of qualitative analysis are familiar to the student, who will find that the reactions made use of in quantitative processes are frequently the same as those employed in qualitative analyses with respect to both precipitation and systematic separation from interfering substances; but it should be noted that the conditions must now be regulated with greater care, and in such a manner as to insure the most complete separation possible. For example, in the qualitative detection of sulphates by precipitation as barium sulphate from acid solution it is not necessary, in most instances, to take into account the solubility of the sulphate in hydrochloric acid, while in the quantitative determination of sulphates by this reaction this solubility becomes an important consideration. The operations of qualitative analysis are, therefore, the more accurate the nearer they are made to conform to quantitative conditions.

The methods of quantitative analysis are subdivided, according to their nature, into those of *gravimetric analysis*, *volumetric analysis*, and *colorimetric analysis*. In *gravimetric* processes the constituent to be determined is sometimes isolated in elementary form, but more commonly in the form of some compound possessing a well-established and definite composition, which can be readily and completely separated, and weighed either directly or after ignition. From the weight of this substance and its known composition, the amount of the constituent in question is determined.

In *volumetric* analysis, instead of weighing a definite body, a well-defined reaction is caused to take place, wherein the reagent is added from an apparatus so designed that the volume of the solution employed to complete the reaction can be accurately measured. The strength of this solution is accurately known, and the volume employed serves, therefore, as a measure of the substance acted upon. An example will make clear the distinction between these two types of analysis. The percentage of chlorine in a sample of sodium chloride may be determined by dissolving a weighed amount of the chloride in dilute acid and precipitating the chloride ions as silver chloride, which is then separated by filtration, ignited, and weighed (a *gravimetric* process); or the sodium chloride may be dissolved in dilute acid, and a solution of silver nitrate containing an accurately known amount of the silver salt in each cubic centimeter may be cautiously added from a measuring device called a burette until precipitation is just complete, when the amount of chlorine may be calculated from the number of cubic centimeters of the silver nitrate solution involved in the reaction (a *volumetric* process).

Volumetric methods are generally more rapid, require less apparatus, and are frequently capable of greater accuracy than gravimetric methods. They are particularly useful when many determinations of the same sort are required.

In a *colorimetric* analysis the substance to be determined is converted into some compound which imparts to its solutions a distinct color, the intensity of which must vary in direct proportion to the amount of the compound in the solution. Such solutions are compared with respect to depth of color with standard solutions containing known amounts of the colored compound, or of other similar color-producing substance which has been found acceptable as a color standard. Colorimetric methods are, in general, restricted to the determinations of very small quantities, since only in dilute solutions are accurate comparisons of color possible.

GENERAL DIRECTIONS

The following paragraphs should be read carefully and thoughtfully. A prime essential for success as an analyst is attention to details and the avoidance of all conditions which could destroy, or even lessen, confidence in the analyses when completed. The suggestions here given are the outcome of much experience, and their adoption will tend to insure permanently work of a high grade, while neglect of them will often lead to disappointment and loss of time.

ACCURACY AND ECONOMY OF TIME

The fundamental conception of quantitative analysis implies a necessity for all possible care in guarding against loss of material or the introduction of foreign matter. The laboratory desk, and all apparatus, should be scrupulously neat and clean at all times. A sponge should always be ready at hand, and desk and filter-stands should be kept dry and in good order. Funnels should never be allowed to drip upon the desk. Glassware should always be wiped with a clean, lintless towel just before use. All filters and solutions should be covered to protect them from dust, just as far as is practicable, and every drop of solution or particle of precipitate must be regarded as invaluable for the success of the analysis.

An economical use of laboratory hours is best secured by acquiring a thorough knowledge of the character of the work to be done before undertaking it, and then by so arranging the work that no time shall be wasted during the evaporation of liquids and other time-consuming operations. To this end the student should read thoughtfully not only the *entire* procedure, but the explanatory notes as well, before any step is taken in the analysis. The explanatory notes furnish, in general, the reasons for particular steps or precautions, but they also occasionally contain details of manipulation not incorporated, for various reasons, in the procedure. These notes follow the procedures at frequent intervals, and the exact points to which they apply are indicated by references. The student should realize that a *failure to study the notes will inevitably lead to mistakes, loss of time, and an inadequate understanding of the subject.*

All analyses should be made in duplicate, and in general a close agreement of results should be expected. It should, however, be remembered that a close concordance of results in "check analyses" is not conclusive evidence of the accuracy of those results, although the probability of their accuracy is, of course, considerably enhanced. The satisfaction in obtaining "check results" in such analyses must never be allowed to interfere with the critical examination of the procedure employed, nor must they ever be regarded as in any measure a substitute for absolute truth and accuracy.

In this connection it must also be emphasized that only the operator himself can know the whole history of an analysis, and only he can know whether his work is worthy of full confidence. No work should be continued for a moment after such confidence is lost, but should be resolutely discarded as soon as a cause for distrust is fully established. The student should, however, determine to put forth his best efforts in each analysis; it is well not to be too ready to condone failures and to "begin again," as much time is lost in these fruitless attempts.

Nothing less than *absolute integrity* is or can be demanded of a quantitative analyst, and any disregard of this principle, however slight, is as fatal to success as lack of chemical knowledge or inaptitude in manipulation can possibly be.

NOTEBOOKS

Notebooks should contain, beside the record of observations, descriptive notes. All records of weights should be placed upon the right-hand page, while that on the left is reserved for the notes, calculations of factors, or the amount of reagents required.

The neat and systematic arrangement of the records of analyses is of the first importance, and is an evidence of careful work, and an excellent credential. Of two notebooks in which the results may be, in fact, of equal value as legal evidence, that one which is neatly arranged will carry with it greater weight.

All records should be dated, and all observations should be recorded at once in the notebook. The making of records upon loose paper is a practice to be deprecated, as is also that of copying original entries into a second notebook. The student should accustom himself to orderly entries at the time of observation. Several sample pages of systematic records are to be found in the Appendix. These are based upon experience, but other arrangements, if clear and orderly, may prove equally serviceable. The student is advised to follow the sample pages until he is in a position to plan out a system of his own.

REAGENTS

The habit of carefully testing reagents, including distilled water, cannot be acquired too early or practiced too constantly; for, in spite of all reasonable precautionary measures, inferior chemicals will occasionally find their way into the stock room, or errors will be made in filling reagent bottles. The student should remember that while there may be others who share the responsibility for the purity of materials in the laboratory of an institution, the responsibility will later be one which he must individually assume.

The stoppers of reagent bottles should never be laid upon the desk, unless upon a clean watch-glass or paper. The neck and mouth of all such bottles should be kept scrupulously clean, and care taken that no confusion of stoppers occurs.

In measuring out a liquid reagent, if more than the desired amount is poured out, it is best to discard the excess rather than to return it to the reagent bottle.

WASH-BOTTLES

Wash-bottles for distilled water should be made from flasks of about one liter capacity and be provided with gracefully bent tubes, which should not be too long. The jet should be connected with the tube entering the wash-bottle by a short piece of rubber tubing in such a way as to be flexible, and should deliver a stream about one millimeter in diameter. The neck of the flask may be wound with cord, or covered with wash-leather, for greater comfort when hot water is used. It is well to provide several small wash-bottles for liquids other than distilled water, which should invariably be clearly labeled.

TRANSFER OF LIQUIDS

Liquids should never be transferred from one vessel to another, nor to a filter, without the aid of a stirring rod held firmly against the side or lip of the vessel. When the vessel is provided with a lip it is not usually necessary to use other means to prevent the loss of liquid by running down the side; whenever loss seems imminent a *very thin* layer of vaseline, applied with the finger to the edge of the vessel, will prevent it. The stirring rod down which the liquid runs should never be drawn upward in such a way as to allow the solution to collect on the under side of the rim or lip of a vessel.

The number of transfers of liquids from one vessel to another during an analysis should be as small as possible to avoid the risk of slight losses. Each vessel must, of course, be completely washed to insure the transfer of all material; but it should be remembered that this can be accomplished better by the use of successive small portions of wash-water (perhaps 5–10 cc.), if each wash-water is allowed to drain away for a few seconds, than by the addition of large amounts which unnecessarily increase the volume of the solutions, causing loss of time in subsequent filtrations or evaporations.

All stirring rods employed in quantitative analyses should be rounded at the ends by holding them in the flame of a burner until they begin to soften. If this is not done, the rods will scratch the inner surface of beakers, causing them to crack on subsequent heating.

EVAPORATION OF LIQUIDS

The greatest care must be taken to prevent loss of solutions during processes of evaporation, either from too violent ebullition, from evaporation to dryness and spattering, or from the evolution of gas during the heating. In general, evaporation upon the steam bath is to be preferred to other methods on account of the impossibility of loss by spattering. If the steam baths are well protected from dust, solutions should be left without covers during evaporation; but solutions which are boiled upon the hot plate, or from which gases are escaping, should invariably be covered. In any case a watch-glass may be supported above the vessel by means of a glass triangle, or other similar device, and the danger of loss of material or contamination by dust thus be avoided. It is obvious that evaporation is promoted by the use of vessels which admit of the exposure of a broad surface to the air.

Liquids which contain suspended matter (precipitates) should always be cautiously heated, since the presence of the solid matter is frequently the occasion of violent " bumping," with consequent risk to apparatus and analysis.

PART II
VOLUMETRIC ANALYSIS

THE processes of volumetric analysis are, in general, simpler than those of gravimetric analysis and accordingly serve best as an introduction to the practice of quantitative analysis. For their execution there are required, first, an accurate balance with which to weigh the material for analysis; second, graduated instruments in which to measure the volumes of the solutions employed; third, standard solutions, that is, solutions the concentrations of which are accurately known; and fourth, indicators, which will furnish accurate evidence of the point at which the desired reaction is completed. The nature of the indicators employed will be explained in connection with the different analyses.

The process whereby a *standard solution* is brought into reaction is called *titration*, and the point at which the reaction is exactly completed is called the *end-point*. The *indicator* should show the *end-point* of the *titration*. The volume of the standard solution used then furnishes the measure of the substance to be determined as truly as if that substance had been separated and weighed.

The processes of volumetric analysis are easily classified, according to their character, into:

I. **Neutralization Methods**; such, for example, as those of acidimetry and alkalimetry.

II. **Oxidation Processes**; as exemplified in the determination of ferrous iron by its oxidation with potassium permanganate.

III. **Precipitation or Saturation Methods**; of which the titration for silver with potassium thiocyanate solution is an illustration.

From a somewhat different standpoint the methods in each case may be subdivided into (a) **Direct Methods,** in which the substance to be measured is directly determined by titration to an end-point with a standard solution; and (b) **Indirect Methods,** in which the substance itself is not measured, but a quantity of reagent is added which is known to be an excess with respect to a specific reaction, and the unused excess determined by titration. Examples of the latter class will be pointed out as they occur in the procedures.

MEASURING INSTRUMENTS

THE ANALYTICAL BALANCE

For a complete discussion of the physical principles underlying the construction and use of balances, and the various methods of weighing, the student is referred to larger manuals of Quantitative Analysis, such as those of Fresenius, or Treadwell-Hall.

The statements and rules of procedure which follow are sufficient for the intelligent use of an analytical balance in connection with processes prescribed in this introductory manual. It is, however, imperative that the student should make himself familiar with these essential features of the balance, and its use. He should fully realize that the analytical balance is a delicate instrument which will render excellent service under careful treatment, but such treatment is an essential condition if its accuracy is to be depended upon. He should also understand that no set of rules, however complete, can do away with the necessity for a sense of personal responsibility, since by carelessness he can render inaccurate not only his own analyses, but those of all other students using the same balance.

Before making any weighings the student should seat himself before a balance and observe the following details of construction:

1. The balance case is mounted on three brass legs, which should preferably rest in glass cups, backed with rubber to prevent slipping. The front legs are adjustable as to height and are used to level the balance case; the rear leg is of permanent length.

2. The front of the case may be raised to give access to the balance. In some makes doors are provided also at the ends of the balance case.

3. The balance beam is mounted upon an upright in the center of the case on the top of which is an inlaid agate plate. To the center of the beam there is attached a steel or agate knife-edge on which the beam oscillates when it rests on the agate plate.

4. The balance beam, extending to the right and left, is graduated along its upper edge, usually on both sides, and has at its extremities two agate or steel knife-edges from which are suspended stirrups. Each of these stirrups has an agate plate which, when the balance is in action, rests upon the corresponding knife-edge of the beam. The balance pans are suspended from the stirrups.

5. A pointer is attached to the center of the beam, and as the beam oscillates this pointer moves in front of a scale near the base of the post.

6. At the base of the post, usually in the rear, is a spirit-level.

7. Within the upright is a mechanism, controlled by a knob at the front of the balance case, which is so arranged as to raise the entire beam slightly above the level at which the knife-edges are in contact with the agate plates. When the balance is not in use the beam must be supported by this device, since otherwise the constant jarring to which a balance is inevitably subjected will soon dull the knife-edges and lessen the sensitiveness of the balance.

8. A small weight, or bob, is attached to the pointer (or sometimes to the beam) by which the center of gravity of the beam and its attachments may be regulated. The center of gravity must lie very slightly below the level of the agate plates to secure the desired sensitiveness of the balance. This is provided for when the balance is set up, and very rarely requires alteration. The student should never attempt to change this adjustment.

9. Below the balance pans are two pan-arrests operated by a button from the front of the case. These arrests exert a very slight upward pressure upon the pans and minimize the displacement of the beam when objects or weights are being placed upon the pans.

10. A movable rod, operated from one end of the balance case, extends over the balance beam and carries a small wire weight, called a rider. By means of this rod the rider can be placed upon any desired division of the scale on the balance beam. Each numbered division on the beam corresponds to one milli-

gram, and the use of the rider obviates the placing of very small fractional weights on the balance pan.

If a new rider is purchased, or an old one replaced, care must be taken that its weight corresponds to the graduations on the beam of the balance on which it is to be used. The weight of the rider in milligrams must be equal to the number of large divisions (5, 6, 10, or 12) between the central knife-edge and the knife-edge at the end of the beam. It should be noted that on some balances the last division bears no number. Each new rider should be tested against a 5 or 10-milligram weight.

In some of the more recent forms of the balance a chain device replaces the smaller weights and the use of the rider as just described. Such a balance is called a *chainomatic* balance.

Before using a balance, it is always best to test its adjustment. This is absolutely necessary if the balance is used by several workers; it is always a wise precaution under any conditions. For this purpose, brush off the balance pans with a soft camel's hair brush. Then note (1) that the balance is level; (2) that the mechanism for raising and lowering the beam works smoothly; (3) that the pan-arrests touch the pans when the beam is lowered; and (4) that the needle swings equal distances on either side of the zero-point when set in motion without any load on the pans. If the latter condition is not fulfilled, the balance should be adjusted by means of the adjusting screw at the end of the beam unless the variation is not more than one division on the scale; it is often better to make a proper allowance for this small zero error than to disturb the balance by an attempt at correction. Unless a student thoroughly understands the construction of a balance he should never attempt to make adjustments, but should apply to the instructor in charge.

The object to be weighed should be placed on the left-hand balance pan and the weights upon the right-hand pan. Every substance which could attack the metal of the balance pan should be weighed upon a watch-glass, and all objects must be dry and at room temperature. A warm body gives rise to air currents which vitiate the accuracy of the weighing.

The weights should be applied in the order in which they occur in the weight-box, beginning with the largest weight which is apparently required. After a weight has been placed upon the pan the beam should be lowered upon its knife-edge, and, if necessary, the pan-arrests depressed. The movement of the pointer will then indicate whether the weight applied is too great or too small. When the weight has been ascertained, by the successive addition of small weights, to the nearest 5 or 10 milligrams, the weighing is completed by the use of the rider. The correct weight is that which causes the pointer to swing an equal number of divisions to the right and left of the zero-point, when the pointer traverses not less than five divisions on either side.

The balance case should always be closed during the final weighing, while the rider is being used, to protect the pans from the effect of air currents.

Before the final determination of an exact weight the beam should always be lifted from the knife-edges and again lowered into place, as it frequently happens that the scale pans are, in spite of the pan-arrests, slightly twisted by the impact of the weights, the beam being thereby virtually lengthened or shortened. Lifting the beam restores the proper alignment.

The beam should never be set in motion by lowering it forcibly upon the knife-edges, nor by touching the pans, but rather by lifting the rider (unless the balance be provided with some of the newer devices for the purpose), and the swing should be arrested only when the needle approaches zero on the scale, otherwise the knife-edges become dull. For the same reason the beam should never be left upon its knife-edges, nor should weights be removed from or placed on the pans without supporting the beam, except in the case of the small fractional weights.

When the process of weighing has been completed, the weight should be recorded in the notebook by first noting the vacant spaces in the weight-box, and then checking the weight by again noting the weights as they are removed from the pan. This practice will often detect and avoid errors. It is obvious that the weights should always be returned to their proper places in the box, and be handled only with pincers.

It should be borne in mind that if the mechanism of a balance is deranged or if any substance is spilled upon the pans or in the balance case, the damage should be reported at once. In many instances serious harm can be averted by prompt action when delay might ruin the balance.

Samples for analysis are sometimes weighed in small tubes with cork stoppers. Since the stoppers are likely to change in weight from the varying amounts of moisture absorbed from the atmosphere, it is necessary to confirm the recorded weight of a tube which has been unused for some time before weighing out a new portion of substance from it. For this reason the use of tubes with ground glass stoppers (*weighing tubes* or *weighing bottles*) is recommended.

WEIGHTS

The set of weights commonly used in analytical chemistry ranges from 50 grams to 5 milligrams. The weights from 50 grams to 1 gram are usually of brass, lacquered or gold plated. The fractional weights are of German silver, gold, platinum or aluminum. The rider is of platinum or aluminum wire.

The sets of weights purchased from reputable dealers are usually sufficiently accurate for analytical work. It is not necessary that such a set should be exact in comparison with the absolute standard of weight, provided they are relatively correct among themselves, and provided the same set of weights is used in all weighings made during a given analysis. The analyst should assure himself that the weights in a set previously unfamiliar to him are relatively correct by a few simple tests. For example, he should make sure that in his set two weights of the same denomination (*i.e.*, two 10-gram weights, or the two 100-milligram weights) are actually equal and interchangeable, or that the 500-milligram weight is equal to the sum of the 200, 100, 100, 50, 20, 20 and 10-milligram weights combined, and so on. If discrepancies of more than a few tenths of a milligram (depending upon the total weight involved) are found, the weights should be returned for correction. The rider should also be compared with a 5 or 10-milligram weight.

In an instructional laboratory appreciable errors should be reported to the instructor in charge for his consideration.

When the highest accuracy is desired, the weights may be calibrated and corrections applied. A calibration procedure is described in a paper by T. W. Richards, *J. Am. Chem. Soc.*, **22,** 144, and in many large text-books.

Weights are inevitably subject to corrosion if not properly protected at all times, and are liable to damage unless handled with great care. It is obvious that anything which alters the weight of a single piece in an analytical set will introduce an error in every weighing made in which that piece is used. This source of error is often extremely obscure and difficult to detect. The only safeguard against such errors is to be found in scrupulous care in handling and protection on the part of the analyst, and an equal insistence that if several analysts use the same set of weights, each shall realize his responsibility for the work of others as well as his own.

EXPERIMENT IN WEIGHING

Procedure. — Test the adjustment of the balance according to the directions above. Place upon the left-hand pan a series of small objects such as coins, crucibles, small flasks, etc., and weigh each accurately to the nearest tenth of a milligram. Record each weighing in the notebook and also record the time required to make each weighing. Continue until such a weighing can be made easily and quickly (at least within 4 minutes).

Also practice weighing out samples of powdered substances. For this purpose fill a weighing tube or weighing bottle with the substance to be weighed. Clean and dry carefully the outside of the tube, taking care to handle it as little as possible after wiping. Weigh the tube accurately to 0.0001 gram and record the weight in the notebook. Hold the tube over the top of a beaker and cautiously remove the stopper, making sure that no particles fall from it or from the tube elsewhere than in the beaker. Pour from the tube a portion of the substance, letting it slide down the inside of the tilted beaker. Replace the stopper, still holding the tube over the beaker, and determine approximately how much has been removed. Continue this procedure until 1.00 to 1.10 grams have been taken from the tube. Then weigh the tube accurately and record the weight under the first weight in the notebook. The difference between the two weights is the weight of the material transferred to the beaker. In the same way, proceed to transfer a second portion to another beaker. Continue until facility is acquired in making such weighings (Note 1).

The latter process is to be used in all future analyses where directions call simply for taking a " 1-gram sample." Such a statement implies weighing out *accurately* a weight of sample of *approximately* one gram. In a similar fashion other weights of sample can be taken (Note 2).

Notes. — 1. The student should appreciate the fact that the time spent in the early acquisition of a reasonable degree of skill in using a balance, weighing samples, and reading burettes is more than compensated by the saving in time attained in future analyses. He should not be content to begin his analyses until he can perform these fundamental operations quickly and accurately.

2. Some analysts prefer to use a tared watch-glass or dish for the purpose of weighing out samples. Two small, light watch-glasses can be made of equal weight by carefully grinding down the heavier by rubbing face down on emery paper. With one watch-glass on each balance pan the weights corresponding to the sample desired are placed on the watch-glass on the right-hand pan, and the substance is transferred to the other watch-glass by means of a small steel spatula. By adding and removing suitable small increments of sample it is possible to weigh out exactly 1.0000 gram of substance, or any other weight desired. Such a method of weighing simplifies calculations and has other advantages, but unless considerable time is spent in making the weighing it is usually of lower degree of precision. Taring a watch-glass or small dish against a small strip of lead or against a tube of sand (which can be hung on the stirrup hook at the top of the balance-pan brace) offers the same advantages and disadvantages.

BURETTES

A burette is made from a glass tube which is as uniformly cylindrical as possible, and of such a bore that the divisions which are etched upon its surface shall correspond closely to actual contents.

The tube is contracted at one extremity, and terminates in either a glass stopcock and delivery-tube, or in such a manner that a piece of rubber tubing may be firmly attached, connecting a delivery-tube of glass. The rubber tubing is closed by means of a glass bead. Burettes of the latter type will be referred to as " plain burettes."

The graduations are usually numbered in cubic centimeters, and the latter are subdivided into tenths.

One burette of each type may be used for the analytical procedures which follow.

PREPARATION OF A BURETTE FOR USE

The inner surface of a burette must be thoroughly cleaned in order that the liquid as drawn out may drain away completely, without leaving drops upon the sides. This is best accomplished by treating the inside of the burette with a warm solution of chromic acid in concentrated sulphuric acid, applied as follows: If the burette is of the " plain " type, first remove the rubber tip and force the lower end of the burette into a medium-sized cork stopper. Nearly fill the burette with the chromic acid solution, close the upper end with a cork stopper and tip the burette backward and forward in such a way as to bring the solution into contact with the entire inner surface. Remove the stopper and pour the solution into a stock bottle to be kept for further use, and rinse out the burette with water several times. Unless the water then runs freely from the burette without leaving drops adhering to the sides, the process must be repeated (Note 1).

If the burette has a glass stopcock, both it and the ground joint should be wiped after the cleaning. The surface of the stopcock should then be smeared with a thin coating of vaseline or stopcock grease and replaced. It should be attached to the burette by means of a wire, or elastic band, to lessen the danger of breakage.

Fill the burettes with distilled water, and allow the water to run out through the stopcock or rubber tip until convinced that no air bubbles are inclosed (Note 2). Fill the burette to a point above the zero-point and draw off the water until the meniscus is just below that mark. It is then ready for calibration.

Notes. — 1. The inner surface of the burette must be absolutely clean if the liquid is to run off freely. Chromic acid in sulphuric acid is usually found to be the best cleansing agent, but the mixture must be warm and concentrated. The solution can be prepared by pouring a little water over a few powdered crystals of potassium bichromate or sodium bichromate and then adding commercial sulphuric acid.

2. It is always necessary to insure the absence of air bubbles in the tips or stopcocks. The treatment described above will usually accomplish this, but, in the case of plain burettes it is sometimes better to allow a little of the liquid to flow out of the tip while it is bent upwards. Any air which may be entrapped then rises with the liquid and escapes.

If air bubbles escape during subsequent calibration or titration, an error is introduced which vitiates the results.

READING THE BURETTE

All liquids when placed in a burette form what is called a meniscus at their upper surfaces. In the case of liquids such as water or aqueous solutions this meniscus is concave, and when the liquids are transparent accurate readings are best obtained by observing the position on the graduated scales of the lowest point of the meniscus. This can best be done as follows: Wrap around the burette a piece of colored paper, the straight, smooth edges of which are held evenly together with the colored side next to the burette (Note 1). Hold the paper about two small divisions below the meniscus and raise or lower the level of the eyes until the edge of the paper at the back of the burette is just hidden from the eye by that in front (Note 2). Note the position of the lowest point of the curve of the meniscus, estimating the tenths of the small divisions, thus reading its position to hundredths of a cubic centimeter.

Notes. — 1. The ends of the colored paper used as an aid to accurate reading may be fastened together by means of a gummed label. The paper may then be left on the burette and be ready for immediate use by sliding it up or down, as required.

2. To obtain an accurate reading the eye must be very nearly on a level with the meniscus. This is secured by the use of the paper as described. The student should observe by trial how a reading is affected when the meniscus is viewed from above or below.

The eye soon becomes accustomed to estimating the tenths of the divisions. If the paper is held as directed, two divisions below the meniscus, one whole division is visible to correct the judgment. It is not well to attempt to bring the meniscus exactly to a division mark on the burette. Such readings are usually less accurate than those in which the tenths of a division are estimated.

CALIBRATION OF GLASS MEASURING DEVICES

If accuracy of results is to be attained, the correctness of all measuring instruments must be tested. None of the apparatus offered for sale can be implicitly relied upon except those more expensive instruments which are accompanied by a certificate from the Bureau of Standards at Washington, or some other equally authentic source.

The process of testing these instruments is called *calibration*. It is usually accomplished by comparing the actual weight of water contained in the instrument with its apparent volume.

A liter is the volume occupied by 1 kilogram of water at the temperature of its maximum density (approximately 4° C.). A *cubic centimeter* (*cc.*) is the volume occupied by a cube 1 centimeter on a side, and is almost one one-thousandth of a liter (Note 1). Since 4° C. is obviously too low a temperature for practical use and since the volume of a given weight of water changes with the temperature, as does the volume of the containing vessel, it is necessary to adopt a more convenient standard working temperature. The Bureau of Standards has specified 20° C. as the *normal temperature*.

To contain a *true liter*, then, a container must be so marked that at 20° C. its capacity will be equal to the volume of water which at 4° C. weighs 1 kilogram in vacuo. Practically all chemical glassware in this country is now calibrated according to this standard. When such apparatus is used at temperatures other than 20° C., a correction must be applied for accurate results, but with volumetric apparatus of less than 100 cc. content, used at temperatures within four or five degrees of 20° C., neglect of this correction is of little consequence in ordinary analytical work. It is best to maintain reasonably uniform temperature in the laboratory, and correction factors should be applied when abnormal conditions prevail. Of all the factors involved in a change in working temperature that of the change in the volume of the solution itself has the greatest effect and is usually the only one that need be corrected for. Data to be used for this purpose are given in the Appendix.

Note. — 1. One liter contains 1000.027 cubic centimeters. The Bureau of Standards now advocates the adoption of the *milliliter* (*ml.*) as the unit for small volumes in place of the cubic centimeter. This is a more logical unit, but the term has not yet come into general use, and the error involved in assuming a liter to be 1000 cubic centimeters is negligibly small.

CALIBRATION OF THE BURETTES

Two burettes, one at least of which should have a glass stop-cock, are required throughout the volumetric work. Both burettes should be calibrated by the student to whom they are assigned.

Procedure. — Weigh a 50 cc., flat-bottomed flask (preferably a light-weight flask), which must be dry on the outside, to the nearest centigram. Record the weight in the notebook. (See Appendix for suggestions as to records.) Place the flask under the burette and draw out into it about 10 cc. of water, removing any drop on the tip by touching it against the inside of the neck of the flask. Do not attempt to stop exactly at the 10 cc. mark, but do not vary more than 0.1 cc. from it. Note the time, and at the expiration of three minutes (or longer) read the burette accurately, and record the reading in the notebook (Note 1). Meanwhile weigh the flask and water to centigrams and record its weight (Note 2). Draw off the liquid from 10 cc. to about

20 cc. into the same flask without emptying it; weigh, and at the expiration of three minutes take the reading, and so on throughout the length of the burette. When this is completed, refill the burette and check the first calibration.

The differences in burette readings represent the apparent volumes; the differences in weights divided by the density of water at the temperature of the water represent the true volumes. For example, if a certain amount of water at 20° C. has (according to the burette) an apparent volume of 10.05 cc. and is found to weigh 10.01 grams, its true volume is $\frac{10.01}{0.998}$, = 10.03 cc., since the density of water at 20° C. is 0.998 (see Appendix). The error is 0.02 cc. That is, 0.02 cc. must be subtracted from a burette reading at or near the 10 cc. mark in order to obtain the true volume.

From the average values obtained calculate the correction for each 10 cc. increment (Note 3). Next tabulate the *total correction* at the 10, 20, 30, 40, and 50 cc. marks. Thus, if the correction for the increment between 0 and 10 is − .02 and between 10 and 20 is − .01, the total correction to be applied at the 20 cc. mark is − .03.

A convenient method of tabulating results is given in the Appendix.

Plot the total corrections against the corresponding cubic centimeters so that when the burette is filled to near the zero mark and its contents used in any titration the correction at any point on the burette can be estimated and applied. Total corrections may also be written on the burette with a diamond or with hydrofluoric acid for permanence of record.

Burettes may also be calibrated by drawing off the liquid in successive portions through a 5 cc. pipette which has been accurately calibrated, as a substitute for weighing. If many burettes are to be tested, this is a more rapid method.

Notes. — 1. A small quantity of liquid at first adheres to the side of even a clean burette. This slowly unites with the main body of liquid, but requires an appreciable time. Three minutes is a sufficient interval, but not too long, and should be adopted in every instance throughout the whole volumetric practice before final readings are recorded.

2. A comparatively rough balance, capable of weighing to centigrams, is sufficiently accurate for use in calibrations, for a moment's reflection will show that it would be useless to weigh the water with an accuracy greater than that of the readings taken on the burette. The latter cannot exceed 0.01 cc. in accuracy, which corresponds to 0.01 gram.

The student should clearly understand that *all other weighings*, except those for calibration, should be made accurately to 0.0001 gram, unless special directions are given to the contrary.

3. Should the error discovered in any interval of 10 cc. on the burette exceed 0.10 cc., it is advisable to weigh small portions (even 1 cc.) to locate the position of the variation of bore in the tube rather than to distribute the correction uniformly over the corresponding 10 cc.

PIPETTES AND MEASURING FLASKS

A pipette usually consists of a narrow tube in the middle of which is a bulb with a capacity a little less than that indicated on the pipette. A line etched on the tube above the bulb denotes the level of the liquid when the pipette contains the specified volume.

In using a pipette first be sure it is clean and dry and that droplets of solution will not adhere to the inside of the glass. Draw the solution into it by sucking at the upper end until the liquid is well above the graduation mark. Quickly place the forefinger over the top of the tube in order to hold the liquid in the pipette. Hold the pipette in a vertical position over a spare beaker and cautiously admit a little air by releasing the pressure of the finger and allow the level of the liquid to fall until the lowest point of the meniscus is at the graduation mark. Remove any hanging droplet of liquid by touching the tip to the side of the beaker and allow the contents of the pipette to run into the desired container. If the pipette is marked to deliver the specified volume (*transfer pipette*), hold it constantly in a vertical position and after it has emptied, allow it to drain for thirty seconds and touch the tip of the pipette to the side of the receiving vessel at the surface of the liquid. The liquid remaining in the tip should not be blown out. If the pipette is marked to *contain* the specified volume (*measuring pipette*), wash the drained pipette out with at least three separate portions of distilled water.

Measuring flasks are usually marked for content and not for delivery. Occasionally the stem of the flask bears two marks, the upper one for delivery and the lower one for content. Flasks used for delivery should be emptied by gradually inclining them until when the continuous stream has ceased they are nearly vertical. After half a minute in this position the mouth is brought in contact with the wet surface of the receiving vessel to remove the adhering drop.

CALIBRATION OF PIPETTES AND MEASURING FLASKS

In order to calibrate a pipette for delivery, proceed as follows: Clean the pipette with cleaning solution, rinse and dry it carefully. Draw distilled water into it and run the water down to the graduation mark, removing any droplet hanging to the tip. Run the water into a small tared or weighed flask, allow to drain in a vertical position for half a minute, and touch the tip of the pipette to the surface of the water in the flask. Weigh the flask and water and, as in the case of the calibration of a burette, from the weight of the water and its density, calculate the necessary correction.

In order to calibrate a flask for *contents*, proceed as follows: Clean and dry the flask outside and inside. Weigh, and then fill with water to the graduation mark. With a piece of filter paper remove any adhering droplets above the mark and weigh again. Calculate the necessary correction as in the case of the pipette or burette.

For more details and directions for calibrating and marking glass measuring apparatus and for correcting for expansion of glass and buoyancy of air which become important factors for larger volumes, the student should consult larger treatises on Quantitative Analysis such as that of Treadwell-Hall.

GENERAL DIRECTIONS FOR VOLUMETRIC ANALYSIS

It cannot be too strongly emphasized that for the success of analyses uniformity of practice must prevail throughout all volumetric work with respect to those factors which can influence the accuracy of the measurement of liquids. For example, whatever conditions are imposed during the calibration of a burette, pipette, or flask (notably the time allowed for draining), must also prevail whenever the flask or burette is used.

The student should also be constantly watchful to insure parallel conditions during both standardization and analysis with respect to the final volume of liquid in which a titration takes place. The value of a standard solution is only accurate under the conditions which prevailed when it was standardized. It is plain that the standard solutions must be scrupulously protected from concentration or dilution, after their value has been established. Accordingly, great care must be taken to rinse out thoroughly all burettes, flasks, etc., with the solutions which they are to contain, in order to remove all traces of water or other liquid which could act as a diluent. It is best to wash out a burette at least three times with small portions of a solution, allowing each to run out through the tip before assuming that the burette is in a condition to be filled and used. It is, of course, possible to dry measuring instruments in a hot closet, but this is tedious and usually unnecessary.

To the same end, all solutions should be kept stoppered and away from direct sunlight or heat. The bottles should be shaken before use to collect any liquid which may have distilled from the solution and condensed on the sides.

The student is again reminded that variations in temperature of volumetric solutions must be carefully noted, and care should always be taken that no source of heat is sufficiently near the solutions to raise the temperature during use.

Much time may be saved by estimating the approximate volume of a standard solution which will be required for a titration (if the data are obtainable) before beginning the operation. It is then usually possible to run in rapidly approximately the required amount, after which it is only necessary to determine the end-point by continuing the titration slowly and carefully with a few drops of titrating solution. In such cases, however, the knowledge of the approximate amount to be required should never be allowed to influence the judgment regarding the actual end-point.

STANDARD SOLUTIONS

The strength or value of a solution for a specific reaction is determined by a procedure called *standardization*, in which the solution is brought into reaction with a definite weight of a substance of known purity. For example, a definite weight of pure sodium carbonate may be dissolved in water, and the volume of a solution of hydrochloric acid to neutralize the carbonate accurately determined. From these data the strength or concentration of the acid can be calculated. It is then a *standard solution*.

NORMAL SOLUTIONS

Standard solutions may be made of a purely empirical strength dictated solely by convenience of manipulation, or the concentration may be chosen with reference to a system which is applicable to all solutions, and based upon chemical equivalents. Such solutions are called *normal solutions* and contain such an amount of the reacting substance per liter as is equivalent in its chemical action to 1.008 grams of hydrogen, or 8.000 grams of oxygen. Solutions containing one half, one tenth, or one one-hundredth of this quantity per liter are called, respectively, half-normal, tenth-normal, or hundredth-normal solutions.

Since normal solutions of various reagents are all referred to a common standard, they have an advantage not possessed by empirical solutions, namely, that they are exactly equivalent to each other. Thus, a liter of a normal solution of an acid will exactly neutralize a liter of a normal alkali solution, and a liter of a normal oxidizing solution will exactly react with a liter of a normal reducing solution, and so on.

Besides the advantage of uniformity, the use of normal solutions simplifies the calculations of the results of analyses. This is particularly true if, in connection with the normal solution, the weight of substance for analysis is chosen with reference to the atomic or molecular weight of the constituent to be determined.

The preparation of an *exactly* normal, half-normal, or tenth-normal solution requires considerable time and care. It is usually carried out only when a large number of analyses are to be made, or when the analyst has some other specific purpose in view. It is, however, a comparatively easy matter to prepare standard solutions which differ but slightly from the normal or half-normal solution, and these have the advantage of practical equality; that is, two approximately half-normal solutions are more convenient to work with than two which are widely different in strength. It is, however, true that some of the advantage which pertains to the use of normal solutions as regards simplicity of calculations is lost when using these approximate solutions.

The application of these general statements will be made clear in connection with the use of normal solutions in the various types of volumetric processes which follow.

PROPER RETENTION OF SIGNIFICANT FIGURES

In any quantitative analysis certain numerical data are obtained and from them numerical results are calculated. The retention of the proper number of significant figures in the data and in the results obtained is a matter of considerable importance, for the number of significant figures used in expressing a given value should give at least an approximate indication of its precision. A numerical result expressed by fewer or more significant figures than are warranted by the various factors involved may give an impression nearly as erroneous as would be given by a result which is entirely inaccurate. The following rules and explanations are from Hamilton and Simpson's *Calculations of Quantitative Chemical Analysis*.

A *number* is an expression of quantity.

A *figure*, or *digit*, is any one of the characters: 0, 1, 2, 3, 4, 5, 6, 7, 8, 9, which, alone or in combination, serve to express numbers.

A *significant figure* is a digit which denotes the amount of the quantity in the place in which it stands. In the case of the number 243, the figures signify that there are two hundreds, four tens, and three units, and are therefore all significant. The character, 0, is used in two ways. It may be used as a significant figure, or it may be used merely to locate the decimal point. It is a significant figure when it indicates that the quantity in the place in which it stands is known to be nearer zero than to any other value. Thus, the weight of a crucible may be found to be 10.603 grams, in which case all five figures, including the zeros, are significant. If the weight in grams of the crucible were found to be 10.610, meaning that the weight as measured was nearer 10.610 than 10.609 or 10.611, both zeros would be significant.

By analysis, the weight of the ash of a quantitative filter-paper is found to be 0.00003 gram. Here, none of the zeros are significant, but merely serve to show that the figure 3 belongs in the fifth place to the right of the decimal point. Any other characters except digits would serve the purpose as well. The same is true of the value 356,000 inches, when signifying the distance between two given points as measured by instruments which are accurate to three figures only. The zeros are not significant.

Rule I. — Retain as many significant figures in a result and in data in general as will give only one uncertain figure. (For very accurate work involving lengthy computations, two uncertain figures may sometimes be retained.) Thus, the value 25.34, representing the reading of an ordinary burette, contains the proper number of significant figures, for the digit 4 is obtained by estimating an ungraduated scale division, and is doubtless uncertain. Another observer would perhaps give a slightly different value for the burette reading, — for example, 25.33 or 25.35. All four figures should be retained.

Rule II. — In rejecting superfluous and inaccurate figures, increase by 1 the last figure retained if the following rejected figure is 5 or over. Thus, in rejecting the last figure of the number 16.279, the new value becomes 16.28.

Rule III. — In adding or subtracting a number of quantities, extend the significant figures in each term and in the sum or difference only to the point corresponding to that uncertain figure occurring farthest to the left relative to the decimal point.

For example, the sum of the following three terms: 0.0121, 25.64, and 1.05782, assuming the last figure in each to be uncertain, is

```
  0.01
 25.64
  1.06
 ─────
 26.71
```

Here it is seen that the second term has its first uncertain figure (the 4) in the hundredths place, the following figures being unknown. Hence it is useless to extend the digits of the other terms beyond the hundredths place even though they are given to the ten thousandths place in the first term and to the hundred thousandths place in the third term. The third digit of the third term is increased by 1 in conformity with Rule II above. The fallacy of giving more than four significant figures in the sum may be shown by substituting x for each unknown figure. Thus,

$$0.0121x$$
$$25.64xxx$$
$$\underline{1.05782}$$
$$26.71xxx$$

Rule IV. — In multiplication or division, the percentage precision of the product or quotient cannot be greater than the percentage precision of the least precise factor entering into the computation. Hence, in computations involving multiplication or division, or both, retain as many significant figures in each factor and in the numerical result as are contained in the factor having the largest percentage deviation. In most cases, as many significant figures may be retained in each factor and in the result as are contained in the factor having the least number of significant figures.

For example, the product of the three terms: 0.0121, 25.64, and 1.05782, assuming the last figure in each to be uncertain, is

$$0.0121 \times 25.6 \times 1.06 = 0.328,$$

for if the first term is assumed to have a possible variation of one in the last place, it has an actual deviation of one unit in every 121 units, and its percentage deviation would be $\frac{1}{121} \times 100$, = 0.8. Similarly, the possible percentage deviation of the second term would be $\frac{1}{2,564} \times 100$, = 0.04, and that of the third term would be $\frac{1}{105,782} \times 100$, = 0.0009. The first term, having the largest percentage deviation, therefore governs the number of significant figures which may be properly retained in the product, for the product cannot have a precision greater than 0.8 per cent. That is, the product may vary by 0.8 parts in every hundred or by nearly three parts in every 328. The last figure in the product as expressed with three significant figures above is therefore doubtful and the proper number of significant figures has been retained.

Rule V. — Computations involving a precision not greater than one fourth of one per cent should be made with a 10-inch slide rule. For greater precision, logarithm tables should be used. If the old style method of multiplication or division must be resorted to, reject all superfluous figures at each stage of the operation.

Rule VI. — In carrying out the operations of multiplication or division by the use of logarithms, retain as many figures in the mantissa of the logarithm of each factor as are properly contained in the factors themselves under Rule IV. Thus, in solving the example given under Rule IV, the logarithms of the factors are expressed as follows:

$$\begin{array}{ll} \log 0.0121 = 8.083 - 10 \\ \log 25.64 = 1.409 \\ \log 1.05782 = \underline{0.024} \\ 9.516 - 10 = \log 0.328 \end{array}$$

In answering problems in this book, it may be assumed that the given data conform to Rule I, above. In problems involving such statements as "a 2-gram sample," or "15 cc. of titrating reagent," the precision obtainable with an ordinary chemical balance, burette, or other measuring apparatus is understood. Under such conditions, these values would be 2.0000 grams and 15.00 cc. respectively, with the last figure uncertain in each case. Similarly, it may be assumed that the normality of a "tenth-normal solution" is known to a precision at least as great as that of the other factors involved.

It should be remembered that the atomic weights of the elements are known only to a limited number of significant figures. The values ordinarily given in atomic weight tables conform to Rule I, above; that is, the last figure in each is usually doubtful. It follows that the same attention must be paid to the reliability of the atomic and molecular weights in computations as to that of any other data.

I. NEUTRALIZATION METHODS

ALKALIMETRY AND ACIDIMETRY

GENERAL DISCUSSION

Standard Acid Solutions are usually prepared from either hydrochloric, sulphuric, or oxalic acids. Hydrochloric acid has the advantage of forming soluble compounds with the alkaline earths, but its solutions cannot be boiled without danger of loss of strength; sulphuric acid solutions may be boiled without loss, but the acid forms insoluble sulphates with three of the alkaline earths; oxalic acid can be accurately weighed for the preparation of solutions, and its solutions may be boiled without loss, but it forms insoluble oxalates with three of the alkaline earths and cannot be used with certain of the indicators.

Standard Alkali Solutions are usually prepared from sodium or potassium hydroxide, sodium carbonate, barium hydroxide, or ammonia. Of sodium and potassium hydroxide, it may be said that they can be used with all indicators, and their solutions may be boiled, but they absorb carbon dioxide readily and attack the glass of bottles, thereby losing strength; sodium carbonate may be weighed directly if its purity is assured, but the presence of carbonic acid from the carbonate is a disadvantage with many indicators; barium hydroxide solutions may be prepared which are entirely free from carbon dioxide, and such solutions immediately show by precipitation any contamination from absorption, but the hydroxide is not freely soluble in water; ammonia does not absorb carbon dioxide as readily as the caustic alkalies, but its solutions cannot be boiled nor can they be used with all indicators. The choice of a solution must depend upon the nature of the work in hand.

INDICATORS

It has already been pointed out that the purpose of an indicator is to mark (usually by a change of color) the point at which just enough of the titrating solution has been added to complete the chemical change which it is intended to bring about. In the neutralization processes which are employed in the measurement of alkalies (*alkalimetry*) or acids (*acidimetry*) the end-point of the reaction should, in the case of strong acids and bases, be that of complete neutrality. Expressed in terms of ionic reactions, it should be the point at which the H^+ ions from an acid unite with a corresponding number of OH^- ions from a base to form water molecules:

$$H^+ + OH^- \rightarrow H_2O.$$

It is not usually possible to realize this condition of exact neutrality, but it is possible to approach it with sufficient exactness for analytical purposes, since substances are known which, in solution, undergo a sharp change of color as soon as even a minute excess of H^+ or OH^- ions are present. Some, as will be seen, react sharply in the presence of H^+ ions, and others with OH^- ions. These substances employed as indicators are usually organic compounds of complex structure and are closely allied to the dyestuffs in character. There are a great many such substances, but only a few are used in analytical work.

The indicators in most common use for acid and alkali titrations are methyl orange, litmus, and phenolphthalein. Of these, methyl orange, as we shall see, is most sensitive to weak bases and is used in titrating such substances as ammonium hydroxide and sodium carbonate. Phenolphthalein is most sensitive to weak acids and is used in the titration of such substances as oxalic acid and acetic acid.

The indicators are usually in themselves either weak acids (*e.g.* phenolphthalein) or weak bases (*e.g.* methyl orange) and the change in color which they undergo can be attributed to the fact that the arrangement of the atoms in their molecules is somewhat different from the arrangement of the atoms in the molecules of their corresponding salts. With a given concentration of indicator, the color change takes place at a point where the hydrogen-ion and the hydroxide-ion concentration in the solution have attained a definite value which is characteristic of the indicator in question. Thus, a solution containing about 0.001 per cent of phenolphthalein turns from colorless to pink when the hydroxide-ion concentration has attained the value of about 1×10^{-5} moles per liter, and the corresponding hydrogen-ion concentration has therefore been reduced to about 1×10^{-9} moles per liter (since in any solution at ordinary temperatures $(H^+)(OH^-) =$ approx. 1×10^{-14}). A table in the Appendix gives the approximate hydrogen-ion and hydroxide-ion concentrations at which dilute solutions of the common indicators change color. From these data it will be seen that of the indicators given, phenolphthalein is the most sensitive to acids, and methyl orange and congo red are the most sensitive to bases.

Since in pure water at room temperature the concentration of the hydrogen ions and the concentration of the hydroxide ions are each approximately 1×10^{-7} moles per liter; and since litmus is of an intermediate color at approximately this concentration, it might be concluded that litmus should be an ideal indicator for all titrations in acidimetry. It should be remembered that except in the titration of strong acids against strong bases forming unhydrolyzed salts, the exact completion of a neutralization titration is rarely in a strictly neutral solution. That is, when acid and alkali have been added in equivalent quantities, the resulting solution is frequently slightly acidic or slightly basic. Thus, when acetic acid is titrated with sodium hydroxide solution, sodium acetate and water are the products of the reaction:

$$HC_2H_3O_2 + NaOH \rightarrow NaC_2H_3O_2 + H_2O.$$

Sodium acetate, however, is somewhat hydrolyzed by water and tends to form a small amount of relatively un-ionized acetic acid, leaving an excess of hydroxide ions in the solution:

$$NaC_2H_3O_2 + H_2O \rightarrow Na^+ + OH^- + HC_2H_3O_2.$$

In other words, the reaction is appreciably reversible, and when the acid and base have been added in equivalent amounts, the solution is slightly alkaline and the titration therefore requires an indicator which changes on the slightly alkaline side of the neutral point. Such an indicator is phenolphthalein (which changes at the point where the hydrogen-ion concentration is about 10^{-9}).

Similarly, the titration of a weak base with an acid like hydrochloric acid gives a salt which by hydrolysis is slightly acidic. That is, when the hydrochloric acid has been added in an amount equivalent to the base titrated, the solution is slightly acidic, and for such a titration an indicator is required which will change color on the slightly acid side of exact neutrality. Such an indicator is methyl orange (which changes when the hydrogen-ion concentration is about 10^{-4}).

In general, other conditions being equal, the correct indicator for a given titration is one of which the color change takes place when the solution has that hydrogen-ion or hydroxide-ion concentration which exists in a solution obtained by dissolving in the same volume of water the salt formed by the neutralization. With strong acids against strong bases the sensitiveness of the indicator is of little importance since the salt formed is not hydrolyzed and a great change in the hydrogen-ion concentration of the solution is brought about by a very slight excess of titrating agent.

From suitable ionization constants it is possible to calculate the exact hydrogen-ion and hydroxide-ion concentration of a solution formed by adding exactly equivalent quantities of a given acid and a given base and hence to determine mathematically which indicator is theoretically best suited for a given titration. Such a procedure is seldom necessary for ordinary analytical work, and except in comparitively rare cases only the following rule need be applied: For the titration of a weak acid with a strong base use phenolphthalein as an indicator; for the titration of a weak base with a strong acid use methyl orange (or methyl red) as an indicator; for the titration of a strong acid with a strong base or the titration of a strong base with a strong acid use either phenolphthalein or methyl orange (or methyl red) as an indicator. The eye is not as sensitive to the changes in color afforded by litmus as it is to many other indicators, and so that common indicator is seldom used in accurate volumetric titrations.

PREPARATION OF STANDARD SOLUTIONS

Hydrochloric Acid and Sodium Hydroxide. Approximate Strength, 0.5 N

Procedure. — Measure out 40 cc. of concentrated, pure hydrochloric acid into a clean liter bottle, and dilute with distilled water to an approximate volume of 1000 cc. Shake the solution vigorously for a full minute to insure uniformity. Be sure that the bottle is not too full to permit of a thorough mixing, since lack of care at this point will be the cause of much wasted time (Note 1).

Weigh out, upon a rough balance, 23 grams of sodium hydroxide (Note 2). Dissolve the hydroxide in water in a beaker. Pour the solution into a liter bottle and dilute, as above, to approximately 1000 cc. This bottle should preferably have a rubber stopper, as the hydroxide solution attacks the glass of the ground joint of a glass stopper, and may cement the stopper to the bottle. Shake the solution as described above.

Notes. — 1. The original solutions are prepared of a strength greater than 0.5 N, as they are more readily diluted than strengthened if later adjustment is desired.

Too much care cannot be taken to insure perfect uniformity of solutions before standardization, and thoroughness in this respect will, as stated, often avoid much waste of time. A solution once thoroughly mixed remains uniform.

2. Commercial sodium hydroxide is usually impure and always contains more or less carbonate; an allowance is therefore made for this impurity by placing the weight taken at 23 grams per liter. If the hydroxide is known to be pure, a lesser amount (say 21 grams) will suffice.

COMPARISON OF ACID AND ALKALI SOLUTIONS

Procedure. — Rinse a previously calibrated burette at least three times with the hydrochloric acid solution, using 10 cc. each time, and allowing the liquid to run out through the tip to displace all water and air from that part of the burette. Then fill the burette with the acid solution. Carry out the same procedure with a second burette, using the sodium hydroxide solution.

The acid solution may be placed in a plain or in a glass-stoppered burette as may be more convenient, but the alkaline solution should never be allowed to remain long in a glass-stoppered burette, as it tends to cement the stopper to the burette, rendering it useless. It is preferable to use a plain burette for this solution. If alkali is used in a glass-stoppered burette, the burette, the stop-cock, and the stop-cock cavity should be thoroughly washed out at the conclusion of the laboratory period.

When the burettes are ready for use and all air bubbles displaced from the tip, note the exact position of the liquid in each, and record the readings in the notebook. Arrange the data essentially as shown in the Appendix. Run out from the burette into a small beaker (or flask) about 40 cc. of the acid and add two drops of a solution of methyl orange; dilute the acid to about 80 cc. and run out alkali solution from the other burette, stirring constantly with a stirring rod, until the pink has given place to yellow. If a flask is used, do not use a stirring rod but gently rotate the flask during the titration. Wash down the sides of the beaker or flask with a little distilled water if the solution has spattered upon them, return the beaker to the acid burette, and add acid to restore the pink; continue these alternations until the point is accurately fixed, at which a single small drop of either solution serves to produce a distinct change of color. Select as the final end-point the appearance of the faintest pink tinge which can be recognized, or the disappearance of this tinge, leaving a pure yellow; but always titrate to the same point (Note 1). If the titration has occupied more than the three minutes required for draining the sides of the burette, the final reading may be taken immediately and recorded in the notebook.

Refill the burettes and repeat the titration. From the records of calibration already obtained, correct the burette readings and make corrections for temperature, if necessary. Obtain the ratio of the sodium hydroxide solution to that of hydrochloric acid by dividing the number of cubic centimeters of acid used by the number of cubic centimeters of alkali required for neutralization. The check results of the two titrations should not vary by more than two parts in one thousand (Note 2). If the variation in results is greater than this, refill the burettes and repeat the titration until satisfactory values are obtained. Use a new page in the notebook for each titration. Inaccurate values should not be erased or discarded. They should be retained and marked " correct " or " incorrect," as indicated by the final outcome of the titrations. This custom should be rigidly followed in all analytical work.

Notes. — 1. The end-point should be chosen exactly at the point of change; any darker tint is unsatisfactory, since it is impossible to carry shades of color in the memory and to duplicate them from day to day.

2. While variation of two parts in one thousand in the values obtained by an inexperienced analyst is not excessive, the idea must be carefully avoided that this is a standard for accurate work to be *generally applied*. In many cases, after experience is gained, the allowable error is less than this proportion. In a few cases a larger variation is permissible, but these are rare and can only be recognized by an experienced analyst. It is essential that the beginner should acquire at least the degree of accuracy indicated if he is to become a successful analyst.

The student should appreciate the distinction between the terms *two parts per thousand* and *two parts in the thousandths decimal place*. The values 0.5010 and 0.5020 differ by about two parts per thousand (*i.e.* by 10 parts in about five thousand), but they differ by one in the thousandths decimal place.

STOICHIOMETRY

In analytical chemistry it is customary to express concentrations of solutions in terms of the *normal solution*. A normal solution is one that contains one equivalent weight expressed in grams (one gram-equivalent weight) of dissolved substance per liter of solution, or one gram-milliequivalent weight per cubic centimeter. A gram-equivalent weight of a substance acting as an acid is that number of grams of the substance which in a neutralization process furnishes one gram-atom (1.008 grams) of replaceable hydrogen. For example, 36.46 grams is the gram-equivalent weight of HCl, since this amount of the acid furnishes in a neutralization process one gram-atom of hydrogen. A normal solution of hydrochloric acid therefore contains 36.46 grams of HCl in a liter of solution, or 0.03646 gram (one gram-milliequivalent weight) per cubic centimeter. The gram-molecular weight of H_2SO_4 is 98.08 grams. The gram-equivalent weight is one half of this value, or 49.04 grams, since this amount furnishes one gram-atom of replaceable hydrogen in a neutralization process. A normal solution contains 49.04 grams of H_2SO_4 per liter of solution.

A normal alkali solution also contains one gram-equivalent weight per liter of solution, or one gram-milliequivalent weight per cubic centimeter. In this case, a gram-equivalent weight is that weight in grams of substance which will neutralize one gram-atom (1.008 grams) of hydrogen in an acid. This quantity is represented by the molecular weight in gram (40.01 grams) of sodium hydroxide (NaOH), but by one half of the gram-molecular weight of barium hydroxide ($Ba(OH)_2$) or of sodium carbonate (Na_2CO_3). A normal solution of sodium hydroxide contains 40.01 grams of the solid NaOH per liter; a normal solution of barium hydroxide contains $\dfrac{Ba(OH)_2}{2}$, = 85.69 grams of the solid $Ba(OH)_2$ per liter; a normal solution of sodium carbonate contains $\dfrac{Na_2CO_3}{2}$, = 53.00 grams of Na_2CO_3 per liter.

Since a normal solution contains one milliequivalent weight in grams of substance per cubic centimeter of solution, it follows that the number of gram-milliequivalents of substance present in a given volume of solution is represented by the product obtained by multiplying the number of cubic centimeters of solution by the normality:

$$cc \times N = \textit{number of gram-milliequivalents.}$$

One milliequivalent of any acid will neutralize one milliequivalent of any base; or more generally, when any acid (A) exactly

ALKALIMETRY AND ACIDIMETRY

neutralizes any base (B), the number of gram-milliequivalents of the two substances involved must be equal:

$$cc_A \times N_A = cc_B \times N_B.$$

Example I. — How many cubic centimeters of 0.2000 normal (also expressed by 0.2000 N, or N/5, or $\frac{1}{5}$ N) hydrochloric acid, and how many cubic centimeters of 0.2000 N sulphuric acid can be neutralized by 20.00 cc. of 0.1500 N sodium hydroxide?

Solution. — Let x = cc. of acid neutralized.
Number of gm.-milliequivalents of acid = $x \times 0.2000$
Number of gm.-milliequivalents of base neutralized = 20.00 × 0.1500

$$x \times 0.2000 = 20.00 \times 0.1500$$
$$x = 15.00 \text{ cc. in both cases.} \quad Ans.$$

It is occasionally desirable to determine the exact volume to which a solution of known normality must be diluted in order to prepare a solution of known lesser normality.

Example II. — To what volume must 1600 cc. of a 0.2050 N solution be diluted in order that the resulting solution shall be 0.2000 N?

Solution. — The number of gm.-milliequivalents present in the original solution is $1600 \times 0.2050 = 328.0$. After dilution to x cc. the same number of gm.-milliequivalents of substance must still be present.

Hence, $\qquad x \times 0.2000 = 328.0$
$$x = 1640 \text{ cc.} \quad Ans.$$

A similar type of problem is that of determining the volume of solution of known normality to be added to a solution of another known normality in order that the resulting solution shall be of given intermediate normality.

Example III. — How many cubic centimeters of 0.3200 N HCl must be added to 100 cc. of 0.1000 N H_2SO_4 in order that the resulting solution shall be 0.1200 N as an acid?

Solution. — Number of gm.-milliequivalents present in 100 cc. of 0.1000 N H_2SO_4 = 100 × 0.1000

Number of gm.-milliequivalents present after adding x cc. of 0.3200 N HCl = $(x \times 0.3200) + (100 \times 0.1000)$

The number of gm.-milliequivalents per cc. is

$$\frac{(x \times 0.3200) + (100 \times 0.1000)}{100 + x}$$

But since the resulting solution is 0.1200 N, the number of gm.-milliequivalents per cc. must be 0.1200.

$$\frac{(x \times 0.3200) + (100 \times 0.1000)}{100 + x} = 0.1200$$

$$x = 10.00 \text{ cc.} \quad Ans.$$

PROBLEMS

1. How many grams of each of the following substances constitute the gram-equivalent weight as an acid, assuming complete neutralization in each case: (a) HNO_3; (b) $KHSO_4$; (c) H_2SO_3; (d) SO_3; (e) P_2O_5; (f) $H_2C_2O_4 \cdot 2 H_2O$ (oxalic acid); (g) $HC_2H_3O_2$ (acetic acid)?

Answer: (a) 63.02 grams; (b) 136.2 grams; (c) 41.04 grams; (d) 40.03 grams; (e) 23.68 grams; (f) 63.03 grams; (g) 60.03 grams.

2. What is the milliequivalent weight of each of the following substances acting as bases? Assume complete neutralization in each case: (a) $Ca(OH)_2$; (b) BaO; (c) $KHCO_3$; (d) Na_2O; (e) Na_2O_2; (f) ZnO; (g) $CaCO_3$.

Answer: (a) 0.03704; (b) 0.07668; (c) 0.1001; (d) 0.03100; (e) 0.03900; (f) 0.0406; (g) 0.05004.

3. A given solution contains 0.1063 gram-equivalents of hydrochloric acid in 976 cc. What is its normal value?

Answer: 0.1089 N.

4. A sample of aqueous hydrochloric acid has a specific gravity of 1.12 and contains 23.81 per cent hydrochloric acid by weight. Calculate the grams and the milliequivalents of hydrochloric acid (HCl) in each cubic centimeter of the aqueous acid.

Answer: 0.2667 gram; 7.314 milliequivalents.

5. Convert 42.75 cc. of 0.5162 normal hydrochloric acid to the equivalent volume of normal hydrochloric acid.

Answer: 22.07 cc.

ALKALIMETRY AND ACIDIMETRY

6. A solution containing 25.27 cc. of 0.1065 normal hydrochloric acid is added to one containing 92.21 cc. of 0.5431 normal sulphuric acid and 50 cc. of exactly normal potassium hydroxide is added from a pipette. Is the solution acid or alkaline? How many cubic centimeters of N/10 acid or alkali must be added to neutralize the solution?

Answer: 27.6 cc. alkali (solution is acid).

7. By experiment the normal value of a sulphuric acid solution is found to be 0.5172. Of this acid 39.65 cc. are exactly equivalent to 21.74 cc. of a standard alkali solution. What is the normal value of the alkali?

Answer: 0.9432 N.

8. How many cubic centimeters of 3 N phosphoric acid must be added to 300 cc. of 0.4 N phosphoric acid in order that the resulting solution may be 0.6 N?

Answer: 25 cc.

9. How many cubic centimeters of 0.3 normal sulphuric acid will be required to neutralize (a) 30 cc. of 0.5 normal potassium hydroxide; (b) to neutralize 30 cc. of 0.5 normal barium hydroxide; (c) to neutralize 20 cc. of a solution containing 10.02 grams of potassium bicarbonate per 100 cc.?

Answer: (a) 50 cc.; (b) 50 cc.; (c) 66.73 cc.

10. Given the following data: 1 cc. of NaOH = 1.117 cc. HCl. The HCl is 0.4876 N. How much water must be added to 100 cc. of the alkali to make it exactly 0.5 N.?

Answer: 9.0 cc.

11. What is the normal value of a sulphuric acid solution which has a specific gravity of 1.839 and contains 95% H_2SO_4 by weight?

Answer: 35.61 N.

12. If 30.00 grams of potassium tetroxalate ($KHC_2O_4 \cdot H_2C_2O_4 \cdot 2 H_2O$) are dissolved and the solution diluted to exactly 1 liter, and 40 cc. are neutralized with 20 cc. of a potassium carbonate solution, what is the normal value of the carbonate solution?

Answer: 0.7084 N.

13. In preparing an alkaline solution for use in volumetric work, an analyst, because of shortage of chemicals, mixed exactly 46.32 grams of pure KOH and 27.64 grams of pure NaOH, and after dissolving in water, diluted the solution to exactly one liter. How many cubic centimeters of 1.022 N hydrochloric acid are necessary to neutralize 50 cc. of the basic solution?

Answer: 74.18 cc.

14. One gram of a mixture of 50% sodium carbonate and 50% potassium carbonate is dissolved in water, and 17.36 cc. of 1.075 N acid is added. Is the resulting solution acid or alkaline? How many cubic centimeters of 1.075 N acid or alkali will have to be added to make the solution exactly neutral?

Answer: Acid; 1.86 cc. alkali.

15. If 30.00 cc. of sulphuric acid are required to neutralize 25.00 cc. of 0.6600 N potassium hydroxide solution, to what volume must 200 cc. of the acid be diluted with water in order that the resulting solution shall be exactly half-normal? What volume of one-normal caustic soda solution should be added to a liter of the potassium hydroxide solution in order that the resulting solution shall be 0.7000 N as a base? How many cubic centimeters of the diluted acid will be neutralized by 25.10 cc. of the alkali mixture?

Answer: 220 cc.; 133.3 cc.; 35.14 cc.

16. A 500 cc. graduated flask contains 150 cc. of 0.2 N sulphuric acid. By adding more concentrated sulphuric acid the solution is brought up to the mark and after mixing is found to be exactly 0.3 N. What was the normality of the acid added? (Assume no change in volume due to chemical or heat effect.)

Answer: 0.343 N.

STANDARDIZATION OF ACID AND BASE

SELECTION OF THE STANDARD

The selection of the best substance to be used as a standard for acid solutions has been the subject of much controversy. Probably the best standard is sodium carbonate, prepared from sodium bicarbonate by heating the latter at a temperature between 270° and 300° C. The bicarbonate is easily prepared in a pure state, and at the temperatures named the decomposition takes place according to the equation

$$2\ HNaCO_3 \rightarrow Na_2CO_3 + H_2O + CO_2$$

and without loss of any carbon dioxide from the sodium carbonate, such as may occur at higher temperatures. The process is carried out as described below.

Calcium carbonate can be obtained pure and has been used as a standard for acid solutions. Its principal disadvantage is its insolubility in water.

There are a greater number of substances which can be used as standards for alkali solutions. Practically all of these are solid organic acids which are soluble in water. Purified oxalic acid ($H_2C_2O_4 \cdot 2\ H_2O$) and the acid oxalates (*e.g.* potassium acid oxalate, $KHC_2O_4 \cdot H_2O$, potassium tetroxalate, $KHC_2O_4 \cdot H_2C_2O_4 \cdot 2\ H_2O$) can be used for this purpose but have the disadvantage of possible loss of some of the water of crystallization. Benzoic acid (C_6H_5COOH) is sometimes used but is fluffy in character and hence hard to transfer from the weighing-tube without loss. Probably the best standard is potassium acid phthalate ($KHC_8H_4O_4$) which can now be obtained sufficiently pure for ordinary analytical work from all chemical supply houses and in a highly purified form from the Bureau of Standards. It is a monobasic acid (*i.e.* one hydrogen is replaceable by a metal). Since the student has determined the ratio existing between his prepared acid and base it is only necessary to standardize one of the solutions. The normality of the other solution can then be calculated from the ratio previously determined.

STANDARDIZATION OF HYDROCHLORIC ACID

Procedure. — Place in a porcelain crucible about 6 grams (roughly weighed) of the purest sodium bicarbonate obtainable. Rest the crucible upon a triangle of iron or copper wire so placed within a large crucible that there is an air space of about three eighths of an inch between them. The larger crucible may be of iron, nickel or porcelain, as may be most convenient. Insert the bulb of a thermometer reading to 350° C. in the bicarbonate, supporting it from a clamp so that the bulb does not rest on the bottom of the crucible. Heat the outside crucible, using a rather small flame, and raise the temperature of the bicarbonate fairly rapidly to 270° C. Then regulate the heat in such a way that the temperature rises *slowly* to 300° C. in the course of a half-hour. The bicarbonate should be frequently stirred with a clean, dry, glass rod, and after stirring, should be heaped up around the bulb of the thermometer in such a way as to cover it. This will require attention during most of the heating, as the temperature should not be permitted to rise above 310° C. for any length of time. At the end of the half-hour remove the thermometer and transfer the porcelain crucible, which now contains sodium carbonate, to a desiccator. When it is cold, transfer the carbonate to a stoppered weighing-tube or weighing-bottle.

Weigh out into small beakers or flasks one-gram samples of the sodium carbonate (see page 15) and record the exact weights in the notebook. Label the beakers or flasks in order to distinguish between them.

Pour over the carbonate in each beaker about 80 cc. of water, stir until solution is complete, and add two drops of methyl orange solution. Fill the burettes with the standard acid and alkali solutions, noting the initial readings of the burettes and temperature of the solutions. Run in acid from the burette, stirring and avoiding loss by effervescence, until the solution has become pink. Wash down the sides of the beaker with a *little* water from a wash-bottle, and then run in alkali from the other burette until the pink is replaced by yellow; then finish the titration as described above. Note the readings of the burettes after the proper interval, and record them in the notebook. Repeat the procedure, using the second portion of sodium carbonate. Apply the necessary calibration corrections to the volumes of the solutions used, and correct for temperature if necessary.

From the data obtained, calculate the volume of the hydrochloric acid solution which is equivalent to the volume of sodium hydroxide solution used in this titration. Subtract this volume from the volume of hydrochloric acid. The difference represents the volume of acid used to react with the sodium carbonate. From this calculate the normality of the acid, and from the known ratio of the two solutions calculate the normality of the sodium hydroxide (Note 1).

Note. — 1. It is also possible to standardize a hydrochloric acid solution by precipitating the chloride ions as silver chloride and weighing the precipitate, as prescribed under the gravimetric analysis of sodium chloride. Sulphuric acid solutions may be standardized by precipitation of the sulphate ions as barium sulphate and weighing the ignited precipitate, but the results are not above criticism on account of the difficulty in obtaining large precipitates of barium sulphate which are uncontaminated by inclosures or are not reduced on ignition.

STANDARDIZATION OF SODIUM HYDROXIDE

Procedure. — Weigh out into small beakers or flasks between 3 and 4 grams of pure potassium acid phthalate ($KHC_8H_4O_4$), accurately weighed to four significant figures (see page 15). Record the weights in the notebook and label the beakers or flasks in order to distinguish between them. Dissolve the acid salt in about 100 cc. of warm water and add two drops of phenolphthalein indicator solution. Fill the burettes with the prepared hydrochloric acid and sodium hydroxide solutions and titrate the potassium acid phthalate with the sodium hydroxide to the first appearance of a delicate pink color, rinsing down the sides of the beaker or flask at or near the end of the titration. If necessary, run back with the hydrochloric acid solution and complete the titration with the sodium hydroxide to the point where one drop of the alkali changes the color of the solution from colorless to faint pink. If hydrochloric acid has been used, calculate the *net* cubic centimeters of sodium hydroxide solution required to neutralize the potassium acid phthalate, and from this value calculate the normality of the sodium hydroxide solution. From the ratio between the two titrating solutions determined in the preceding experiment calculate also the normality of the hydrochloric acid solution.

STOICHIOMETRY

When a known weight of pure solid basic substance is completely neutralized by a solution of given acid, the number of milliequivalents of the substance neutralized is identical to the number of milliequivalents of acid required. The same is true of the neutralization of an acid substance by a solution of an alkali. Since the number of gram-milliequivalents of a given solid (x) is found by dividing its weight in grams by its milliequivalent weight (me), and since the number of gram-milliequivalents of substance in a solution (s) is the product of the number of cubic centimeters and the normality,

$$cc_s \times N_s = \frac{grams_x}{me_x}$$

or, $$cc_s \times N_s \times me_x = grams_x$$

Example I. — What is the normality of a solution of potassium hydroxide if 45.18 cc. are required to neutralize 0.3000 gram of pure oxalic acid ($H_2C_2O_4 \cdot 2\ H_2O$)?

Solution. — The milliequivalent weight of oxalic acid is $\frac{H_2C_2O_4 \cdot 2\ H_2O}{2000} = 0.06303$. The number of gram-milliequivalents of oxalic acid present is $\frac{0.3000}{0.06303}$. The number of gram-milliequivalents of potassium hydroxide solution required = $45.18 \times N$.

$$45.18 \times N = \frac{0.3000}{0.06303}$$

$$N = 0.1053. \ Ans.$$

STANDARDIZATION OF ACID AND BASE

Example II. — A 0.5000-gram sample of pure $CaCO_3$ is dissolved in water to which 50.00 cc. of HCl solution has been added. The solution then requires 6.20 cc. of NaOH solution of which 1 cc. ⇌ 1.010 cc. of the HCl. What is the normality of each of the two solutions?

Solution. — Number of gram-milliequivalents of $CaCO_3$ = $\dfrac{0.5000}{\dfrac{CaCO_3}{2000}}$; 6.20 cc. NaOH ⇌ 6.20 × 1.010 ⇌ 6.26 cc. HCl. Net cc. HCl = 50.00 − 6.26, = 43.74 cc.

$$43.74 \times N = \dfrac{0.5000}{\dfrac{CaCO_3}{2000}}$$

N = 0.2287 (normality of the HCl). *Ans.*

0.2287 × 1.010 = 0.2310 (normality of the NaOH). *Ans.*

PROBLEMS

17. In standardizing a hydrochloric acid solution it is found that 47.26 cc. of hydrochloric acid are exactly equivalent to 1.216 grams of pure sodium carbonate, using methyl orange as an indicator. What is the normal value of the hydrochloric acid?

Answer: 0.4855 N.

18. A solution of sulphuric acid is standardized against a sample of calcium carbonate which has been previously accurately analyzed and found to contain 92.44% $CaCO_3$ and no other basic material. The sample weighing 0.7423 gram was titrated by adding an excess of acid (42.42 cc.) and titrating the excess with sodium hydroxide solution (11.22 cc.). 1 cc. of acid is equivalent to 0.9976 cc. of sodium hydroxide. Calculate the normal value of each.

Answer: Acid 0.4398 N; alkali 0.4409 N.

19. It is desired to dilute a solution of sulphuric acid of which 1 cc. is equivalent to 0.1027 gram of pure sodium carbonate to make it exactly 1.250 normal. 700 cc. of the solution are available. To what volume must it be diluted?

Answer: 1084 cc.

48 VOLUMETRIC ANALYSIS

20. A sample of Rochelle Salt (KNaC₄H₄O₆·4 H₂O), after ignition in platinum to convert it to the double carbonate, is titrated with sulphuric acid, using methyl orange as an indicator. From the following data calculate the percentage purity of the sample:

$$\text{Wt. sample} = 0.9500 \text{ gram}$$
$$\text{H}_2\text{SO}_4 \text{ used} = 43.65 \text{ cc.}$$
$$\text{NaOH used} = 1.72 \text{ cc.}$$
$$1 \text{ cc. H}_2\text{SO}_4 = 1.064 \text{ cc. NaOH}$$
$$\text{Normal value NaOH} = 0.1321 \text{ N.}$$

Answer: 87.72 cc.

21. It is desired to dilute a solution of hydrochloric acid to exactly 0.05 N. The following data are given: 44.97 cc. of the hydrochloric acid are equivalent to 43.76 cc. of the NaOH solution. The NaOH is standardized against a pure potassium tetroxalate (KHC₂O₄·H₂C₂O₄·2 H₂O) weighing 0.2162 gram and requires 49.14 cc. How many cc. of water must be added to 1000 cc. of the aqueous hydrochloric acid?

Answer: 25 cc.

22. 60.00 cc. NaOH ⇔ 2.54 grams potassium tetroxalate (KHC₂O₄·H₂C₂O₄·2 H₂O); 50.00 cc. HCl ⇔ 40.00 cc. of the NaOH solution. How many cubic centimeters of 2 N HNO₃ must be added to 100 cc. of the above HCl in order to make a mixture which is one normal as an acid?

Answer: 60.0 cc.

23. Solutions of potassium hydroxide and of hydrochloric acid are prepared. The acid is of such strength that 20.00 cc. are equivalent to 0.1121 gram of CaO. 30.00 cc. KOH ⇔ 20.00 cc. HCl. What is the normality of the alkali solution and what is the value of 1 cc. of it in terms of pure benzoic acid (*i.e.* how many grams of benzoic acid will be neutralized by 1 cc. of the alkali)? Benzoic acid is a mono-basic acid with the formula C₆H₅COOH.

Answer: 0.1333 N; 0.01627 gm.

24. What is the equivalent weight of a certain organic acid if 44.00 cc. of NaOH solution (1 cc. ⇔ 1.100 cc. HCl ⇔ 0.01001 gram CaCO₃) are required to neutralize 0.5192 gram of the pure acid?

Answer: 59.00.

25. In standardizing a solution of caustic soda against 1.431 grams of pure potassium acid phthalate the analyst uses 35.50 cc. of the alkali and is obliged to run back with 5.12 cc. of acid (1 cc. ⇔ 0.003100 gram Na₂O). What is the normality of the caustic soda solution?

Answer: 0.2118 N

STANDARDIZATION OF ACID AND BASE

26. Potassium hydroxide which has been exposed to the air is found on analysis to contain 7.62% water, 2.38% K_2CO_3, and 90% KOH. What weight of residue will be obtained if one gram of this sample is added to 46 cc. of normal hydrochloric acid and the resulting solution, after exact neutralization with 1.070 N potassium hydroxide solution, is evaporated to dryness?

Answer: 3.47 grams.

27. What volume of a solution of sodium hydroxide (1 cc. $\doteq$ 0.0821 gram $KHC_2O_4 \cdot 2 H_2O$) must be added to 100 cc. of a solution of potassium hydroxide (1 cc. contains the equivalent of 0.00471 gram of K_2O) in order that the resulting solution shall be of such basic strength that 10.0 cc. will be equivalent to the nitrogen in one gram-millimole of urea $CO(NH_2)_2$ (by the Kjeldahl method whereby the urea is converted into $(NH_4)_2SO_4$ and the NH_3 subsequently evolved and titrated)?

Answer: 33.3 cc.

DETERMINATION OF THE TOTAL ALKALINE STRENGTH OF SODA ASH

Soda ash is crude sodium carbonate. If made by the ammonia process it may contain also sodium chloride, sulphate, and hydroxide; when made by the Le Blanc process it may contain sodium sulphide, silicate, and aluminate, and other impurities. Some of these, notably the hydroxide, combine with acids and contribute to the total alkaline strength, but it is customary to calculate this strength in terms of sodium carbonate; *i.e.* as though no other alkali were present.

The analysis of soda ash is chosen merely as a typical alkalimetric process and the student should bear in mind that there are many other types of commercial products which are alkaline in nature and which can be analyzed by a process essentially the same as that given below. Among these products can be included pearl ash (impure K_2CO_3), limestone ($CaCO_3$), quick lime (CaO), commercial caustic soda (NaOH), washing powder, and ammonium hydroxide solutions.

Procedure. — Weigh out accurately to four significant figures two samples of soda ash of about one gram each into beakers or flasks of about 200 cc. capacity. Dissolve the ash in 75 cc. of water, warming gently, and filter off the insoluble residue; wash the filter by filling it at least three times with distilled water, allowing it to drain, and adding the washings to the main filtrate. Cool the filtrate, add two drops of methyl orange (Note 1) and titrate for the alkali with the standard hydrochloric acid solution, using the standard alkali to complete the titration as already prescribed.

From the volumes of acid and alkali employed, corrected for burette errors and temperature changes, and the data derived from the standardization, calculate the percentage of alkali present, assuming it all to be present as sodium carbonate (Note 2). Also calculate the alkaline strength of the ash in terms of per cent Na_2O (Note 3).

Notes. — 1. The hydrochloric acid sets free carbonic acid which is unstable and breaks down into water and carbon dioxide, most of which escapes from the solution. Carbonic acid is a weak acid and, as such, does not yield a sufficient concentration of H^+ ions to cause the indicator to change to a pink.

2. A determination of the alkali present as hydroxide in soda ash may be determined by precipitating the carbonate by the addition of barium chloride, removing the barium carbonate by filtration, and titrating the alkali in the filtrate.

The caustic alkali may also be determined by first using phenolphthalein as an indicator, which will show by its change from pink to colorless the point at which the caustic alkali has been neutralized and the carbonate has been converted to bicarbonate, and then adding methyl orange and completing the titration. The amount of acid necessary to change the methyl orange to pink is a measure of one half of the carbonate present. The results of the double titration furnish the data necessary for the determination of the caustic alkali and of the carbonate in the sample.

3. It is common practice in certain analyses to express percentages in terms of the oxides of the elements. This is particularly convenient in mineral analyses where the exact combinations of the various constituents are often unknown.

DETERMINATION OF THE ACID STRENGTH OF OXALIC ACID

The analysis of oxalic acid represents a typical acidimetric process and the student should bear in mind that a great many other substances are acidic in nature and can be analyzed by a process essentially the same as that given below.

Procedure. — Weigh out to four significant figures two portions of the acid of about 1 gram each. Dissolve these in 100 cc. of warm water. Add two drops of phenolphthalein solution, and run in alkali from the burette until the solution is pink; add acid from the other burette until the pink is just destroyed, and then add 0.3 cc. (not more) in excess. Heat the solution to boiling for three minutes. If the pink returns during the boiling, discharge it with acid and again add 0.3 cc. in excess and repeat the boiling (Note 1). If the color does not then reappear, add alkali until it does, and a *drop or two* of acid in excess and boil again for one minute (Note 2). If no color reappears during this time, complete the titration in the hot solution. The end-point should be the faintest visible shade of color (or its disappearance), as the same difficulty would exist here as with methyl orange if an attempt were made to match shades of pink.

From the corrected volume of alkali, calculate the percentage of acid in the sample in terms of hydrated oxalic acid ($H_2C_2O_4 \cdot 2 H_2O$) (Note 3).

Notes. — 1. All commercial caustic soda such as that from which the standard solution was made contains some sodium carbonate. This reacts with the oxalic acid, setting free carbonic acid, which, in turn, forms sodium bicarbonate with the remaining carbonate:

$$H_2CO_3 + Na_2CO_3 \rightarrow 2\ NaHCO_3.$$

This compound does not hydrolyze sufficiently to furnish enough OH^- ions to cause phenolphthalein to remain pink; hence, the color of the indicator is discharged in cold solutions at the point at which bicarbonate is formed. If, however, the solution is heated to boiling, the bicarbonate loses carbon dioxide and water, and reverts to sodium carbonate, which causes the indicator to become pink again:

$$2\ NaHCO_3 \rightarrow Na_2CO_3 + H_2O + CO_2.$$

ACID STRENGTH OF OXALIC ACID

By adding successive portions of hydrochloric acid and boiling, the carbonate is ultimately all brought into reaction.

The student should make sure that the difference in behavior of the two indicators, methyl orange and phenolphthalein, is understood.

2. Hydrochloric acid is volatilized from aqueous solutions, except such as are very dilute. If the directions in the procedure are strictly followed, no loss of acid need be feared, but the amount added in excess should not be greater than 0.3–0.4 cc.

3. Attention has already been called to the fact that the color changes in the different indicators occur at varying concentrations of H^+ or OH^- ions. They do not indicate exact theoretical neutrality, but a particular indicator always shows its color change at a particular concentration of H^+ or OH^- ions. Strictly speaking, the results of an analysis with a given indicator are correct only if the previous standardization and ratio were made using the same indicator. In cases where both methyl orange and phenolphthalein have been used, the error involved is very small, however, and for our present purposes can be neglected.

STOICHIOMETRY

Just as the normality of a solution can be found from the volume required to react with a definite weight of substance of known purity, the percentage purity of a substance can be determined from the volume of a solution of known normality required to react with a definite weight of the substance. The product of the number of cubic centimeters of the titrating solution used (cc_s) and the normality of the solution (N_s) represents the number of gram-milliequivalents in the solution used. This is the same as the number of gram-milliequivalents of pure substance neutralized (x). If the number of gram-milliequivalents of substance is multiplied by the value in grams of one milliequivalent weight (me), the product is the number of grams of substance present in the sample. The percentage purity of the sample is then simply 100 times the weight of pure substance divided by the weight of sample taken for analysis:

$$\frac{cc_s \times N_s \times me_x}{wt.\ sample} \times 100 = \%_{ox}$$

Example I. — What is the percentage of total acid expressed as acetic acid ($HC_2H_3O_2$) in a sample of vinegar if 3.000 grams of the vinegar require 20.50 cc. of 0.1150 N KOH solution for neutralization?

Solution. — Gram-milliequivalents of KOH used = 20.50 × 0.1150 = 2.358.

Number of gram-milliequivalents of $HC_2H_3O_2$ present = 2.358.

Value of one gram-milliequivalent weight of $HC_2H_3O_2 = \dfrac{HC_2H_3O_2}{1000}$, = 0.0600 gram.

Grams of $HC_2H_3O_2$ present = 2.358 × 0.0600 = 0.1415 gram.

Percentage $HC_2H_3O_2 = \dfrac{0.1415}{3.000} \times 100 = 4.717\%$ *Ans.*

Example II. — Calculate the alkaline strength of pearl ash (impure potassium carbonate) in terms of per cent K_2O from the following data: Sample = 0.3500 gram; HCl used = 48.03 cc.; NaOH used for back titration = 2.02 cc.; 1 cc. HCl ≎ 0.005300 gram Na_2CO_3; 1 cc. NaOH ≎ 0.02192 gram $KHC_2O_4 \cdot H_2O$.

Solution. — Normality of HCl = $\dfrac{0.005300}{1 \times \dfrac{Na_2CO_3}{2000}}$, = 0.1000.

Normality of NaOH = $\dfrac{0.02192}{1 \times \dfrac{KHC_2O_4 \cdot H_2O}{1000}}$, = 0.1500

2.02 cc. NaOH ≎ 2.02 × $\dfrac{0.1500}{0.1000}$, = 3.03 cc. HCl

Net cc. HCl = 48.03 − 3.03 = 45.00 cc.
(or net gram-milliequivs. = (48.03 × 0.1000) − (2.02 × 0.1500), = 4.500)

% $K_2O = \dfrac{45.00 \times 0.1000 \times \dfrac{K_2O}{2000}}{0.3500} \times 100 = 60.56\%$ *Ans.*

ACID STRENGTH OF OXALIC ACID

Example III. — What weight of a sample of impure oxalic acid should be taken for titration by $\frac{N}{2}$ alkali so that the percentage of $H_2C_2O_4 \cdot 2H_2O$ will be twice the burette reading?

Solution. —
$$\frac{cc_s \times N_s \times \frac{H_2C_2O_4 \cdot 2H_2O}{2000}}{\text{wt. sample}} \times 100 = \%_{ox}$$

$$\frac{A \times 0.5000 \times 0.06302}{\text{wt. sample}} \times 100 = 2A$$

Wt. sample = 1.575 grams. *Ans.*

Example IV. — A sample consisting entirely of pure lithium carbonate and pure barium carbonate weighs 1.000 gram and requires 30.00 cc. of $\frac{N}{2}$ HCl for neutralization. Calculate the percentage of Li_2CO_3 in the sample.

Solution. — Let x = grams Li_2CO_3 present

Then $1.000 - x$ = grams $BaCO_3$ present

Number of gram-milliequivs. $Li_2CO_3 = \dfrac{x}{\dfrac{Li_2CO_3}{2000}}$

Number of gram-milliequivs. $BaCO_3 = \dfrac{1.000 - x}{\dfrac{BaCO_3}{2000}}$

Number of gram-milliequivs. HCl required = 30.00×0.5000.

$$\dfrac{x}{\dfrac{Li_2CO_3}{2000}} + \dfrac{1.000 - x}{\dfrac{BaCO_3}{2000}} = 30.00 \times 0.5000$$

$x = 0.2876$ gram Li_2CO_3 *Ans.*

DOUBLE INDICATOR TITRATIONS

The fact that certain indicators change color at different stages of a neutralization is sometimes made use of in volumetric work to determine the proportions of the components of certain mixtures by making use of two end-points in a single titration. For example, in the titration of sodium carbonate by acid the neutralization takes place in two stages of which the first is the formation of sodium bicarbonate:

$$Na_2CO_3 + H^+ \to NaHCO_3 + Na^+$$
$$NaHCO_3 + H^+ \to Na^+ + H_2O + CO_2.$$

It is obvious from the molar relationships of these two equations that if a certain volume of acid is required to convert a given weight of Na_2CO_3 into $NaHCO_3$, an additional equal volume of the same acid will be required to effect complete neutralization.

When sodium carbonate is titrated in the cold using phenolphthalein as the indicator, the solution turns colorless when the sodium carbonate has been converted only to the bicarbonate. With methyl orange as the indicator, however, the color of the solution does not change until the complete neutralization has taken place. The practical use of this is illustrated in the following two examples.

Example V. — A 1.200-gram sample of a mixture of NaOH and Na_2CO_3 with inert impurity is dissolved and titrated cold with $\frac{N}{2}$ HCl. With phenolphthalein as the indicator, the solution turns colorless after the addition of 30.00 cc. of the acid. Methyl orange is then added and 5.00 cc. more of the acid are required for the color to change to pink. What is the percentage of NaOH and of Na_2CO_3 in the sample?

Solution. — If the acid is added slowly, the stronger base (NaOH) is neutralized first. After this reaction is complete the Na_2CO_3 is converted to $NaHCO_3$ at which point the phenolphthalein changes color. All this requires 30.00 cc. of the acid. Since the further neutralization of the bicarbonate formed requires 5.00 cc. of the acid, of the total 35.00 cc. used, 10.00 cc. must have reacted with the Na_2CO_3, and therefore 25.00 cc. with the NaOH.

$$\% \text{ NaOH} = \frac{25.00 \times 0.5000 \times \frac{\text{NaOH}}{1000}}{1.200} \times 100 = 41.68\%$$

Ans.

$$\% \text{ Na}_2\text{CO}_3 = \frac{10.00 \times 0.5000 \times \frac{\text{Na}_2\text{CO}_3}{2000}}{1.200} \times 100 = 22.08\% \quad Ans.$$

Example VI. — A 1.200-gram sample containing Na_2CO_3, NaHCO_3, and inert impurities is titrated cold with $\frac{N}{2}$ HCl. With phenolphthalein as the indicator the solution turns colorless after the addition of 15.00 cc. of the acid. Methyl orange is then added and 22.00 cc. more of the acid are required to change the color of this indicator. What is the percentage of Na_2CO_3 and of NaHCO_3 in the sample?

Solution. — Na_2CO_3 is first converted into NaHCO_3 requiring 15.00 cc. of the acid. Of the 22.00 cc. of additional acid added, 15.00 cc. must have been required to complete the neutralization of this NaHCO_3 formed, and 7.00 cc. to neutralize the NaHCO_3 originally present.

$$\% \text{ Na}_2\text{CO}_3 = \frac{30.00 \times 0.5000 \times \frac{\text{Na}_2\text{CO}_3}{2000}}{1.2000} \times 100 = 66.25\% \quad Ans.$$

$$\% \text{ NaHCO}_3 = \frac{7.00 \times 0.5000 \times \frac{\text{NaHCO}_3}{1000}}{1.2000} \times 100 = 24.50\% \quad Ans.$$

PROBLEMS

28. One gram of crude ammonium salt is treated with strong potassium hydroxide solution. The ammonia liberated is distilled and collected in 50 cc. of 0.5000 N acid and the excess titrated with 1.55 cc. of 0.5000 N sodium hydroxide. Calculate the percentage of NH_3 in the sample.

Answer: 41.17%.

29. In the analysis of a one-gram sample of soda ash, what must be the normality of the acid in order that the number of cubic centimeters of acid used shall represent the percentage of carbon dioxide present?

Answer: 0.4544 N.

30. What weight of pearl ash must be taken for analysis in order that the number of cubic centimeters of 0.5000 N acid used may be equal to one third the percentage of K_2CO_3?

Answer: 1.152 grams.

VOLUMETRIC ANALYSIS

31. What weight of cream of tartar must have been taken for analysis in order to have obtained 97.60% $KHC_4H_4O_6$ in an analysis involving the following data: NaOH used = 30.06 cc.; H_2SO_4 solution used = 0.50 cc.; 1 cc. $H_2SO_4 \backsimeq 0.0255$ gram $CaCO_3$; 1 cc. $H_2SO_4 \backsimeq 1.02$ cc. NaOH?
Answer: 2.846 grams.

32. Calculate the alkaline strength of an impure sample of potassium carbonate in terms of per cent potassium oxide from the following data: Weight of sample = 1.00 gram; HCl used = 55.90 cc.; NaOH used = 0.42 cc.; 1 cc. NaOH $\backsimeq$ 0.008473 gram of $KHC_2O_4 \cdot H_2C_2O_4 \cdot 2H_2O$; 2 cc. HCl $\backsimeq$ 5 cc. NaOH.
Answer: 65.68%.

33. Calculate the percentage purity of a sample of calcite ($CaCO_3$) from the following data: (Standardization) Weight of $H_2C_2O_4 \cdot 2 H_2O$ = 0.2460 gram; NaOH solution used = 41.03 cc.; HCl solution used = 0.63 cc.; 1 cc. NaOH solution = 1.190 cc. HCl solution. (Analysis) Weight of sample = 0.1200 gram; HCl used = 36.38 cc.; NaOH used = 6.20 cc.
Answer: 97.97%.

34. The same volume of carbon dioxide at the same temperature and the same pressure is liberated from a 1 gram sample of dolomite, by adding an excess of hydrochloric acid, as can be liberated by the addition of 35 cc. of 0.5 N hydrochloric acid to an excess of any pure or impure carbonate. Calculate the percentage of CO_2 in the dolomite. *Answer:* 38.5%.

35. In the analysis of a 2.000-gram sample of lime by titration with H_2SO_4, what must be the normality of the acid so that the percentage of calcium may be found by dividing the net volume of acid required by 4?
Answer: 0.2500 N.

36. Calculate the percentage of acetic acid ($HC_2H_3O_2$) in a sample of vinegar from the following data: Sample = 15.00 grams; cc. NaOH used = 43.00; cc. 0.600 N H_2SO_4 used for back titration = 2.50 cc.; 1 cc. NaOH $\backsimeq$ 0.0315 gram oxalic acid ($H_2C_2O_4 \cdot 2 H_2O$). *Answer:* 8.00%.

37. What weight of soda ash must be taken for analysis so that by using 0.5 N HCl for titrating, (*a*) the burette reading shall equal the percentage of Na_2O; (*b*) three times the burette reading shall equal the percentage of Na_2O; (*c*) every three cubic centimeters shall represent 1 per cent Na_2O; (*d*) each cubic centimeter shall represent 3 per cent Na_2O; (*e*) the burette reading and the percentage of Na_2O shall be in the respective ratio of 2 to 3?
Answer: (*a*) 1.550 grams. (*b*) 0.5167 gram. (*c*) 4.650 grams.
(*d*) 0.5167 gram. (*e*) 1.033 grams.

38. A sample of fuming sulphuric acid containing only SO_3 and H_2SO_4 weighs 1.4000 grams and requires 36.10 cc. of 0.8050 normal NaOH for neutralization. What is the percentage of each constituent in the sample?

Answer: 91.98 per cent H_2SO_4; 8.02 per cent SO_3.

39. A mixture of pure sodium carbonate and pure barium carbonate weighing 0.2000 gram requires 30.00 cc. of $\frac{N}{10}$ acid for complete neutralization. What is the percentage of each constituent in the mixture?

Answer: 55.7% Na_2CO_3; 44.3% $BaCO_3$.

40. What weight of barium carbonate must be added to one gram of lithium carbonate so that the mixture will require the same volume of standard acid for neutralization as would the same weight of pure calcium carbonate? *Answer:* 0.716 gram.

41. A mixture of pure lithium carbonate and pure strontium carbonate weighs 0.7920 gram and requires 29.73 cc. of 0.5060 N acid for neutralization. What is the percentage of Li_2O and SrO in the sample?

Answer: Li_2O = 16.3%; SrO = 41.8%.

42. The combined weight of LiOH, KOH, and $Ba(OH)_2$ in a mixture is 0.5000 gram and 25.44 cc. of $\frac{N}{2}$ acid are required for neutralization. The same amount of material with CO_2 gives a precipitate of $BaCO_3$ which when filtered is found to require 5.27 cc. of the above acid for neutralization. Calculate the weights of LiOH, KOH, and $Ba(OH)_2$ in the original sample.

Answer: LiOH = 0.2174 gram.   KOH = 0.0567 gram.
$Ba(OH)_2$ = 0.2259 gram.

43. If all of the nitrogen in a 0.600-gram sample of urea, $CO(NH_2)_2$, were converted by concentrated H_2SO_4 into ammonium salt, and with excess NaOH solution the NH_3 were liberated and absorbed in 50.00 cc. of H_2SO_4 (1 cc. ⇔ 0.01550 gram Na_2O), how much NaOH solution (1 cc. ⇔ 0.01220 gram benzoic acid, C_6H_5COOH) would be required to complete the titration?

Answer: 50.0 cc.

44. The percentage of protein in organic nitrogenous matter is found by multiplying the percentage of nitrogen by the factor 6.25. A sample of meat scrap weighing 2.000 grams is digested with concentrated H_2SO_4 and mercury until the nitrogen in the sample is converted to ammonium sulphate. By means of excess NaOH solution the ammonium salt is decomposed and the liberated ammonia is absorbed in 50.00 cc. of H_2SO_4 and the

excess acid then requires 22.14 cc. of 0.6190 N NaOH solution. A separate 50.00 cc. portion of the H$_2$SO$_4$ is neutralized by 40.23 cc. of the NaOH titrating solution. Calculate the percentage of protein in the meat scrap.

Answer: 48.99%.

45. From the following data, calculate the percentages of Na$_2$CO$_3$ and NaOH in an impure mixture. Weight of sample, 1.500 grams; HCl (0.5 N) required for phenolphthalein end-point, 28.85 cc.; HCl (0.5 N) required to complete the titration after adding methyl orange, 23.85 cc.

Answer: 6.67% NaOH; 84.28% Na$_2$CO$_3$.

46. A sample of sodium carbonate containing sodium hydroxide weighs 1.179 grams. It is titrated with 0.3000 N hydrochloric acid, using phenolphthalein in cold solution as an indicator and becomes colorless after the addition of 48.16 cc. Methyl orange is added and 24.08 cc. are needed for complete neutralization. What is the percentage of NaOH and Na$_2$CO$_3$?

Answer: 24.50% NaOH; 64.92% Na$_2$CO$_3$.

47. From the following data, calculate the percentages of Na$_2$CO$_3$ and NaHCO$_3$ in an impure mixture. Weight of sample = 1.000 gram; volume of 0.25 N hydrochloric acid required for phenolphthalein end-point = 26.40 cc.; after adding an excess of acid and boiling out the carbon dioxide, the total volume of 0.25 N hydrochloric acid required for phenolphthalein end-point = 67.10 cc.

Answer: 69.95% Na$_2$CO$_3$; 30.02% NaHCO$_3$.

48. A chemist received four different solutions, with the statement that they contained either pure NaOH; pure Na$_2$CO$_3$; pure NaHCO$_3$, or mixtures of these substances. From the following data identify them:

Sample I. On adding phenolphthalein to a solution of the substance, it gave no color to the solution.

Sample II. On titrating with standard acid, it required 15.26 cc. for a change in color, using phenolphthalein, and 17.90 cc. additional, using methyl orange as an indicator.

Sample III. The sample was titrated with hydrochloric acid until the pink of phenolphthalein disappeared, and on the addition of methyl orange the solution was colored pink.

Sample IV. On titrating with hydrochloric acid, using phenolphthalein, 15.00 cc. were required. A new sample of the same weight required exactly 30 cc. of the same acid for neutralization, using methyl orange.

Answer: (a) NaHCO$_3$; (b) NaHCO$_3$ + Na$_2$CO$_3$; (c) NaOH; (d) Na$_2$CO$_3$.

49. A one-gram sample of sodium hydroxide which has been exposed to the air for some time, is dissolved in water and diluted to exactly 500 cc. One hundred cubic centimeters of the solution, when titrated with 0.1062 N hydrochloric acid, using methyl orange as an indicator, require 38.60 cc. for complete neutralization. Barium chloride in excess is added to a second portion of 100 cc. of the solution, which is diluted to exactly 250 cc., allowed to stand and filtered. Two hundred cubic centimeters of this filtrate require 29.62 cc. of 0.1062 N hydrochloric acid for neutralization, using phenolphthalein as an indicator. Calculate percentage of NaOH and of Na_2CO_3.

Answer: 78.63% NaOH; 4.45% Na_2CO_3.

II. OXIDATION PROCESSES

GENERAL DISCUSSION

In the oxidation processes of volumetric analysis standard solutions of oxidizing agents and of reducing agents take the place of the acid and alkali solutions of the neutralization processes already studied. Just as an acid solution was the principal reagent in alkalimetry, and the alkali solution used only to make certain of the end-point, the solution of the oxidizing agent is the principal reagent for the titration of substances exerting a reducing action. It is, in general, true that oxidizable substances are determined by *direct* titration, while oxidizing substances are determined by *indirect* titration.

The important oxidizing agents employed in volumetric solutions are potassium bichromate, potassium permanganate, potassium ferricyanide, iodine, ferric chloride, and sodium hypochlorite.

The important reducing agents which are used in the form of standard solutions are ferrous sulphate (or ferrous ammonium sulphate), oxalic acid, sodium thiosulphate, stannous chloride, arsenious acid, and potassium cyanide. Other reducing agents, as sulphurous acid, hydrogen sulphide, and zinc (nascent hydrogen), may take part in the processes, but not as standard solutions.

The most important combinations among the foregoing are: potassium bichromate and ferrous salts; potassium permanganate and ferrous salts; potassium permanganate and oxalic acid; iodine and sodium thiosulphate; hypochlorites and arsenious acid.

OXIDATION AND REDUCTION EQUIVALENTS

As in acidimetry, a normal oxidizing or reducing solution is one containing one gram-equivalent weight (one equivalent weight expressed in grams) of substance per liter of solution, or one gram-milliequivalent weight per cubic centimeter. The equivalent weight is again based on the hydrogen equivalent but from a somewhat different point of view. It is assumed that the student has a clear understanding of the mechanism of determining the valence of an element in a given compound; that he understands, for example, that the valence of iron in ferrous compounds is $+2$ and in ferric compounds is $+3$, that the valence of manganese in permanganate (*e.g.* $KMnO_4$) is $+7$ and in manganous salts (*e.g.* $MnSO_4$) is $+2$. The reduction of ferric compounds to ferrous compounds can be expressed as taking place by the action of hydrogen atoms, as follows:

$$FeCl_3 + H^0 \rightarrow FeCl_2 + HCl.$$

Similarly the reduction of permanganate to manganous salt can be expressed by the hypothetical equation:

$$KMnO_4 + 5\,H^0 + 3\,HCl \rightarrow MnCl_2 + KCl + 4\,H_2O.$$

It is seen above that iron changes by one unit in valence and involves the equivalent of one hydrogen; the manganese in permanganate changes by 5 units in valence ($+7$ to $+2$) and the equivalent of 5 hydrogen atoms are involved. By writing other reductions in the same way the student can verify the fact that the number of changes in valence which a substance undergoes represent directly the number of equivalents of hydrogen atoms involved. Hence a gram-equivalent weight of an oxidizing or reducing agent is the gram-molecular weight divided by the number of changes in valence which the substance undergoes when it is involved in an oxidation or reduction reaction. It is the weight of substance which involves in reaction the oxidizing or reducing equivalent of one gram atom (1.008 grams) of hydrogen (or 8.000 grams of oxygen). As in acidimetry, a normal solution contains one gram-equivalent per liter, or one gram-milliequivalent per cubic centimeter.

A normal solution of potassium permanganate contains $\frac{KMnO_4}{5} = 31.61$ grams (= one gram-equivalent weight) of the salt per liter of solution or 0.03161 gram (one gram-milliequivalent weight) per cubic centimeter; a normal solution of ferrous sulphate contains $\frac{FeSO_4 \cdot 7\,H_2O}{1} = 278.0$ grams of $FeSO_4 \cdot 7\,H_2O$ per liter. One cubic centimeter of 1-normal $KMnO_4$ will just oxidize one cubic centimeter of 1-normal ferrous sulphate solution ($MnO_4^- + 5\,Fe^{++} + 8\,H^+ \rightarrow Mn^{++} + 5\,Fe^{+++} + 4\,H_2O$), or of any 1-normal reducing agent, since they are each equal to one gram-milliatom of hydrogen. The product of the number of cubic centimeters of solution and its normality gives the number of gram-milliequivalents of dissolved substance present, and when solution A of oxidizing normality N_A exactly oxidizes solution B of reducing normality N_B:

$$cc_A \times N_A = cc_B \times N_B \text{(cf. acidimetry)}.$$

It is important to note that the equivalent weight of an oxidizing or reducing agent depends upon the reaction in which it is involved. Thus, as seen above, the gram-equivalent weight of potassium permanganate as an oxidizing agent in any reaction in which the manganese is reduced to manganous salt is $\frac{KMnO_4}{5}$ = 31.61 grams. In acid solution the reduction of permanganate is always by 5 units of valence, but occasionally $KMnO_4$ is used in neutral or basic solution where the manganese is reduced to MnO_2. In this particular case the equivalent weight of $KMnO_4$ is $\frac{KMnO_4}{3}$, = 52.68 grams, since the valence of manganese changes by only 3 units (from $+\,7$ to $+\,4$).

It is also true that a given substance may have a certain equivalent weight when it is used as an acid or as a salt and a

OXIDATION AND REDUCTION EQUIVALENTS

different equivalent weight when it is used as an oxidizing or reducing agent. The equivalent weight of HNO_3 is $\dfrac{HNO_3}{1} = 63.00$ when used as an acid, but as an oxidizing agent in a reaction where it is reduced to NO, the equivalent weight is $\dfrac{HNO_3}{3} = 21.00$ (valence change from $+5$ to $+2$).

Example. — What is the normality as an oxidizing agent of a solution of potassium bichromate ($K_2Cr_2O_7$) containing 9.806 grams per liter and what volume of $\dfrac{N}{10}$ ferrous ammonium sulphate will 30.00 cc. of the bichromate oxidize in the presence of acid ($Cr_2O_7^= + 6\ Fe^{++} + 14\ H^+ \rightarrow Cr^{+++} + 6\ Fe^{+++} + 7\ H_2O$)? How many grams of $FeSO_4 \cdot (NH_4)_2SO_4 \cdot 6\ H_2O$ are contained in each cubic centimeter of the ferrous solution?

Solution. — A normal solution of potassium bichromate contains one gram-equivalent weight per liter $= \dfrac{K_2Cr_2O_7}{6} = 49.03$ grams (since there are two chromium atoms in the bichromate molecule, each of which changes by 3 units of valence, from $+6$ to $+3$). Normality of the given solution $= \dfrac{9.806}{49.03} = 0.2000\ N$. *Ans.*

$$30 \times 0.2000 = x \times 0.1000$$
$$x = 60.00 \text{ cc. of ferrous solution. } Ans.$$

One cubic centimeter of 1-normal ferrous ammonium sulphate contains $\dfrac{FeSO_4 \cdot (NH_4)_2SO_4 \cdot 6\ H_2O}{1000} = 0.3920$ gram of salt. One cubic centimeter of $\dfrac{N}{10}$ solution contains 0.03920 gram. *Ans.*

PROBLEMS

50. In the reactions expressed by the following equations, what fraction of the molecular weights of the initial oxidizing and reducing substances represents the equivalent weight in each case? (*a*) $2\ FeCl_3 + SO_2 + 2\ H_2O \rightarrow 2\ FeCl_2 + 2\ HCl + H_2SO_4$; (*b*) $2\ Na_2S_2O_3 + I_2 \rightarrow 2\ NaI + Na_2S_4O_6$;

(c) $Mn(NO_3)_2 + 5 BiO_2 + 13 HNO_3 \to HMnO_4 + 5 Bi(NO_3)_3 + 6 H_2O$;
(d) $2 Cr(NO_3)_3 + 3 NaBiO_3 + 4 HNO_3 \to Na_2Cr_2O_7 + 3 Bi(NO_3)_3 + NaNO_3 + 2 H_2O$; (e) $KBrO_3 + 6 KI + 3 H_2SO_4 \to 3 I_2 + KBr + 3 K_2SO_4 + 3 H_2O$; (f) $I_2 + H_2S \to 2 HI + S$; (g) $NaOCl + Na_3AsO_3 \to NaCl + Na_3AsO_4$.

Answer: (a) $1, \tfrac{1}{2}$; (b) $1, \tfrac{1}{2}$; (c) $\tfrac{1}{5}, 1$; (d) $\tfrac{1}{3}, \tfrac{1}{2}$; (e) $\tfrac{1}{6}, 1$; (f) $\tfrac{1}{2}, \tfrac{1}{2}$; (g) $\tfrac{1}{2}, \tfrac{1}{2}$.

51. In the following reactions what fraction of the molecular weights of the initial oxidizing and reducing substances represents the equivalent weight in each case? (a) $2 MnO_4^- + 10 I^- + 16 H^+ \to 5 I_2 + 2 Mn^{++} + 8 H_2O$; (b) $IO_3^- + 5 I^- + 6 H^+ \to 3 I_2 + 3 H_2O$; (c) $Cr_2O_7^- + 3 H_2S + 8 H^+ \to 2 Cr^{+++} + 3 S + 7 H_2O$; (d) $10 Cr^{+++} + 6 MnO_4^- + 11 H_2O \to 5 Cr_2O_7^- + 6 Mn^{++} + 22 H^+$; (e) $2 MnO_4^- + 5 C_2O_4^- + 16 H^+ \to 10 CO_2 + 2 Mn^{++} + 8 H_2O$; (f) $2 Mn^{++} + 5 S_2O_8^- + 8 H_2O \to 10 SO_4^- + 2 MnO_4^- + 16 H^+$.

Answer: (a) $\tfrac{1}{5}, 1$; (b) $\tfrac{1}{5}, 1$; (c) $\tfrac{1}{6}, \tfrac{1}{2}$; (d) $\tfrac{1}{3}, \tfrac{1}{5}$; (e) $\tfrac{1}{5}, \tfrac{1}{2}$; (f) $\tfrac{1}{5}, \tfrac{1}{2}$.

52. The following reactions take place in acid solution. Complete each equation by adding acid (or H^+ ion) and water wherever necessary and balance by the change of valence method. In the case of each oxidizing and reducing agent state what fraction of the molecular weight gives the equivalent weight. (a) $MnO_2 + H_2O_2 \to Mn^{++} + O_2$; (b) $Cr_2O_7^- + I^- \to I_2 + Cr^{+++}$; (c) $NO_2^- + MnO_4^- \to Mn^{++} + NO_3^-$; (d) $Cu + NO_3^- \to Cu^{++} + NO$; (e) $SO_3^- + Br_2 \to SO_4^- + Br^-$; (f) $Fe^{++} + ClO_3^- \to Fe^{+++} + Cl^-$; (g) $VO^{++} + MnO_4^- \to VO_3^- + Mn^{++}$.

53. The following reactions take place in acid solution. Complete each equation by adding acid and water wherever necessary and balance by change of valence. In the case of each oxidizing and reducing agent state what fraction of the molecular weight gives the equivalent weight. (a) $Mn(NO_3)_2 + NaBiO_3 \to HMnO_4 + Bi(NO_3)_3$; (b) $KMnO_4 + H_2O_2 + H_2SO_4 \to MnSO_4 + K_2SO_4 + O_2$; (c) $K_2CrO_4 + KI + HCl \to I_2 + CrCl_3 + KCl$; (d) $Sn + HNO_3 \to H_2SnO_3 + NO + H_2O$; (e) $K_2Cr_2O_7 + FeCl_2 + HCl \to KCl + FeCl_3 + CrCl_3$.

54. How much water must be added to 50 cc. of a solution of nitric acid which is 2 N as an acid to make the resulting solution 2 N as an oxidizing agent? Assume reduction of the HNO_3 to NO? *Answer*: 100 cc.

55. A solution contains 50 grams of $KHC_2O_4 \cdot H_2C_2O_4 \cdot 2 H_2O$ per liter. What is the normal value of the solution (a) as an acid, and (b) as a reducing agent? (Oxalate is oxidized to CO_2.)

Answer: (a) 0.5903 N; (b) 0.7872 N.

OXIDATION AND REDUCTION EQUIVALENTS

56. From the following data, calculate the ratio of the nitric acid as an oxidizing agent to the tetroxalate solution as a reducing agent: 1 cc. HNO_3 = 1.246 cc. NaOH solution; 1 cc. NaOH = 1.743 cc. $KHC_2O_4 \cdot H_2C_2O_4 \cdot 2 H_2O$ solution; Normal value NaOH = 0.1200. (Oxalate is oxidized to CO_2.) *Answer:* 4.885.

57. How many grams of KNO_2 per cubic centimeter does a solution of potassium nitrite contain if it is tenth normal as a reducing agent? How many grams of SO_2 per liter does a sulphurous acid solution contain which is 0.05860 N as a reducing agent? *Answer:* 0.004256 gram; 1.876 grams.

58. If 100 cc. of a solution contain 0.158 gram of pure $KMnO_4$ and 0.490 gram of pure $K_2Cr_2O_7$, what is its normality as an oxidizing agent? How many cubic centimeters of $\frac{N}{10}$ ferrous sulphate solution will 40.0 cc. of the oxidizing solution oxidize in acid solution? How many grams of $FeSO_4 \cdot 7 H_2O$ are in each cubic centimeter of the ferrous solution?
Answer: 0.150 N; 60.0 cc.; 0.0278 gram.

59. Which is the stronger oxidizing agent, a solution containing 0.3200 gram of $KMnO_4$ per 100 cc. or one containing 0.7200 gram of $K_2Cr_2O_7$ per 150 cc.? How many cubic centimeters of $\frac{N}{10}$ stannous salt solution will 50.00 cc. of each of the oxidizing agents react with in acid solution to form stannic salt? How many grams of tin are present in each liter of the stannous salt?
Answer: Permanganate; 50.62 cc.; 48.96 cc.; 5.935 grams.

60. What is the normality of a nitric acid solution to be used as an oxidizing agent (reduced to NO) if it contains 55.5 per cent by weight of HNO_3 and has a specific gravity of 1.350? *Answer:* 35.67 N.

61. If 10 grams of $K_4Fe(CN)_6 \cdot 3 H_2O$ are dissolved in water and the volume made up to 600 cc., what is the normality of the solution as a reducing agent? (10 $K_4Fe(CN)_6$ + 2 $KMnO_4$ + 8 $H_2SO_4 \rightarrow$ 10 $K_3Fe(CN)_6$ + 6 K_2SO_4 + 2 $MnSO_4$ + 8 H_2O). *Answer:* 0.05683 N.

62. If 100 cc. of potassium bichromate solution (10 gram $K_2Cr_2O_7$ per liter), 5 cc. of 6 N sulphuric acid, and 75 cc. of ferrous sulphate solution (80 grams $FeSO_4 \cdot 7 H_2O$ per liter) are mixed, and the resulting solution titrated with 0.2121 N $KMnO_4$, how many cubic centimeters of the $KMnO_4$ solution will be required? *Answer:* 5.70 cc.

PERMANGANATE PROCESS

Potassium permanganate is a very powerful oxidizing agent and is capable of oxidizing quantitatively such substances as ferrous iron, stannous tin, mercurous mercury, oxalic acid, nitrites, sulphites, hydrogen sulphide, etc. These substances and many others can therefore be determined by titration with a standard solution of permanganate. In such titrations in acid solution permanganate is reduced to a manganous salt which, in dilute solution, is colorless. One drop of excess permanganate colors the solution a very definite pink and the appearance of such a color is taken as the end-point. The intense coloring power of permanganate and the fact that no auxiliary indicator is needed makes potassium permanganate the most commonly used standard oxidizing solution in volumetric analysis. Its greatest disadvantage is its tendency to decompose slowly.

The reaction of potassium permanganate with ferrous salts takes place quantitatively in the cold, acid solution as follows: $5\ Fe^{++} + MnO_4^- + 8\ H^+ \rightarrow 5\ Fe^{+++} + Mn^{++} + 4\ H_2O$. The reaction of potassium permanganate with oxalate takes place quantitatively in the hot, acid solution as follows: $5\ C_2O_4^= + 2\ MnO_4^- + 16\ H^+ \rightarrow 10\ CO_2 + 2\ Mn^{++} + 8\ H_2O$. These two are the most common reactions of permanganate in quantitative analysis and are the fundamental reactions in the determinations by the permanganate process in this book.

In determinations of iron, hydrochloric acid is the most effective solvent for dissolving iron ores, but permanganate is reduced by hydrochloric acid. This action, although slow in cold, dilute solutions is much more rapid in the presence of iron salts, which appear to act as catalysts. Two general procedures are used to overcome this difficulty. One is to heat to fumes with an excess of sulphuric acid, which serves to drive off all of the hydrochloric acid by volatilization. The other procedure is to titrate in cold, dilute solution in the presence of a large excess of manganous sulphate. The presence of manganous ions causes the permanganate to oxidize the ferrous ions without acting appreciably on the hydrochloric acid. The latter method is less time consuming but the end-point is less permanent ("fugitive" end-point). The details of both procedures are given below under the determination of iron in limonite.

A standard solution of ferrous sulphate or of ferrous ammonium sulphate is commonly used for back titrations in case the permanganate end-point is overstepped. Directions for preparing the ferrous solution and for determining its ratio to permanganate are given below, but it is possible to dispense with such a solution. In titrating any reducing solution with potassium permanganate, as each drop of permanganate falls into the solution there is a local coloration which almost immediately disappears as the solution is stirred or shaken. As the end-point is approached and the reducing agent is almost completely oxidized, the time required for the local pink coloration to disappear becomes greater, and with a little experience the analyst can tell when the end-point is nearly reached. The titration is then continued very slowly to an exact end-point. An experienced analyst almost never prepares a back-titrating solution for permanganate titrations. The beginner can also dispense with such a solution if he titrates slowly and carefully. It is recommended in such cases that he titrate a few solutions of unweighed ferrous salt before proceeding with the standardizations and analyses.

PREPARATION OF STANDARD SOLUTIONS

Approximate Strength 0.1 N

As mentioned above, permanganate in acid solution is always reduced to a manganous salt and the valence of the manganese changes by five units, from $+7$ to $+2$. One fifth of the gram-molecular weight of potassium permanganate $= \dfrac{KMnO_4}{5} =$ 31.61 grams therefore constitutes one gram-equivalent weight and this amount in one liter of solution constitutes a normal solution as an oxidizing agent. Ferrous salt is oxidized in acid solution to ferric salt, involving a one-unit change in valence, from $+ 2$ to $+ 3$. The gram-molecular weight of $FeSO_4 \cdot 7 H_2O$ ($= 278.0$ grams) or of $FeSO_4 \cdot (NH_4)_2SO_4 \cdot 6 H_2O$ ($= 392.0$ grams) therefore constitutes one gram-equivalent weight of each of these two commonly used ferrous compounds, and this amount when dissolved in one liter of solution gives a one-normal solution in each case.

Procedure. — Dissolve about 3.25 grams of potassium permanganate crystals in approximately 1000 cc. of distilled water in a large beaker, or casserole. Heat slowly and when the crystals have dissolved, boil the solution for 10–15 minutes. Cover the solution with a watch-glass; allow it to stand until cool, or preferably over night. Filter the solution through a layer of asbestos. Transfer the filtrate to a liter bottle and mix thoroughly (Note 1).

To prepare a solution of ferrous salt, pulverize about 28 grams of ferrous sulphate ($FeSO_4 \cdot 7 H_2O$) or about 40 grams of ferrous ammonium sulphate ($FeSO_4 \cdot (NH_4)_2SO_4 \cdot 6 H_2O$), moisten with 30 cc. of 6 N sulphuric acid (Note 2) and dissolve in distilled water. Transfer the solution to a liter bottle, make up to about 1000 cc. and shake vigorously to insure uniformity.

Notes. — 1. Potassium permanganate solutions are not usually stable for long periods, and change more rapidly when first prepared than after standing several days. This change is probably caused by interaction with the organic matter contained in all distilled water, except that redistilled from an alkaline permanganate solution. The solutions should be protected from light and heat as far as possible, since both induce decomposition with a deposition of manganese dioxide, and it has been shown that decomposition proceeds with considerable rapidity, with the evolution of oxygen, after the dioxide has begun to form. As commercial samples of the permanganate are likely to be contaminated by the dioxide, it is advisable to boil and filter solutions through asbestos before standardization, as prescribed above. Such solutions are relatively stable.

2. Ferrous salts in aqueous solution tend to hydrolyze and precipitate out as basic salts. The presence of sulphuric acid prevents this hydrolysis.

COMPARISON OF PERMANGANATE AND FERROUS SOLUTIONS

Procedure. — Fill a glass-stoppered burette with the permanganate solution, observing the usual precautions, and fill a second burette with the ferrous sulphate solution. The permanganate solution cannot be used in burettes with rubber tips, as a reduction takes place upon contact with the rubber. The solution has so deep a color that the lower line of the meniscus cannot be detected; readings must therefore be made from the upper edge.

Run out into a beaker about 40 cc. of the ferrous solution, dilute to about 100 cc., add 10 cc. of dilute sulphuric acid, and run in the permanganate solution to a slight permanent pink. Repeat, until the ratio of the two solutions is satisfactorily established.

STANDARDIZATION OF POTASSIUM PERMANGANATE SOLUTION

Commercial potassium permanganate is rarely sufficiently pure to admit of its direct weighing as a standard. On this account, and because of the uncertainties as to the permanence of its solutions, it is advisable to standardize them against substances of known value. Those in most common use are iron wire, ferrous ammonium sulphate, sodium oxalate, oxalic acid, and some other derivatives of oxalic acid. With the exception of sodium oxalate, the salts all contain water of crystallization which may be lost on standing. They should, therefore, be freshly prepared, and with great care. At present, sodium oxalate is considered to be one of the most satisfactory standards.

Procedure. — Weigh out to four significant figures two portions of pure sodium oxalate of 0.25–0.30 gram each into beakers of about 500 cc. capacity. Add about 400 cc. of boiling water and 20 cc. of manganous sulphate solution (Note 1). When the solution of the oxalate is complete, run in the standard permanganate drop by drop from a burette, stirring constantly until an end-point is reached (Note 2). Do not allow the temperature of the solution to fall below 75° C. Make a blank test with 20 cc. of manganous sulphate solution and a volume of distilled water equal to that of the titrated solution to determine the volume of the permanganate solution required to produce a very slight pink. Deduct this volume from the amount of permanganate solution used in the titration.

From the data obtained, calculate the relation of the permanganate solution to the normal. The reaction involved is:

$$5\ Na_2C_2O_4 + 2\ KMnO_4 + 8\ H_2SO_4 \rightarrow 5\ Na_2SO_4 + K_2SO_4 \\ + 2\ MnSO_4 + 10\ CO_2 + 8\ H_2O$$

Notes. — 1. The manganous sulphate titrating solution is made by dissolving 20 grams of $MnSO_4$ in 200 cubic centimeters of water and adding 40 cc. of concentrated sulphuric acid (sp. gr. 1.84) and 40 cc. of phosphoric acid (85%). Manganous ions catalyze the oxidation of oxalate by permanganate. The phosphoric acid present in the reagent is of no effect in this titration but is essential when the reagent is used as a catalyst in the titration of ferrous salts in hydrochloric acid solution.

2. The reaction between oxalates and permanganates takes place quantitatively only in hot acid solutions.

STOICHIOMETRY

In the titration of a pure substance like sodium oxalate by potassium permanganate solution, the number of gram-milli-equivalents (as an oxidizing agent) of potassium permanganate in the solution used must be equal to the number of gram-milliequivalents (as a reducing agent) of substance oxidized. As in acidimetry,

$$cc_s \times N_s = \frac{grams_x}{me_x}$$

or,
$$cc_s \times N_s \times me_x = grams_x.$$

Example I. — What is the normality of a solution of $KMnO_4$ if 40.00 cc. will oxidize 0.3000 gram of $Na_2C_2O_4$? What is the value of 1 cc. of the permanganate in terms of $FeSO_4 \cdot 7\ H_2O$ and of Fe?

Solution. — Permanganate oxidizes oxalate to carbon dioxide (see equation above). The average electrical valence of each carbon atom in sodium oxalate is $+\ 3$; in carbon dioxide it is $+\ 4$. Each carbon changes by one unit of valence and as each molecule of $Na_2C_2O_4$, contains 2 carbon atoms, there is a total

PERMANGANATE PROCESS

change of 2 units of valence. The gram-milliequivalent weight of sodium oxalate is $\dfrac{Na_2C_2O_4}{2000} = 0.06700$ gram. The number of gram-milliequivalent weights in 0.3000 gram of sodium oxalate is $\dfrac{0.3000}{0.06700} = 4.477$. This must be the same as the number of gram-milliequivalent weights of permanganate in the 40.00 cc. of solution used. Therefore, $40.00 \times N = 4.477$.

$$N = 0.1119. \text{ Ans.}$$

The expression "the value of 1 cc. of the permanganate in terms of $FeSO_4 \cdot 7 H_2O$" means the number of grams of $FeSO_4 \cdot 7 H_2O$ capable of being oxidized by 1 cc. of the permanganate.

$$1 \times 0.1119 \times \dfrac{FeSO_4 \cdot 7 H_2O}{1000} = 0.03110 \text{ gram of } FeSO_4 \cdot 7 H_2O.$$
Ans.

When iron wire is used to standardize permanganate it is dissolved in H_2SO_4 and titrated from the ferrous to the ferric state, or through a valence change of one unit.

$$1 \times 0.1119 \times \dfrac{Fe}{1000} = 0.006246 \text{ gram of Fe. } \text{Ans.}$$

Example II. — What is the normality of a solution of $KMnO_4$ if 40.00 cc. will oxidize that weight of potassium tetroxalate, $KHC_2O_4 \cdot H_2C_2O_4 \cdot 2 H_2O$, which requires 30.00 cc. of $\dfrac{N}{2}$ NaOH solution for neutralization? How many cubic centimeters of potassium binoxalate ($KHC_2O_4 \cdot H_2O$) solution which is $\dfrac{N}{4}$ as an acid will 25.00 cc. of the above $KMnO_4$ oxidize?

Solution. — Weight of potassium tetroxalate neutralized by 30.00 cc. of $\dfrac{N}{2}$ NaOH = $30.00 \times \dfrac{1}{2} \times \dfrac{KHC_2O_4 \cdot H_2C_2O_4 \cdot 2 H_2O}{3000}$.
Weight of potassium tetroxalate oxidized by 40.00 cc. of x-normal $KMnO_4 = 40.00 \times x \times \dfrac{KHC_2O_4 \cdot H_2C_2O_4 \cdot 2 H_2O}{4000}$.

VOLUMETRIC ANALYSIS

Therefore: $30.00 \times \dfrac{1}{2} \times \dfrac{KHC_2O_4 \cdot H_2C_2O_4 \cdot 2\,H_2O}{3000} =$

$40.00 \times x \times \dfrac{KHC_2O_4 \cdot H_2C_2O_4 \cdot 2\,H_2O}{4000}$.

$$x = 0.5000 \text{ N}. \quad Ans.$$

Potassium binoxalate which is $\dfrac{N}{4}$ as an acid (one hydrogen equivalent) is $\dfrac{N}{2}$ as a reducing agent (two hydrogen equivalents).

$$25.00 \times \tfrac{1}{2} = x \times \tfrac{1}{2}$$
$$x = 25.00 \text{ cc.} \quad Ans.$$

PROBLEMS

63. Calculate the value of 1 cc. of 0.1242 N $KMnO_4$ in terms of (a) Fe; (b) Fe_2O_3; (c) $FeSO_4 \cdot 7\,H_2O$.

Answer: (a) 0.006934 gram; (b) 0.009917 gram; (c) 0.03451 gram.

64. One cubic centimeter $KHC_2O_4 \cdot H_2C_2O_4 \cdot 2\,H_2O \backsimeq 0.2000$ cc. $KMnO_4$. One cubic centimeter $KMnO_4 \backsimeq 0.1117$ gram Fe.

What is the normality of the tetroxalate solution when used as a reducing agent? *Answer:* 0.4000 N.

65. Calcium may be precipitated as $CaC_2O_4 \cdot H_2O$, the precipitate filtered, washed, and dissolved in dilute H_2SO_4. The oxalic acid formed may be titrated with potassium permanganate. If a $\dfrac{N}{10}$ solution of $KMnO_4$ is used, calculate the value of 1 cc. in terms of (a) Ca; (b) CaO; (c) $CaCO_3$.

Answer: (a) 0.002004 gram; (b) 0.002804 gram; (c) 0.005004 gram.

66. A solution of potassium permanganate is of such concentration that 20.00 cc. $\backsimeq 0.2192$ gram of $KHC_2O_4 \cdot H_2O$. What is the normality of the permanganate, what is the value of 1 cc. in terms of Fe, and how many grams of manganese are contained in each cubic centimeter of the permanganate? *Answer:* 0.1500 N; 0.008376 gram; 0.001648 gram.

67. How many grams of $KMnO_4$ are contained in a liter of potassium permanganate if a certain volume of it will oxidize a weight of potassium tetroxalate requiring one half that volume of $\dfrac{N}{5}$ potassium hydroxide solution for neutralization? *Answer:* 4.214 grams.

PERMANGANATE PROCESS

68. What is the normality of a solution of potassium permanganate if 100.26 cc. will oxidize that weight of KHC_2O_4 which requires 43.42 cc. of 0.3010 N sodium hydroxide for neutralization?

Answer: 0.2607 N.

69. What weight of iron ore containing 56.2% Fe should be taken to standardize an approximately 0.1 N oxidizing solution, if not more than 47 cc. are to be used?

Answer: 0.467 gram.

70. Given two permanganate solutions. Solution A contains 0.01507 gram of $KMnO_4$ per cubic centimeter. Solution B is of such strength that 20 cc. ≎ 0.1200 gram Fe. In what proportion must the two solutions be mixed in order that the resulting solution shall have the same oxidizing power in the presence of acid as $\frac{N}{3}$ $K_2Cr_2O_7$?

Answer: $\frac{Vol. A}{Vol. B} = 1.576.$

71. One tenth gram of iron wire, 99.78% pure, is dissolved in hydrochloric acid and the iron oxidized completely with bromine water. How many grams of $SnCl_2$ are there in a liter of solution if it requires 9.47 cc. to just reduce the iron in the above? What is the normal value of the stannous chloride solution as a reducing agent?

Answer: 17.92 grams; 0.1888 N.

DETERMINATION OF IRON IN LIMONITE

Method A

Reduction with Zinc

The procedures, as here prescribed, are applicable to iron ores in general, provided these ores contain no constituents which are reduced by zinc or stannous chloride and reoxidized by permanganates. Many iron ores contain titanium, and this element among others interferes with the determination of iron by the process described. If, however, the solutions of such ores are treated with hydrogen sulphide or sulphurous acid, instead of zinc or stannous chloride to reduce the iron, and the excess reducing agent removed by boiling, an accurate determination of the iron can be made.

Procedure. — Grind the mineral (Note 1) to a fine powder. Weigh out accurately two portions of about 0.5 gram each into small porcelain crucibles. Roast the ore at dull redness for ten minutes (Note 2), allow the crucibles to cool, and place them and their contents in casseroles containing 30 cc. of dilute hydrochloric acid (sp. gr. 1.12). Heat the covered casseroles at a temperature just below boiling until the undissolved residue is white, or until solvent action has ceased. If the residue is white or known to be free from iron, it may be neglected and need not be removed by filtration. If a dark residue containing iron remains, collect it on a filter, wash free from hydrochloric acid, and ignite the filter in a platinum crucible (Note 3). Mix the ash with five times its weight of sodium carbonate and heat to fusion; cool, and disintegrate the fused mass with boiling water in the crucible. Unite this solution and precipitate (if any) with the acid solution, taking care to avoid loss by effervescence. Add 6 cc. of concentrated sulphuric acid to each casserole, and evaporate on the steam bath until the solution is nearly colorless (Note 4). Cover the casseroles and heat over the flame of the burner, holding the casserole in the hand and rotating it slowly to hasten evaporation and prevent spattering, until the heavy white fumes of sulphuric anhydride are freely evolved (Note 5). Cool, add 100 cc. of water, and boil gently until the ferric sulphate is dissolved.

The dissolved iron must be reduced to the ferrous condition before it can be titrated with permanganate. This reduction can be accomplished with sulphurous acid or with hydrogen sulphide, afterwards boiling out the excess of the reducing agent in an inert atmosphere to prevent reoxidation of the iron. By far the most efficient and convenient reducing agent is metallic zinc, but for prompt and complete reduction it is essential that the iron solution should be brought into intimate contact with the metal. This is brought about by the use of a modified Jones reductor, as shown in Figure 1. This reductor is a standard apparatus and is used in other quantitative processes.

The tube A has an inside diameter of 18 mm. and is 300 mm. long; the small tube has an inside diameter of 6 mm. and extends 100 mm. below the stopcock. At the base of the tube A are placed some pieces of broken glass or porcelain, covered by a plug of glass wool about 8 mm. thick, and upon this is placed a thin layer of asbestos, such as is used for Gooch filters, 1 mm. thick. The tube is then filled with the amalgamated zinc (Note 6) to within 50 mm. of the top, and on the zinc is placed a plug of glass wool. If the top of the tube is not already shaped like the mouth of a thistle-tube (B), a 60 mm. funnel is fitted into the tube with a rubber stopper and the reductor is connected with a suction bottle, F. The bottle D is a safety bottle to prevent contamination of the solution by water from the pump. After preparation for use, or when left standing, the tube A should be filled with water, to prevent clogging of the zinc.

Prepare the reductor for use as follows: Connect the vacuum bottle with the suction pump and pour into the funnel at the top warm, dilute sulphuric acid, prepared by adding 5 cc. of concentrated sulphuric acid to 100 cc. of distilled water. See that the stopcock (C) is open far enough to allow the acid to run through slowly. Continue to pour in acid until 200 cc. have passed through, then close the stopcock *while a small quantity of liquid is still left in the funnel*. Discard the filtrate, and again pass through 100 cc. of the warm, dilute acid. Test this with the permanganate solution. A single drop should color it permanently; if it does not, repeat the washing, until assured that the zinc is not contaminated with appreciable quantities of reducing substances. Be sure that no air enters the reductor (Note 7).

Pour the iron solution while hot (but not boiling) through the reductor at a rate not exceeding 50 cc. per minute (Notes 8 and 9). Wash out the beaker with dilute sulphuric acid, and follow the iron solution without interruption with 175 cc. of the warm acid and finally with 75 cc. of distilled water, leaving the funnel partially filled. Remove the filter bottle and cool the solution quickly under the water tap (Note 10), avoiding unnecessary exposure to the oxygen of the air. Add 10 cc. of dilute sulphuric acid and titrate to a faint pink with the permanganate solution, adding it directly to the contents of the suction flask.

From the volume of permanganate solution used, calculate the iron content of the limonite in terms of the percentage of Fe and also in terms of the percentage of Fe_2O_3.

Notes. — 1. Limonite is selected as a representative of iron ores in general. It is a native, hydrated oxide of iron. It frequently occurs in or near peat beds and contains more or less organic matter which, if brought into solution, would be acted upon by the potassium permanganate.

2. The preliminary roasting is usually necessary because, even though the sulphuric acid would subsequently char the carbonaceous matter,

certain nitrogenous bodies are not thereby rendered insoluble in the acid, and would be oxidized by the permanganate.

3. A platinum crucible may be used for the roasting of the limonite and must be used for the fusion of the residue. When used, it must not be allowed to remain in the acid solution of ferric chloride for any length of time, since the platinum is attacked and dissolved.

4. The temperature of the steam bath is not sufficient to volatilize sulphuric acid. Solutions may, therefore, be left to evaporate overnight without danger of evaporation to dryness.

5. The hydrochloric acid, both free and combined, is displaced by the less volatile sulphuric acid at its boiling point. Ferric sulphate separates at this point, since there is no water to hold it in solution and care is required to prevent bumping. The ferric sulphate usually has a silky appearance and is easily distinguished from the flocculent silica which often remains undissolved.

6. The use of fine zinc in the reductor is not necessary and tends to clog the tube. Particles which will pass a 10-mesh sieve, but are retained by one of 20 meshes to the inch, are most satisfactory.

The zinc can be amalgamated by stirring or shaking it in a mixture of 25 cc. of normal mercuric chloride solution, 25 cc. of hydrochloric acid (sp. gr. 1.12), and 250 cc. of water for two minutes. The solution should then be poured off and the zinc thoroughly washed. It is then ready for bottling and preservation under water. A small quantity of glass wool is placed in the neck of the funnel to hold back foreign material when the reductor is in use.

7. The funnel of the reductor must never be allowed to empty. If it is left partially filled with water the reductor is ready for subsequent use after a very little washing; but a preliminary test is always necessary to safeguard against error.

If more than a small drop of permanganate solution is required to color 100 cc. of the dilute acid after the reductor is well washed, an allowance must be made for the iron in the zinc. *Great care* must be used to prevent the access of air to the reductor after it has been washed out ready for use. If air enters, hydrogen peroxide forms, which reacts with the permanganate, and the results are worthless.

8. The iron is reduced to the ferrous condition by contact with the zinc. The rate at which the iron solution passes through the zinc should not exceed that prescribed, but the rate may be increased somewhat when the wash-water is added. It is well to allow the iron solution to run nearly, but not entirely, out of the funnel before the wash-water is added. If it is necessary to interrupt the process, the complete emptying of the funnel can always be avoided by closing the stopcock.

It is also possible to reduce the iron by treatment with zinc in a flask from which air is excluded. The zinc must be present in excess of the quantity necessary to reduce the iron and is finally completely dissolved. This method is, however, less convenient and more tedious than the use of the reductor.

9. The dilute sulphuric acid for washing must be warmed ready for use before the reduction of the iron begins, and it is of the first importance that the volume of acid and of wash-water should be measured. The volume used should always be the same in the standardizations and all subsequent analyses.

10. The end-point is more permanent in cold than hot solutions, possibly because of a slight action of the permanganate upon the manganous sulphate formed during titration. If the solution turns brown, it is an evidence of insufficient acid, and more should be immediately added. The results are likely to be less accurate in this case, however, as a consequence of secondary reactions between the ferrous iron and the manganese dioxide thrown down. It is wiser to discard such solutions and repeat the process.

Method B

Reduction with Stannous Chloride

(Zimmermann-Reinhardt Procedure)

It has already been noted that potassium permanganate oxidizes hydrochloric acid slowly in cold solution but by adding a large excess of manganese sulphate and titrating the very dilute, cold solution slowly, it is possible to titrate iron with permanganate even in the presence of chlorides. Stannous chloride can therefore be used for the reduction of ferric iron previous to the oxidation with permanganate. The explanation of the part played by manganous sulphate is somewhat obscure. It is possible that an intermediate manganic compound is formed which reacts rapidly with the ferrous compounds, — thus in effect catalyzing the oxidation process.

After reducing the iron with stannous chloride the excess of the latter must be removed, since otherwise it would be acted upon by the potassium permanganate. This is accomplished by adding mercuric chloride which oxidizes the excess stannous salt and is itself reduced to mercurous chloride. The latter is insoluble and has no effect upon permanganate.

Procedure. — Grind the mineral to a fine powder. Weigh out two portions of about 0.5 gram each into small porcelain crucibles. Proceed with the solution of the ore as in Method A above, fusing the residue if necessary. To the hot hydrochloric acid solution add *from a dropper* a solution of stannous chloride until the ferric chloride has been reduced to ferrous chloride as indicated by the disappearance of the yellow color. *Do not add more than a drop or two in excess.* Cool completely and add rapidly about 30 cc. of mercuric chloride solution (Note 1). A white silky precipitate should be formed. If there is no precipitate, insufficient stannous chloride was used; if the precipitate is at all gray in color, too much stannous chloride was used and the solution should be discarded (Note 2). Allow the solution to stand for 5 minutes, dilute to about 400 cc. with cold water, add 25 cc. of manganous sulphate titrating solution (Note 3), and titrate the cold solution at once with standard potassium permanganate solution. From the standardization data and the values obtained in the above titration calculate the percentage of iron (Fe) in the limonite. Also express in terms of the percentage of Fe_2O_3.

Notes. — 1. The reactions taking place on adding stannous chloride and mercuric chloride are as follows:

$$2\ FeCl_3 + SnCl_2 \rightarrow 2\ FeCl_2 + SnCl_4$$
$$SnCl_2 + 2\ HgCl_2 \rightarrow SnCl_4 + Hg_2Cl_2.$$

The mercurous chloride, Hg_2Cl_2, is precipitated as a fine white silky precipitate.

2. If stannous chloride is in too great an excess, a secondary reaction takes place resulting in a reduction of the mercurous chloride to metallic mercury: $$SnCl_2 + Hg_2Cl_2 \rightarrow SnCl_4 + 2\ Hg.$$

The occurrence of this secondary reaction is indicated by the darkening of the precipitate; and, since potassium permanganate oxidizes this mercury slowly, solutions in which it has been precipitated are worthless for iron determinations.

3. For the preparation of manganous sulphate titrating solution see Note 1 on page 72. The phosphoric acid, by forming a relatively un-ionized ferric phosphate, serves to destroy the yellow color of

ferric chloride which is formed by the titration and which tends to obscure the end-point color.

The solution should be allowed to stand about five minutes after the addition of mercuric chloride to permit the complete deposition of mercurous chloride. It should then be titrated without delay to avoid possible reoxidation of the iron by the oxygen of the air.

STOICHIOMETRY

When a substance (x) is analyzed by oxidation with potassium permanganate the product of the number of cubic centimeters of titrating solution (s) and its normality gives the number of gram-milliequivalents of permanganate used and hence of the reducing agent present in the sample. Multiplying this by the value in grams of one milliequivalent weight of the substance oxidized gives the number of grams of that substance present. Dividing by the weight of sample and multiplying by 100 gives the percentage of the required substance:

$$\frac{cc_s \times N_s \times me_x}{wt.\ sample} \times 100 = \%_{ox}.$$

Example I. — What is the percentage of iron in terms of Fe and of Fe_2O_3 in an iron ore if 0.5000 gram of the ore after solution in acid and complete reduction of the iron requires 25.50 cc. of $KMnO_4$ (1 cc. $\backsimeq$ 0.01260 gram $H_2C_2O_4 \cdot 2\ H_2O$) for oxidation? What volume of this $KMnO_4$ would be required for a 10.0-gram sample of 3.00% (by weight) hydrogen peroxide solution (5 H_2O_2 + 2 MnO_4^- + 6 H^+ → 2 Mn^{++} + 5O_2 + 8 H_2O)?

Solution. —

$$\text{Normality of } KMnO_4 = \frac{0.01260}{1 \times \dfrac{H_2C_2O_4 \cdot 2\ H_2O}{2000}} = 0.2000\ N$$

$$\frac{25.50 \times 0.2000 \times \dfrac{Fe}{1000}}{0.5000} \times 100 = 56.96\%. \quad Ans.$$

$$\frac{25.50 \times 0.2000 \times \dfrac{Fe_2O_3}{2000}}{0.5000} \times 100 = 81.44\%. \quad Ans.$$

(each atom of iron changes in valence by one unit)

DETERMINATION OF IRON IN LIMONITE

$$\frac{x \times 0.2000 \times \frac{H_2O_2}{2000}}{10.0} \times 100 = 3.00$$

$$x = 88.2 \text{ cc.} \quad Ans.$$

In H_2O_2 one oxygen atom may be considered to have an electrical valence of -2; the other an electrical valence of zero: $H^+ - {}^-O^+ - {}^-O^- - {}^+H$.

When H_2O_2 is reduced the zero charged oxygen atom changes in valence from 0 to -2 (*i.e.* forms water); when H_2O_2 is oxidized the negatively charged oxygen atom changes in valence from -2 to 0 (*i.e.* forms oxygen gas). The milliequivalent weight of H_2O_2 as an oxidizing agent or as a reducing agent is therefore $\frac{H_2O_2}{2000}$.

Example II. — A $KMnO_4$ solution has an "iron value" of 0.005584 (*i.e.* 1 cc. will oxidize 0.005584 gram of iron from the ferrous to the ferric state). A sample of steel weighing 5.00 grams is dissolved in acid and the manganese is titrated in *neutral* solution with the above $KMnO_4$ by the Volhard method ($3 \text{ Mn}^{++} + 2 \text{ MnO}_4^- + H_2O \rightarrow 5 \text{ MnO}_2 + 4 \text{ H}^+$). If 20.0 cc. are required, what is the percentage of manganese in the steel?

Solution. — Normality of $KMnO_4 = \dfrac{0.005584}{1 \times \dfrac{Fe}{1000}} = 0.1000 \text{ N}.$

When $KMnO_4$ is used in neutral solution, however, the change in valence of the manganese is not 5 but 3 (from $+7$ in $KMnO_4$ to $+4$ in MnO_2). *In this particular case* therefore the normality of the $KMnO_4$ is $0.1000 \times \tfrac{3}{5}$. Since the titrated manganese changes in valence by 2 units (from $+2$ to $+4$) its milliequivalent weight is $\dfrac{Mn}{2000}$.

$$\frac{20.0 \times 0.1000 \times \frac{3}{5} \times \frac{Mn}{2000}}{5.00} \times 100 = 0.66\%. \quad Ans.$$

DETERMINATION OF THE OXIDIZING POWER OF PYROLUSITE

INDIRECT OXIDATION

Pyrolusite, when pure, consists of manganese dioxide. Its value as an oxidizing agent, and for the production of chlorine, depends upon the percentage of MnO_2 in the sample. This percentage is usually determined by an indirect method, in which the manganese dioxide is reduced and dissolved by an excess of ferrous sulphate or oxalic acid in the presence of sulphuric acid, and the unused excess determined by titration with standard permanganate solution.

The method for pyrolusite also applies to several other oxidizing agents, for example, to the very similar PbO_2 and to Pb_2O_3 ($= PbO_2 \cdot PbO$) and Pb_3O_4 ($= PbO_2 \cdot 2\, PbO$).

Procedure. — Grind the mineral in an agate mortar until no grit whatever can be detected under the pestle (Note 1). Weigh out accurately two portions of about 0.5 gram each into 500 cc. beakers. Calculate in each case the weight of oxalic acid ($H_2C_2O_4 \cdot 2\, H_2O$) or of sodium oxalate ($Na_2C_2O_4$) theoretically required to react with the weights of pyrolusite taken:

$$MnO_2 + C_2O_4^= + 4\, H^+ \rightarrow Mn^{++} + 2\, CO_2 + 2\, H_2O.$$

Weigh out about 0.2 gram in excess of this quantity of *pure* oxalic acid or sodium oxalate into the corresponding beakers, weighing accurately and recording the weight in the notebook. Pour into each beaker 25 cc. of water and 50 cc. of 6 N sulphuric acid, cover and warm the beaker and its contents gently until the evolution of carbon dioxide ceases (Note 3). If a residue remains which is sufficiently colored to obscure the end-reaction of the permanganate, it must be removed by filtration.

Finally, dilute the solution to 200–300 cc., heat the solution to a temperature just below boiling, add 15 cc. of a manganese sulphate solution and while hot, titrate for the excess of oxalic acid with standard permanganate solution (Note 4).

From the data obtained calculate the percentage of MnO_2 in the pyrolusite.

Notes. — 1. The success of the analysis is largely dependent upon the fineness of the powdered mineral. If properly ground, solution should be complete in fifteen minutes or less.

2. A moderate excess of oxalic acid above that required to react with the pyrolusite is necessary to promote solution; otherwise the residual quantity of oxalic acid would be so small that the last particles of the mineral would scarcely dissolve. It is also desirable that a sufficient excess of the acid should be present to react with a considerable volume of the permanganate solution during the titration, thus increasing the accuracy of the process. On the other hand, the excess of oxalic acid should not be so large as to react with more of the permanganate solution than is contained in a 50 cc. burette. If the pyrolusite under examination is known to be of high grade, say 80 per cent pure, or above, the calculation of the oxalic acid needed may be based upon an assumption that the mineral is all MnO_2. If the quality of the mineral is unknown, it is better to weigh out three portions instead of two and to add to one of these the amount of oxalic prescribed, assuming complete purity of the mineral. Then run in the permanganate solution from a pipette or burette to determine roughly the amount required. If the volume exceeds the contents of a burette, the amount of oxalic acid added to the other two portions is reduced accordingly.

3. Care should be taken that the sides of the beaker are not overheated, as oxalic acid would be decomposed by heat alone if crystallization should occur on the sides of the vessel. Strong sulphuric acid also decomposes the oxalic acid. The dilute acid should, therefore, be prepared before it is poured into the beaker.

4. Ferrous ammonium sulphate, ferrous sulphate, or iron wire may be substituted for the oxalic acid. The reaction is then the following:

$$2\ FeSO_4 + MnO_2 + 2\ H_2SO_4 \rightarrow Fe_2(SO_4)_3 + MnSO_4 + 2\ H_2O,$$
or $2\ Fe^{++} + MnO_2 + 4\ H^+ \rightarrow 2\ Fe^{+++} + Mn^{++} + 2\ H_2O.$

The excess of ferrous iron may also be determined by titration with potassium bichromate, if desired. Care is required to prevent the oxidation of the iron by the air, if ferrous salts are employed.

STOICHIOMETRY

The determination of the oxidizing power of pyrolusite in terms of manganese dioxide is an indirect process in that the manganese dioxide or its equivalent is not titrated directly. Other things being equal, the less the percentage of manganese dioxide in the sample, the greater the burette reading. The reducing agent (oxalate or ferrous salt) can be weighed out and added in crystalline form as in the directions above, or a solution of these reducing agents can be prepared and a definite volume can be added to the sample. In either case, the calculation of the percentage of manganese dioxide is best made by calculating or experimentally determining the volume of the permanganate equivalent to all of the reducing agent added and subtracting the volume of permanganate used for the excess. This difference is equal to the volume of permanganate equivalent to the manganese dioxide in the sample.

In calculating analyses of Pb_2O_3 (= $PbO_2 \cdot PbO$) and of Pb_3O_4 (= $PbO_2 \cdot 2\,PbO$) it should be noted that the milliequivalent weight of each of these substances is the molecular weight divided by 2000, even though more than one atom of lead is present in the molecule. Only one atom of lead in the molecule in each case is reduced by the reducing agent (from $+\,4$ to $+\,2$). The remaining lead is already in the divalent state.

Example I. — A sample of pyrolusite weighs 0.5000 gram. To this is added 0.8500 gram of oxalic acid and dilute sulphuric acid. After solvent action has ceased, the excess oxalic acid is titrated with 45.00 cc. of $\dfrac{N}{10}$ $KMnO_4$. Calculate the oxidizing power of the pyrolusite in terms of % MnO_2.

Solution. — Volume of $\dfrac{N}{10}$ $KMnO_4$ equivalent to 0.8500 cc.

of oxalic acid = $\dfrac{0.8500}{0.1000 \times \dfrac{H_2C_2O_4 \cdot 2\,H_2O}{2000}}$ = 135.0 cc.

Volume $KMnO_4$ used = 45.00 cc.

Net volume of $KMnO_4$ = volume equivalent to the oxalic acid which in turn is equivalent to the MnO_2 present = 135.0 − 45.00 = 90.00 cc.

THE OXIDIZING POWER OF PYROLUSITE

$$\frac{90.00 \times 0.1000 \times \dfrac{MnO_2}{2000}}{0.5000} \times 100 = 78.23\%. \quad Ans.$$

Or, number of gram-milliequivalents of oxalic acid added =
$$\frac{0.8500}{\dfrac{H_2C_2O_4 \cdot 2\,H_2O}{2000}} = 13.50.$$

Number of gram-milliequivalents of $KMnO_4$ used = 45.00 × 0.1000 = 4.500.

Net number of gram-milliequivalents = 13.50 − 4.500 = 9.000 = number of gram-milliequivalents of MnO_2 present.

$$\frac{9.000 \times \dfrac{MnO_2}{2000}}{0.5000} \times 100 = 78.23\%. \quad Ans.$$

Example II. — A sample of red lead (Pb_3O_4) containing only inert impurities weighs 3.500 grams. To this is added a pipetteful of a solution of ferrous ammonium sulphate and a sufficient volume of dilute sulphuric acid. After solvent action has ceased, the excess ferrous salt requires 3.05 cc. of $\dfrac{N}{5}$ $KMnO_4$. A similar pipetteful of the above ferrous solution when titrated directly with the $KMnO_4$ requires 48.05 cc. Calculate the percentage of Pb_3O_4 in the red lead.

Solution. — 48.05 − 3.05 = 45.00 = net cc. of $KMnO_4$ equivalent to that part of the ferrous solution which is equivalent to the Pb_3O_4.

$$\frac{45.00 \times \dfrac{1}{5} \times \dfrac{Pb_3O_4}{2000}}{3.500} \times 100 = 88.15\%. \quad Ans.$$

PROBLEMS

72. In the analysis of an iron ore containing 60.0% Fe_2O_3, a sample weighing 0.5000 gram is taken and the iron is reduced with sulphurous acid. On account of failure to boil out all the excess SO_2, 38.60 cubic centimeters of 0.1 N $KMnO_4$ were required to titrate the solution. What was the error, percentage error, and what weight of sulphur dioxide was in the solution?

Answer: (a) 1.60%; (b) 2.67%; (c) 0.00322 gram.

VOLUMETRIC ANALYSIS

73. If a 0.5000 gram sample of limonite containing 59.50 per cent Fe_2O_3 requires 40 cc. of $KMnO_4$ to oxidize the iron, what is the value of 1 cc. of the permanganate in terms of (a) Fe, (b) $H_2C_2O_4 \cdot 2 H_2O$?

Answer: (a) 0.005189 gram; (b) 0.005859 gram.

74. Determine the percentage of iron in a sample of limonite from the following data: Sample = 0.5000 gram. $KMnO_4$ used = 50.00 cc. 1 cc. $KMnO_4 \approx$ 0.005317 gram Fe. $FeSO_4$ used = 6.00 cc. 1 cc. $FeSO_4 \approx$ 0.009200 gram FeO. *Answer:* 44.60%.

75. If 1 gram of a silicate yields 0.5000 gram of Fe_2O_3 and Al_2O_3 and the iron present requires 25.00 cc. of 0.2 N $KMnO_4$, calculate the percentage of FeO and Al_2O_3 in the sample.

Answer: 35.89% FeO; 10.03% Al_2O_3.

76. A sample of ore is analyzed for calcium by precipitating as calcium oxalate, dissolving the precipitate in H_2SO_4, and titrating the resulting oxalic acid with $KMnO_4$. What weight of ore must be taken so that one half the number of cubic centimeters of $\frac{N}{10}$ $KMnO_4$ required, shall be twice the percentage of CaO in the sample? *Answer:* 1.121 grams.

77. A sample of hydrogen peroxide weighing 2.50 grams is titrated with $\frac{N}{10}$ $KMnO_4$ (5 H_2O_2 + 2 MnO_4^- + 6 H^+ = 2 Mn^{++} + 5 O_2 + 8 H_2O). If the volume (measured under standard conditions) of oxygen evolved is 50.4 cc., what volume of $KMnO_4$ was used and what is the percentage of H_2O_2 in the sample? *Answer:* 45.0 cc.; 3.06%.

78. A sample of potassium binoxalate ($KHC_2O_4 \cdot H_2O$) containing inert impurities requires the same volume of titrating solution whether it is titrated with a certain solution of KOH or with a solution of $KMnO_4$ (of which 40.00 cc. are required for a half-gram sample of limonite containing 79.84% Fe_2O_3). What volume of the KOH solution would be required to neutralize 60.00 cc. of potassium tetroxalate ($KHC_2O_4 \cdot H_2C_2O_4 \cdot 2 H_2O$) solution which is 0.04000 Normal as a reducing agent?

Answer: 28.80 cc.

79. What should be the value of one cubic centimeter of a solution of potassium permanganate in terms of iron so that when the permanganate is used to titrate a 0.2000-gram sample of impure Na_2SO_3 (sulphite is oxidized to sulphate), the percentage of SO_2 in the sample can be found by multiplying the burette reading by 2? *Answer:* 0.006974 gram.

80. In analyzing a sample of ore containing manganese by titrating the latter in neutral solution (Volhard method) with standard KMnO$_4$ (3 Mn^{++} + 2 MnO$_4^-$ + 2 H$_2$O → 5 MnO$_2$ + 4 H$^+$) what weight of ore should be taken so that the percentage of manganese will be one tenth of the burette reading? The KMnO$_4$ is of such normality that in titrating one gram of any sample of impure NaNO$_2$ in acid solution the volume required is the same as the percentage of NaNO$_2$ in the sample.

Answer: 4.776 grams.

81. The determination of manganese in steel can be carried out by several methods. In one such method (persulphate method) the manganese in the steel is oxidized by excess ammonium persulphate to permanganate, the excess persulphate is destroyed by boiling, a pipetteful of ferrous sulphate is added, and the excess ferrous solution titrated with standard permanganate. In another method (Volhard method) the manganese in the steel is titrated directly in neutral solution with standard permanganate: 3 Mn^{++} + 2 MnO$_4^-$ + H$_2$O → 5 MnO$_2$ + 4 H$^+$. If with a 2.00-gram sample of steel, analyzed by the persulphate method, a 50 cc. pipetteful of $\frac{N}{20}$ ferrous sulphate solution is used and the volume of KMnO$_4$ (1 cc. ≏ 0.005584 gram Fe) required is 15.0 cc., what is the percentage of manganese in the steel? Using the same weight of sample and the same KMnO$_4$ what would be the burette reading if the Volhard method were used? *Answer:* 0.55%; 6.66 cc.

82. A sample of pyrolusite weighing 0.6000 gram is treated with 0.9000 gram of oxalic acid. The excess oxalic acid requires 23.95 cc. of permanganate (1 cc. ≏ 0.03038 gram FeSO$_4$ · 7 H$_2$O). What is the percentage of MnO$_2$ in the sample? *Answer:* 84.47%.

83. To a sample of pyrolusite weighing 0.2500 gram a certain weight of pure oxalic acid (H$_2$C$_2$O$_4$ · 2H$_2$O) is added and after reaction in acid solution is complete, the excess oxalic acid requires 30.00 cc. of KMnO$_4$ (1 cc. ≏ 0.01960 gram FeSO$_4$ · (NH$_4$)$_2$SO$_4$ · 6 H$_2$O) for oxidation. If the pyrolusite is known to contain 86.93% MnO$_2$, what weight of oxalic acid was added?

Answer: 0.4095 gram.

84. In the analysis of a 0.300-gram sample of pyrolusite, 60.0 cc. of a solution of ferrous ammonium sulphate were used and after reaction was complete, 15.0 cc. of KMnO$_4$ were required for the excess ferrous iron. The original ferrous solution contained 0.0392 gram of the pure hydrated crystals per cubic centimeter. 40.0 cc. of the KMnO$_4$ will oxidize 30.00 cc. of KHC$_2$O$_4$ solution which is $\frac{N}{10}$ as an acid. Calculate the percentage of Mn in the pyrolusite. *Answer:* 34.4%.

VOLUMETRIC ANALYSIS

85. A 2.00-gram sample of lead sesquioxide (= Pb_2O_3 = $PbO_2 \cdot PbO$) containing only inert impurities is treated with 20.0 cc. of 6 N H_2SO_4, and one 50 cc. pipetteful of oxalic acid solution (containing 0.0126 gram $H_2C_2O_4 \cdot 2 H_2O$ per cc.) is added. After complete reaction, the solution requires that volume of $\frac{N}{10}$ $KMnO_4$ which would oxidize 30.0 cc. of potassium tetroxalate solution (40.0 cc. $KHC_2O_4 \cdot H_2C_2O_4 \cdot 2 H_2O$ solution ≎ 20.0 cc. $\frac{N}{10}$ NaOH). Calculate the purity of the sample in terms of the percentage of Pb and also of Pb_2O_3. *Answer:* 82.8% Pb; 92.4% Pb_2O_3.

86. Calculate the normality of the $KMnO_4$ and express the percentage of lead (Pb) in a sample of red lead (Pb_3O_4) from the following data: Sample = A grams; $H_2C_2O_4 \cdot 2 H_2O$ used to reduce the quadrivalent lead = B grams; $KMnO_4$ used for the excess oxalic acid = C cc. The $KMnO_4$ is of such strength that when titrating hydrogen peroxide, the burette reading is equal to the volume of oxygen gas (standard conditions) liberated. ($5 H_2O_2 + 2 MnO_4^- + 6 H^+ \rightarrow 2 Mn^{++} + 5 O_2 + 8 H_2O$).

Answer: 0.08930 N; $\dfrac{\left[\dfrac{B}{0.06300} - (C \times 0.08930)\right] \times \dfrac{3\,Pb}{2000} \times 100}{A}$.

BICHROMATE PROCESS

Like potassium permanganate, potassium bichromate is a powerful oxidizing agent, but it has certain advantages over permanganate, especially in the titration of ferrous iron. One advantage is its stability and another is that ferrous iron can be titrated in cold, dilute hydrochloric acid solution without danger of oxidizing any of the chloride. The reaction is as follows: $6\ Fe^{++} + Cr_2O_7^= + 14\ H^+ \rightarrow 6\ Fe^{+++} + 2\ Cr^{+++} + 7\ H_2O$. The principal disadvantage is that there has not yet been found an entirely satisfactory internal indicator to indicate the completion of the oxidation. Instead, an outside indicator is usually used, namely a dilute solution of potassium ferricyanide which, when tested with minute amounts of the solution, gives a blue color only so long as ferrous ions are present: $3\ Fe^{++} + 2\ Fe(CN)_6^{---} \rightarrow Fe_3[Fe(CN)_6]_2$. Its limited applicability due to lack of convenient indicator lessens the general usefulness of the bichromate process, but for the determination of iron and indirectly of certain oxidizing agents, the bichromate process is capable of excellent results.

Since it is usually impossible to reach the end-point directly without overstepping, a solution of ferrous salt must be used for back titration.

As shown by the equation above, when bichromate is reduced in acid solution the chromium is reduced in valence from $+6$ in the bichromate radical to $+3$ in the chromic compound formed. The change in valence of each chromium is therefore 3 units, and of the whole bichromate molecule is 6 units. The gram-equivalent weight of potassium bichromate is $\dfrac{K_2Cr_2O_7}{6} = 49.03$ grams, and this amount in a liter of solution constitutes a normal solution as an oxidizing agent.

As in the permanganate process the gram-equivalent weight of ferrous sulphate and of ferrous ammonium sulphate is equal to the gram-molecular weight.

The calculations involving ratios of solution, standardization, and analyses are in principle the same as under the permanganate process.

PREPARATION OF SOLUTIONS

Approximate Strength 0.1 N

It is possible to purify commercial potassium bichromate by recrystallization from hot water. It must then be dried and cautiously heated to fusion to expel the last traces of moisture, but not sufficiently high to expel any oxygen. The pure salt thus prepared, may be weighed out directly, dissolved, and the solution diluted in a graduated flask to a definite volume. In this case no standardization is made, as the normal value can be calculated directly. It is, however, customary to standardize a solution of the commercial salt by comparison with some substance of definite composition, as described below.

Procedure. — Pulverize about 5 grams of potassium bichromate of good quality. Dissolve the bichromate in distilled water, transfer the solution to a liter bottle, and dilute to approximately 1000 cc. Shake thoroughly until the solution is uniform.

To prepare the solution of the reducing agent, pulverize about 28 grams of ferrous sulphate ($FeSO_4 \cdot 7\ H_2O$) or about 40 grams of ferrous ammonium sulphate ($FeSO_4 \cdot (NH_4)_2SO_4 \cdot 6\ H_2O$), moisten with 30 cc. of 6 N H_2SO_4 and dissolve in distilled water. Transfer the solution to a liter bottle, make up to about 1000 cc. and shake vigorously to insure uniformity.

INDICATOR SOLUTION

As stated above, no satisfactory indicator is known which, like methyl orange, can be used within the solution, to show when the titration process is complete. Instead, an outside indicator solution is employed to which drops of the titrated solution are transferred for testing. The reagent used is potassium ferricyanide, which produces a blue precipitate (or color) with ferrous compounds as long as there are unoxidized ferrous ions in the titrated solution. Drops of the indicator solution are placed upon a glazed porcelain tile, or upon white cardboard which has been coated with paraffin to render it waterproof, and drops of the titrated solution are transferred to the indicator on the end of a stirring rod. When the oxidation is nearly completed only very small amounts of the ferrous compounds remain unoxidized and the reaction with the indicator is no longer instantaneous. It is necessary to allow a brief time to elapse before determining that no blue color is formed. Thirty seconds is a sufficient interval, and should be adopted throughout the analytical procedure. If left too long, the combined effect of light and dust from the air will cause a reduction of the ferric compounds already formed and a resultant blue will appear which misleads the observer with respect to the true end-point.

The indicator solution must be highly diluted, otherwise its own color interferes with accurate observation. Prepare a fresh solution, as needed each day, by dissolving a crystal of potassium ferricyanide about the size of a pin's head in 25 cc. of distilled water. The salt should be carefully tested with ferric chloride for the presence of ferrocyanides, which give a blue color with ferric salts.

In case of need, the ferricyanide can be purified by adding to its solution a little bromine water and recrystallizing the compound.

COMPARISON OF OXIDIZING AND REDUCING SOLUTIONS

Procedure. — Fill the burettes, observing the general procedure with respect to cleaning and rinsing already prescribed. The bichromate solution is preferably to be placed in a glass-stoppered burette.

Run out from a burette into a beaker of about 300 cc. capacity nearly 40 cc. of the ferrous solution, add 15 cc. of dilute hydrochloric acid (sp. gr. 1.12) and 150 cc. of water and run in the bichromate solution from another burette. Since both solutions are approximately tenth-normal, 35 cc. of the bichromate solution may be added without testing. Test at that point by removing a very small drop of the iron solution on the end of a stirring rod, mixing it with a drop of indicator on the tile (Note 1). If a blue precipitate appears at once, 0.5 cc. of the bichromate solution may be added before testing again. The stirring rod which has touched the indicator should be dipped in distilled water before returning it to the iron solution. As soon as the blue appears to be less intense, add the bichromate solution in small portions, finally a single drop at a time, until the point is reached at which no blue color appears after the lapse of thirty seconds from the time of mixing solution and indicator. At the close of the titration a large drop of the iron solution should be taken for the test. To determine the end-point beyond any question, as soon as the thirty seconds have elapsed remove another drop of the solution of the same size as that last taken and mix it with the indicator, placing it beside the last previous test. If this last previous test shows a blue tint in comparison with the fresh mixture, the end-point has not been reached; if no difference can be noted, the reaction is complete. Should the end-point be overstepped, a little more of the ferrous solution may be added and the end-point definitely fixed.

From the volumes of the solutions used, after applying corrections for burette readings, and, if need be, for the temperature of solutions, calculate the value of the ferrous solution in terms of the oxidizing solution.

Note. — 1. The accuracy of the work may be much impaired by the removal of unnecessarily large quantities of solution for the tests. At the beginning of the titration, while much ferrous iron is still present, the end of the stirring rod need only be moist with the solution; but at the close of the titration drops of considerable size may properly be taken for the final tests. The stirring rod should be washed to prevent transfer of indicator to the main solution. This cautious removal of solution does not seriously affect the accuracy of the determination, as it will be noted that the volume of the titrated solution is about 200 cc. and the portions removed are very small. Moreover, if the procedure is followed as prescribed, the concentration of unoxidized iron decreases very rapidly as the titration is carried out so that when the final tests are made, though large drops may be taken, the amount of ferrous iron is not sufficient to produce any appreciable error in results.

If the end-point is determined as prescribed, it can be as accurately fixed as that of other methods; and if a ferrous solution is at hand, the titration need consume hardly more time than that of the permanganate process.

STANDARDIZATION OF POTASSIUM BICHROMATE SOLUTIONS

Selection of a Standard

As in the permanganate process, a substance which will serve satisfactorily as a standard must be of accurately known composition and definite in its behavior as a reducing agent, and it must be permanent against oxidation in the air, at least for considerable periods. Such standards may take the form of pure crystalline salts, such as ferrous ammonium sulphate, or may be in the form of iron wire or an iron ore of known iron content. It is not necessary that the standard should be of 100 per cent purity, provided the content of the active reducing agent is known and no interfering substances are present.

The two substances most commonly used as standards for a bichromate solution are ferrous ammonium sulphate and iron wire. A standard wire can be purchased in the market which answers the purpose well, and its iron content may be determined for each lot purchased by a number of gravimetric determinations. It may best be preserved in tubes containing calcium chloride, but this must not be allowed to come into contact with the wire. It should, however, even then be examined carefully for rust before use.

If pure ferrous ammonium sulphate is used as the standard, clear crystals only should be selected. It is perhaps even better to determine by gravimetric methods once for all the iron content of a large commercial sample which has been ground and well mixed. This salt is permanent over long periods if kept in stoppered containers.

STANDARDIZATION

Method A

Against Iron Wire

Procedure. — Weigh out accurately two portions of iron wire of about 0.24–0.26 gram each, examining the wire carefully for rust. It should be handled and wiped with filter paper (not touched by the fingers), should be weighed on a watch-glass, and be bent in such a way as not to interfere with the movement of the balance.

Place 30 cc. of hydrochloric acid (sp. gr. 1.12) in each of two 300 cc. Erlenmeyer flasks, cover them with watch-glasses, and bring the acid just to boiling. Remove them from the flame and drop in the portions of wire, taking great care to avoid loss of liquid during solution. Boil for two or three minutes, keeping the flasks covered (Note 1), then wash the sides of the flasks and the watch-glass with a little water and add stannous chloride and mercuric chloride exactly as in the determination of iron in limonite by the permanganate process, page 81. (Read the notes covering this determination.) Very little stannous chloride will be used in this case since most of the iron is already in the ferrous condition. After the addition of mercuric chloride allow the solution to stand five minutes, dilute with 150 cc. of water, and then (without adding manganous sulphate solution) titrate without further delay. Add about 35 cc. of the standard solution at once and finish the titration as prescribed above.

From the corrected volumes of the bichromate solution required to oxidize the iron actually known to be present in the wire, calculate the relation of the standard solution to the normal.

Repeat the standardization until the results are concordant within at least two parts in one thousand.

Note. — 1. The hydrochloric acid is added to the ferrous solution to insure the presence of at least sufficient free acid for the titration, as expressed by the equation on page 64.

The solution of the wire in hot acid and the short boiling insure the removal of compounds of hydrogen and carbon which are formed from the small amount of carbon in the iron. These might be acted upon by the bichromate if not expelled.

Method B

Against Ferrous Sulphate

Weigh out accurately about 0.8 gram of pure ferrous sulphate ($FeSO_4 \cdot 7 H_2O$), or about 1.2 grams of pure ferrous ammonium sulphate ($FeSO_4 \cdot (NH_4)_2SO_4 \cdot 6 H_2O$) into 250 cc. beakers.

Moisten with 10 cc. of dilute sulphuric acid and dissolve in 100 cc. of water. Titrate without delay, adding about 35 cc. of the bichromate at once and finishing the titration as prescribed above.

From the corrected volume of the bichromate solution required to oxidize the iron in the salt calculate the normality of the bichromate.

Repeat the standardization until the results are concordant to at least two parts per thousand.

DETERMINATION OF IRON IN LIMONITE

Procedure. — Grind the mineral to a fine powder and proceed with its solution in hydrochloric acid as in the analysis of limonite by the Zimmermann-Reinhardt permanganate process (page 80). Add stannous chloride and mercuric chloride exactly as given in that procedure and after letting the solution stand five minutes, dilute to 200 cc. and titrate at once with the standard bichromate. No manganous sulphate solution is necessary.

From the standardization data and the titration values calculate the iron content of the limonite in terms of the percentage of Fe and of Fe_2O_3. Read the notes pertaining to the analysis of limonite by the permanganate process.

STOICHIOMETRY

The calculations involved in the analysis of limonite by the bichromate process are essentially the same as in the permanganate process.

DETERMINATION OF CHROMIUM IN CHROME IRON ORE

Chromite ("chrome iron ore") is essentially ferrous chromite, $Fe(CrO_2)_2$ or $FeO \cdot Cr_2O_3$. When fused with a strong oxidizing alkaline flux like sodium peroxide, leached with water and acidified, the iron is in solution as ferric salt and the chromium as bichromate:

$2\ FeO + Na_2O_2 \rightarrow 2\ NaFeO_2$
$Cr_2O_3 + 3\ Na_2O_2 \rightarrow 2\ Na_2CrO_4 + Na_2O$
$NaFeO_2 + 2\ H_2O \rightarrow Fe(OH)_3 + NaOH$
$2\ Fe(OH)_3 + 3\ H_2SO_4 \rightarrow Fe_2(SO_4)_3 + 6\ H_2O$
$2\ Na_2CrO_4 + H_2SO_4 \rightarrow Na_2Cr_2O_7 + Na_2SO_4 + H_2O.$

By adding an excess of ferrous solution the value of which is known in terms of standard bichromate solution, the bichromate ions are reduced to chromic ions ($Cr_2O_7^= + 6\ Fe^{++} + 14\ H^+ \rightarrow 2\ Cr^{+++} + 6\ Fe^{+++} + 7\ H_2O$) and the excess ferrous solution can be titrated with standard bichromate solution using ferricyanide as an outside indicator in the usual way. This is therefore an indirect process similar in principle to the analysis of pyrolusite.

Chromite could be analyzed by the permanganate process, *i.e.* by titrating the excess ferrous solution with standard potassium permanganate were it not for the deep color of the solution which would mask the end-point of the permanganate titration. Chromite can, as we shall see, be analyzed by a direct iodimetric process.

Procedure. — Grind the chrome iron ore (Note 1) in an agate mortar until no grit is perceptible under the pestle. Weigh out two portions of 0.5 gram each into iron crucibles which have been scoured inside until bright (Note 2). Weigh out on a watch-glass (Note 3), using the rough balances, 5 grams of dry sodium peroxide for each portion, and pour about three quarters of the peroxide upon the ore. Mix the ore and flux by thorough stirring with a dry glass rod. Then cover the mixture with the remainder of the peroxide. Place the crucible on a triangle and raise the temperature *slowly* to the melting point of the flux, using a low flame, and holding the lamp in the hand (Note 4). Maintain the fusion for five minutes, and stir constantly with a stout iron wire, but do not raise the temperature above moderate redness (Notes 5 and 6).

Allow the crucible to cool until it can be comfortably handled (Note 7) and then place it in a 300 cc. beaker, and cover it with distilled water (Note 8). The beaker must be carefully covered to avoid loss during the disintegration of the fused mass. When the evolution of gas ceases, rinse off and remove the crucible; then heat the solution *while still alkaline* to boiling for fifteen minutes. Allow to cool for a few minutes; then acidify with dilute sulphuric acid (1 : 5), adding 10 cc. in excess of the amount necessary to dissolve the ferric hydroxide (Note 9). Filter if a dark-colored residue is present (Note 10). Dilute to 200 cc., cool, add from a burette an excess of a standard ferrous solution, and titrate the excess with a standard solution of potassium bichromate, using the outside indicator (Note 11).

From the corrected volumes of the two standard solutions, and their relations to normal solutions, calculate the percentage of chromium in the ore.

Notes. — 1. Chrome iron ore must be reduced to a state of fine subdivision to ensure a prompt reaction with the flux.

2. The scouring of the iron crucible is rendered much easier if it is first heated to bright redness and plunged into cold water. In this process oily matter is burned off and adhering scale is caused to chip off when the hot crucible contracts rapidly in the cold water.

3. Sodium peroxide must be kept away from balance pans and should not be weighed out on paper, as is the usual practice in the rough weighing of chemicals. If paper to which the peroxide is adhering is exposed to moist air, it is likely to take fire as a result of the absorption of moisture, and consequent evolution of heat and liberation of oxygen.

4. The lamp should never be allowed to remain under the crucible, as this will raise the temperature to a point at which the crucible itself is rapidly attacked by the flux and burned through.

5. The sodium peroxide acts as both a flux and an oxidizing agent. The chromic oxide is dissolved by the flux and oxidized to chromic

anhydride (CrO_3) which combines with the alkali to form sodium chromate. The iron is oxidized to the ferric condition.

6. The sodium peroxide cannot be used in porcelain, platinum, or silver crucibles. It attacks iron and nickel as well; but crucibles made from these metals may be used if care is exercised to keep the temperature as low as possible. Preference is here given to iron crucibles, because the resulting ferric hydroxide is more readily brought into solution than the nickelic oxide from a nickel crucible. The peroxide must be dry, and must be protected from any admixture of dust, paper, or of organic matter of any kind, otherwise explosions may ensue.

7. When an iron crucible is employed it is desirable to allow the fusion to become nearly cold before it is placed in water, otherwise scales of magnetic iron oxide may separate from the crucible, which by slowly dissolving in acid form ferrous sulphate, which reduces the chromate.

8. Upon treatment with water the chromate passes into solution, the ferric hydroxide remains undissolved, and the excess of peroxide is decomposed with the evolution of oxygen. The subsequent boiling insures the complete decomposition of the peroxide. Unless this is complete, hydrogen peroxide is formed when the solution is acidified, and this reacts with the bichromate, reducing it and introducing a serious error.

9. The addition of the sulphuric acid converts the sodium chromate to bichromate, which behaves exactly like potassium bichromate in acid solution.

10. If manganese is present in the ore it will form MnO_2 after fusing and acidifying. If this MnO_2 is not filtered off, it will be reduced by the ferrous sulphate and will therefore give a high chromium value for the ore.

11. If a standard solution of a ferrous salt is not at hand, a weight of iron wire somewhat in excess of the amount which would be required if the chromite were pure $FeO \cdot Cr_2O_3$ may be weighed out and dissolved in sulphuric acid; after reduction of all the iron by stannous chloride and the addition of mercuric chloride, this solution may be poured into the chromate solution and the excess of iron determined by titration with standard bichromate solution.

STOICHIOMETRY

The analysis of chromite by the bichromate process is an indirect process in that the excess of ferrous solution over that required to react with the desired constituent is titrated. The gram-milliequivalent weight of chromium is one third the gram-atomic weight since in the titration the valence of the chromium changes by 3 units (from $+6$ to $+3$).

Example. — What is the percentage of Cr in a sample of chromite if a 0.5000-gram sample after fusion in the regular way is treated with 50.00 cc. of 0.1200 N ferrous ammonium sulphate solution and the excess requires 15.05 cc. of $K_2Cr_2O_7$ solution (1 cc. $\backsimeq$ 0.006000 gram Fe)? Express also in terms of per cent Cr_2O_3.

Solution. — Normality of $K_2Cr_2O_7 = \dfrac{0.006000}{1 \times \dfrac{Fe}{1000}} = 0.1075$ N

50.00 cc. of 0.1200 N ferrous soln. $\backsimeq 50.00 \times \dfrac{0.1200}{0.1075}$

$= 55.81$ cc. $K_2Cr_2O_7$

$\dfrac{(55.81 - 15.05)0.1075 \times \dfrac{Cr}{3000}}{0.5000} \times 100 = 15.20\%$ Cr. *Ans.*

$\dfrac{(55.81 - 15.05)0.1075 \times \dfrac{Cr_2O_3}{6000}}{0.5000} \times 100 = 22.20\%$ Cr_2O_3. *Ans.*

PROBLEMS

87. In the standardization of a $K_2Cr_2O_7$ solution against iron wire, 99.85% pure, 42.42 cc. of the solution were added. The weight of the wire used was 0.2200 gram. 3.27 cc. of a ferrous sulphate solution having a normal value as a reducing agent of 0.1011 were added to complete the titration. Calculate the normal value of the $K_2Cr_2O_7$. *Answer:* 0.1006 N.

88. One gram of a pure oxide of iron is fused with potassium acid sulphate and the fusion dissolved in acid. The iron is reduced with stannous chloride, mercuric chloride is added, and the iron titrated with a normal $K_2Cr_2O_7$ solution. 12.94 cc. were used. What is the formula of the oxide, FeO, Fe_2O_3, or Fe_3O_4? *Answer:* Fe_3O_4.

89. If an element has 98 for its atomic weight, and after reduction with stannous chloride can be oxidized by bichromate to a state corresponding to an XO_4^- anion, compute the oxide, or valence, corresponding to the reduced state from the following data: 0.3266 gram of the pure element, after being dissolved, was reduced with stannous chloride and oxidized by 40 cc. of $K_2Cr_2O_7$, of which 1.00 cc. ≎ 0.1960 gram of $FeSO_4 \cdot (NH_4)_2SO_4 \cdot 6 H_2O$. *Answer:* Monovalent.

90. In the analysis of a sample of limonite by potassium bichromate solution (1 cc. ≎ 0.01116 gram Fe) what weight of sample should be taken so that the percentage of Fe_2O_3 will be found by multiplying the burette reading by 4? How many grams of $K_2Cr_2O_7$ are in each cubic centimeter of the above bichromate solution?
Answer: 0.3992 gram; 0.009806 gram.

91. A half-gram sample of chromite is fused with Na_2O_2, leached with water, and acidified with H_2SO_4. The chromium is reduced by the addition of 2.78 grams of $FeSO_4 \cdot 7 H_2O$ crystals. The excess ferrous iron then requires 10.0 cc. of $K_2Cr_2O_7$ solution (1 cc. ≎ 0.0160 gram Fe_2O_3). Calculate the percentage of Cr in the chromite. *Answer:* 27.7%.

92. What must be the "iron value" of one cubic centimeter of potassium bichromate solution if in the titration of 0.4000 gram of limonite, the net number of cubic centimeters of bichromate and the percentage of Fe_2O_3 in the limonite are equal? *Answer:* 0.002797 gram.

93. What is the percentage of chromium in a sample of chrome iron ore if 0.2000 gram of the ore after oxidation with Na_2O_2 and treatment of the acidified solution with 5 gram-millimoles of ferrous sulphate requires one sixth of a gram-millimole of bichromate solution for the excess iron.
Answer: 34.68%.

94. From the following data calculate the purity of a sample of chrome iron ore in terms of the percentage of Cr and of Cr_2O_3: Weight of sample = 0.2500 gram; $FeSO_4$ solution = 53.40 cc.; $K_2Cr_2O_7$ solution used = 8.00 cc.; 100 cc. $FeSO_4$ solution ≎ 80.00 cc. $K_2Cr_2O_7$ solution; 40.00 cc. $K_2Cr_2O_7$ solution are required to titrate the iron in a half-gram sample of limonite containing 79.84% Fe_2O_3. *Answer:* 30.08% Cr; 43.97% Cr_2O_3.

95. A sample of chromite weighing 0.2000 gram is fused with Na_2O_2, leached, and acidified with H_2SO_4. To the solution is added a certain weight of $FeSO_4 \cdot 7 H_2O$ crystals which is in excess of that required to reduce the chromium present. The excess ferrous sulphate is titrated with 10.10 cc. of $K_2Cr_2O_7$ (1 cc. ≎ 0.005584 gram Fe) and 0.20 cc. of ferrous ammonium sulphate solution (containing 19.60 grams $FeSO_4(NH_4)_2SO_4 \cdot 6 H_2O$ per liter). If the percentage of Cr_2O_3 in the ore is 50.66%, what weight of $FeSO_4 \cdot 7 H_2O$ crystals was added? *Answer:* 1.390 grams.

IODIMETRY

The titration of iodine against sodium thiosulphate, with starch as an indicator, may perhaps be regarded as the most accurate of volumetric processes.

The fundamental reaction upon which iodimetric processes are based is the following:

$$I_2 + 2 Na_2S_2O_3 \rightarrow 2 NaI + Na_2S_4O_6,$$
or, $$I_2 + 2 S_2O_3^= \rightarrow 2 I^- + S_4O_6^=.$$

This reaction between iodine and sodium thiosulphate, resulting in the formation of the compound $Na_2S_4O_6$, called sodium tetrathionate, is quantitatively exact, and differs in that respect from the action of chlorine or bromine, which oxidize the thiosulphate, but not quantitatively.

The usual indicator for iodimetric titrations is a solution of starch which with even a minute excess of free iodine gives a deep blue product of unknown composition (Note 1). Occasionally either chloroform or carbon tetrachloride is used as an indicator. Each of these liquids settles to the bottom of the aqueous solution and dissolves out most of the free iodine, giving a deep purple solution.

In the titration equation above it is seen that each iodine atom changes in valence by one unit (from 0 to -1). The equivalent weight of iodine is therefore $\frac{I}{1} = 126.93$ and a normal solution contains 126.9 grams of iodine crystals per liter of solution. The average valence of sulphur in thiosulphate is $+2$ and in tetrathionate is $+2\frac{1}{2}$. The average change in valence of each sulphur atom is therefore $\frac{1}{2}$, and since the thiosulphate molecule contains two sulphur atoms, the total change is 1. The equivalent weight of sodium thiosulphate is therefore equal to the molecular weight and a normal solution contains $\frac{Na_2S_2O_3 \cdot 5 H_2O}{1} =$ 248.1 grams of the hydrated crystals per liter of solution.

The iodimetric process can be applied in two ways. Such reducing substances as hydrogen sulphide, sulphites, and arsenites can be titrated directly with standard iodine solution to an endpoint with starch as an indicator. The titration of ferrous salts and of several other reducing agents with iodine is not practicable, due usually to incompleteness of reaction, and so iodine is less commonly used as a direct standard oxidizing agent than is potassium permanganate.

On the other hand, one of the best methods of analyzing oxidizing substances is by the iodimetric process. The method makes use of the fact that practically all oxidizing agents oxidize potassium iodide in dilute acid solution to free iodine, which in turn can be titrated with standard sodium thiosulphate. From the analytical view-point, this is not an indirect process even though the oxidizing agent itself is not titrated. The volume of titrating solution (thiosulphate) used is a direct measure of the amount of oxidizing substance present, since the amount of iodine liberated from the potassium iodide is a direct measure of the oxidizing power of the substance analyzed.

Note. — 1. The blue color which results when free iodine and starch are brought together is probably not due to the formation of a true chemical compound. It is regarded as a "solid solution" of iodine in starch. Although it is unstable, and easily destroyed by heat, it serves as an indicator for the presence of free iodine of remarkable sensitiveness, and makes the iodimetric processes the most satisfactory of any in the field of volumetric analysis.

PREPARATION OF STANDARD SOLUTIONS

Approximate Strength, 0.1 N

Procedure. — Weigh out on the rough balances 13 grams of commercial iodine. Place it in a mortar with 18 grams of potassium iodide and triturate with small portions of water until all is dissolved (Note 1). Dilute the solution to 1000 cc. and transfer to a liter bottle and mix thoroughly (Notes 2 and 3).

Weigh out 25 grams of sodium thiosulphate, dissolve it in water which has been previously boiled and cooled, and dilute to 1000 cc., also with boiled water. Transfer the solution to a liter bottle and mix thoroughly (Note 4).

Notes. — 1. Iodine does not dissolve appreciably in water but does dissolve in a solution of potassium iodide, probably forming $KI \cdot I_2$. This compound is very unstable and the iodine is so loosely bound to the potassium iodide that the resulting solution behaves chemically as if it were a true solution of iodine.

2. Iodine solutions react with water to form hydriodic acid under the influence of the sunlight, and even at low room temperatures the iodine tends to volatilize from solution. They should, therefore, be protected from light and heat. Iodine solutions are not stable for long periods under the best of conditions and cannot be used in burettes with rubber tips, since they attack the rubber.

3. It will be found more economical to have a considerable quantity of the solution prepared by a laboratory attendant, and to have all unused solutions returned to the common stock.

4. Sodium thiosulphate ($Na_2S_2O_3 \cdot 5\ H_2O$) is rarely wholly pure as sold commercially, but may be purified by recrystallization. If unboiled water is used to dissolve the crystals, the carbonic acid in the water will on standing partially decompose the thiosulphate forming sulphurous acid and free sulphur.

$$S_2O_3^= + 2\ H^+ \rightarrow H_2S_2O_3$$
$$H_2S_2O_3 \rightarrow H_2SO_3 + S.$$

It has been suggested that bacterial action may also play an important part in this decomposition. In either case a stable solution results from dissolving thiosulphate crystals in water which has been boiled and cooled out of contact with the air.

INDICATOR SOLUTION

The starch solution must be freshly prepared since on standing it becomes mouldy and unsuitable for use as an indicator. A soluble starch is obtainable which serves well, and a solution of 1.0 gram of this starch in 100 cc. of boiling water is sufficient. First grind the starch thoroughly in a small mortar with a small amount of water until a smooth paste is formed, then pour slowly into the boiling water. If necessary let the solution stand and decant the supernatant liquid. About 5 cc. should be used for a titration.

COMPARISON OF IODINE AND THIOSULPHATE SOLUTIONS

Procedure. — Place the solutions in burettes (the iodine in a glass-stoppered burette), observing the usual precautions. Run out 40 cc. of the thiosulphate solution into a beaker, dilute with 150 cc. of water, add 5 cc. of the soluble starch solution, and titrate with the iodine to the appearance of the blue of the iodo-starch. Repeat until the ratio of the two solutions is established, remembering all necessary corrections for burettes and for temperature changes.

STANDARDIZATION OF SOLUTIONS

Commercial iodine is usually not sufficiently pure to permit of its use as a standard for thiosulphate solutions or the direct preparation of a standard solution of iodine. It is likely to contain, besides moisture, some iodine chloride, if chlorine was used to liberate the iodine when it was prepared. It may be purified by sublimation after mixing it with a little potassium iodide, which reacts with the iodine chloride, forming potassium chloride and setting free the iodine. The sublimed iodine is then dried by placing it in a closed container over concentrated sulphuric acid. It may then be weighed in a stoppered weighing-tube and dissolved in a solution of potassium iodide in a stoppered flask to prevent loss of iodine by volatilization.

An iodine solution made from commercial iodine may also be standardized against arsenious oxide (As_2O_3). This substance also usually requires purification by sublimation before use.

Substances which can be obtained sufficiently pure to serve for the standardization of sodium thiosulphate are potassium bromate ($KBrO_3$), potassium iodate (KIO_3), potassium biiodate ($KIO_3 \cdot HIO_3$), potassium bichromate ($K_2Cr_2O_7$), and metallic copper. If necessary the salts can be purified by recrystallization. All of these substances in acid solution will liberate iodine from an excess of potassium iodide and the liberated iodine can be titrated with the thiosulphate solution.

Two methods for the direct standardization of the sodium thiosulphate solution are here described, and one for the direct standardization of the iodine solution.

Method A

Procedure. — Weigh out accurately into 500 cc. beakers two portions of about 0.15–0.18 gram of pure potassium bromate, or pure potassium iodate, or pure potassium biiodate (Note 1). Dissolve in 50 cc. of water, and add 10 cc. of a potassium iodide solution containing 3 grams (roughly weighed) of the salt in that volume (Note 2). Add to the mixture 10 cc. of 6 N sulphuric acid, allow the solution to stand for three minutes, and dilute to 150 cc. (Note 3). Run in thiosulphate solution from a burette until the color of the liberated iodine is nearly destroyed, and then add 5 cc. of starch solution, titrate to the disappearance of the iodo-starch blue, and finally add iodine solution until the color is just restored. Make a blank test for the amount of thiosulphate solution required to react with the iodine liberated by the iodate which is generally present in the potassium iodide solution, and deduct this from the total volume used in the titration (Note 2).

From the data obtained, calculate the relation of the thiosulphate solution to a normal solution, and subsequently calculate the similar value for the iodine solution.

Notes. — 1. Potassium bichromate crystals can be used for the standardization of sodium thiosulphate, but the deep green color of the resulting chromic ions makes it difficult to estimate the iodo-starch end-point.

If solutions of bichromate or permanganate of known normality are available, they too can be used to standardize a sodium thiosulphate solution. In this case run out about 35 cc. of the standard solution (which should be approximately $\frac{N}{10}$ in concentration) into a beaker or flask, and add the potassium iodide and acid, and continue exactly as in the above standardization against potassium bromate.

2. Potassium iodide usually contains small amounts of potassium iodate as impurity which, when the iodide is brought into an acid solution, liberates iodine, just as does the potassium bromate used as a standard. It is necessary to determine the amount of thiosulphate which reacts with the iodine thus liberated by making a "blank test" with the iodide and acid alone. As the iodate is not always uniformly distributed throughout the iodide, it is better to make up a sufficient

IODIMETRY

volume of a solution of the iodide for the purposes of the work in hand, and to make the blank test by using the same volume of the iodide solution as is added in the standardizing process. The iodide solution should contain about 3 grams of the salt in 10 cc.

3. The color of the iodo-starch is somewhat less satisfactory in concentrated solutions of alkali salts, notably the iodides. The dilution prescribed obviates this difficulty.

Method B

Procedure. — Weigh out two portions of 0.25–0.27 gram of clean copper wire into 250 cc. Erlenmeyer flasks (Note 1). Add to each 5 cc. of concentrated nitric acid (sp. gr. 1.42) and 25 cc. of water, cover, and warm until solution is complete. Add 5 cc. of bromine water and boil until the excess of bromine is expelled. Cool, and add strong ammonia (sp. gr. 0.90) drop by drop until a deep blue color indicates the presence of an excess. Boil the solution until the deep blue is replaced by a light bluish green, or a brown stain appears on the sides of the flask (Note 2). Add 10 cc. of strong acetic acid (sp. gr. 1.04), cool under the water tap, and add a solution of potassium iodide (Note 3) containing about 3 grams of the salt, and titrate with thiosulphate solution until the color of the liberated iodine is nearly destroyed. Then add 5 cc. of freshly prepared starch solution, and add thiosulphate solution, drop by drop, until the blue color is discharged.

From the data obtained, including the "blank test" of the iodide, calculate the relation of the thiosulphate solution to the normal.

Notes. — 1. While copper wire of commerce is not absolutely pure, the requirements for its use as a conductor of electricity are such that the impurities constitute only a few hundredths of one per cent and are negligible for analytical purposes.

2. Ammonia neutralizes the free nitric acid. It should be added in slight excess only, since the excess must be removed by boiling, which is tedious. If too much ammonia is present when acetic acid is added, the resulting ammonium acetate is hydrolyzed, and the ammonium hydroxide reacts with the iodine set free.

3. A considerable excess of potassium iodide is necessary for the prompt liberation of iodine.

Method C

Procedure. — Weigh out into 500 cc. beakers two portions of 0.175–0.200 gram each of pure arsenious oxide. Dissolve each of these in 10 cc. of sodium hydroxide solution, with stirring. Dilute the solutions to 150 cc. and add dilute hydrochloric acid until the solutions contain a few drops in excess, and finally add to each a concentrated solution of 5 grams of pure sodium bicarbonate ($NaHCO_3$) in water. Cover the beakers before adding the bicarbonate, to avoid loss. Add the starch solution and titrate with the iodine to the appearance of the blue of the iodostarch, taking care not to pass the end-point by more than a few drops (Note 1).

From the corrected volume of the iodine solution used to oxidize the arsenious oxide, calculate its relation to the normal. From the ratio between the solutions, calculate the similar value for the thiosulphate solution.

Note. — 1. Arsenious oxide dissolves more readily in caustic alkali than in a bicarbonate solution, but the presence of caustic alkali during the titration is not admissible. It is therefore destroyed by the addition of acid, and the solution is then made neutral with the solution of bicarbonate, part of which reacts with the acid, the excess remaining in solution. The reaction during titration is the following:

$$Na_3AsO_3 + I_2 + 2\ NaHCO_3 \rightarrow Na_3AsO_4 + 2\ NaI + 2\ CO_2 + H_2O.$$

As the reaction between sodium thiosulphate and iodine is not always free from secondary reactions in the presence of even the weakly alkaline bicarbonate, it is best to avoid the addition of any considerable excess of iodine. Should the end-point be passed by a few drops, the thiosulphate may be used to correct it.

STOICHIOMETRY

In the standardization of iodine solution against pure arsenious oxide, the solution of the weighed oxide in sodium hydroxide is expressed by the equation: $As_2O_3 + 6\ NaOH \rightarrow 2\ Na_3AsO_3 + 3\ H_2O$, and that of the resulting titration by the equation: $Na_3AsO_3 + I_2 + 2\ NaHCO_3 \rightarrow Na_3AsO_4 + 2\ NaI + 2\ CO_2 + H_2O$. In calculating the normality of the iodine, the milliequivalent weight of As₂O₃ is the molecular weight divided by 4000 since each arsenic atom changes in valence by two units (from $+3$ to $+5$).

In the standardization of sodium thiosulphate solution against a pure solid oxidizing agent like potassium bromate, potassium iodate, potassium bichromate, or copper, the oxidizing agent reacts with an added excess of potassium iodide liberating as many equivalents of iodine as there are of the oxidizing agent present:

$$BrO_3^- + 6\,I^- + 6\,H^+ \rightarrow Br^- + 3\,I_2 + 3\,H_2O$$
$$IO_3^- + 5\,I^- + 6\,H^+ \rightarrow 3\,I_2 + 3\,H_2O$$
$$Cr_2O_7^= + 6\,I^- + 14\,H^+ \rightarrow 3\,Cr^{+++} + 3\,I_2 + 7\,H_2O$$
$$2\,Cu^{++} + 4\,I^- \rightarrow Cu_2I_2 + I_2.$$

Although it is the liberated iodine that is titrated by the thiosulphate, the volume required and hence the calculations involved are the same as if the original oxidizing agent were directly titrated by the thiosulphate, with the oxidation of the latter to tetrathionate.

As mentioned above, if a solution of potassium permanganate or of potassium bichromate of known normality is at hand, the thiosulphate can be standardized by determining the ratio between them. To do this, a measured volume of the standard permanganate of bichromate is run out, an excess of potassium iodide is added, the solution is acidified and the liberated iodine is titrated with the sodium thiosulphate solution. Again the calculations are the same as if the two solutions were directly titrated against each other.

Example. — Given a solution of iodine (1 cc. ≈ 0.004947 gram As₂O₃) and a solution of sodium thiosulphate (20.0 cc. ≈ 0.08340 gram KBrO₃). What is the normality of each solution and what is the value of the thiosulphate in terms of metallic copper? What volume of $\frac{N}{10}$ KMnO₄ would liberate an amount of iodine from excess potassium iodide to require 40.00 cc. of the above thiosulphate for reduction?

$$\text{Normality of } I_2 = \frac{0.004947}{1 \times \dfrac{As_2O_3}{4000}} = 0.1000 \text{ N.} \quad Ans.$$

$$\text{Normality of } Na_2S_2O_3 = \frac{0.08340}{20 \times \dfrac{KBrO_3}{6000}} = 0.1500 \text{ N}$$

$$1 \text{ cc. } Na_2S_2O_3 = 1 \times 0.1500 \times \frac{Cu}{1000}$$
$$= 0.009535 \text{ gram Cu.} \quad Ans.$$
$$x \times 0.1000 = 40.00 \times 0.1500$$
$$x = 60.00 \text{ cc.} \quad Ans.$$

DETERMINATION OF ANTIMONY IN STIBNITE

Stibnite is native antimony sulphide. Nearly pure samples of this mineral are easily obtainable and should be used for this analysis, since many impurities, notably iron, seriously interfere with the accurate determination of the antimony by iodimetric methods. It is, moreover, essential that the directions with respect to amounts of reagents employed and concentration of solutions should be followed closely.

Procedure. — Grind the mineral with great care, and weigh out two portions of 0.35–0.40 gram into small, dry beakers (250 cc.). Add about 0.3 gram of solid potassium chloride, cover the beakers and pour over the stibnite 5 cc. of concentrated hydrochloric acid (sp. gr. 1.20) and warm gently on the water bath (Note 1). When the residue is white, add to each beaker 2 grams of powdered tartaric acid (Note 2). Warm the solution on the water bath for ten minutes longer, dilute the solution very cautiously by adding water in portions of 5 cc., stopping if the solution turns red. It is possible that no coloration will appear, in which case cautiously continue the dilution to 125 cc. If a red precipitate or coloration does appear, warm the solution until it is colorless, and again dilute cautiously to a total volume of 125 cc. and boil for a minute (Note 3).

If a white precipitate of the oxychloride separates during dilution (which should not occur if the directions are followed), it is best to discard the determination and to start anew.

Carefully neutralize most of the acid with sodium hydroxide solution, but leave it distinctly acid (Note 4). Dissolve 3 grams of sodium bicarbonate in 200 cc. of water in a 500 cc. beaker, and pour the cold solution of the antimony chloride into this, avoiding loss by effervescence. Make sure that the solution contains an excess of the bicarbonate, and then add 5 cc. of starch solution and titrate with iodine solution to the appearance of the blue, avoiding an excess (Note 5).

From the corrected volume of the iodine solution required to oxidize the antimony, calculate the percentage of antimony (Sb) in the stibnite.

Notes. — 1. Antimony chloride is volatile with steam from its concentrated solutions; hence these solutions must not be boiled until they have been diluted. Potassium chloride lessens the volatility of the antimony chloride.

2. Antimony salts, such as the chloride, are readily hydrolyzed, and compounds such as SbOCl are formed which are often relatively insoluble; but in the presence of tartaric acid compounds with complex ions are formed, and these are soluble. An excess of hydrochloric acid also prevents precipitation of the oxychloride because the H^+ ions from the acid lessen the dissociation of the water and thus prevent any considerable hydrolysis.

3. The action of hydrochloric acid upon the sulphide sets free hydrogen sulphide, a part of which is held in solution by the acid. This is usually expelled by the heating upon the water bath; but if it is not wholly driven out, a point is reached during dilution at which the antimony sulphide, being no longer held in solution by the acid, separates. If the dilution is immediately stopped and the solution warmed, this sulphide is again brought into solution and at the same time more of the hydrogen sulphide is expelled. This procedure must be continued until the hydrogen sulphide is all removed, since it reacts with iodine. If no precipitation of the sulphide occurs, it is an indication that the hydrogen sulphide was all expelled on solution of the stibnite.

4. Sodium hydroxide is added to neutralize most of the acid, thus lessening the amount of sodium bicarbonate to be added. The NaOH should not neutralize all of the acid; if too much base is added, immediately acidify with HCl.

5. If the end-point is not permanent, that is, if the blue of the iodostarch is discharged after standing a few moments, the cause may be an insufficient quantity of sodium bicarbonate, leaving the solution slightly acid, or a very slight precipitation of an antimony compound which is slowly acted upon by the iodine when the latter is momentarily present in excess. In either case it is better to discard the analysis and to repeat the process, using greater care in the amounts of reagents employed.

STOICHIOMETRY

The reaction which takes place during the titration of antimony in stibnite may be expressed by the equation:

$$Na_3SbO_3 + 2\ NaHCO_3 + I_2 \rightarrow Na_3SbO_4 + 2\ NaI + 2\ CO_2 + H_2O.$$

It is seen that this reaction closely resembles that involved in the titration of arsenious oxide in the standardization of iodine (see above). The change of valence of antimony is two and hence the equivalent weight of Sb is one half of the atomic weight.

A common determination made by direct titration with standard iodine solution is that of sulphide. In the determination of sulphur in steel, the addition of hydrochloric acid to the steel liberates the sulphur as hydrogen sulphide which can be titrated with standard iodine solution: $H_2S + I_2 \rightarrow 2\,HI + S$. The equivalent weight of sulphur is obviously $\dfrac{S}{2} = 16.03$.

Example I. — A solution of iodine is of such concentration that 20.00 cc. are required to titrate the antimony in a 0.1000-gram sample of stibnite containing 84.95% of Sb_2S_3. This iodine is used for the analysis of sulphur in a 5.00-gram sample of steel. The steel is dissolved in hydrochloric acid and the H_2S evolved is caught in an ammoniacal solution of cadmium chloride. The resulting CdS is filtered, dissolved in acid, and the H_2S formed in the solution is titrated with 4.00 cc. of the iodine solution. Calculate the percentage of sulphur in the steel.

Solution. —

$$\dfrac{20.00 \times N \times \dfrac{Sb_2S_3}{4000}}{0.1000} \times 100 = 84.95$$

Whence, $N = 0.05000 =$ normality of I_2 soln.

$$\dfrac{4.00 \times 0.0500 \times \dfrac{S}{2000}}{5.00} \times 100 = 0.064\%. \quad Ans.$$

DETERMINATION OF COPPER IN ORES

Copper ores vary widely in composition from the nearly pure copper minerals, such as malachite and copper sulphide, to very low grade materials which contain such impurities as silica, lead, iron, silver, sulphur, arsenic, and antimony. In nearly all varieties there will be found a siliceous residue insoluble in acids. The method here given, which is a modification of that described by A. H. Low (*J. Am. Chem. Soc.* (1902), **24**, 1082), provides for the extraction of the copper from commonly occurring ores, and for the presence of their common impurities. For practice analyses it is advisable to select an ore of a fair degree of purity.

Procedure. — Weigh out two portions of about 0.5 gram each of the ore (which should be ground until no grit is detected) into 250 cc. Erlenmeyer flasks or small beakers. Add 10 cc. of concentrated nitric acid (sp. gr. 1.42) and heat very gently until the ore is decomposed and the acid evaporated nearly to dryness (Note 1). Add 5 cc. of concentrated hydrochloric acid (sp. gr. 1.2) and warm gently. Then add about 7 cc. of concentrated sulphuric acid (sp. gr. 1.84) and evaporate over a free flame until the sulphuric acid fumes freely (Note 2). It has then displaced nitric and hydrochloric acids from their salts.

Cool the flask or beaker, add 25 cc. of water, heat the solution to boiling, and boil for two minutes. Filter to remove insoluble sulphates, silica, and any silver that may have been precipitated as silver chloride, and receive the filtrate in a small beaker, washing the precipitate and filter paper with warm water until the filtrate and washings amount to 75 cc. Bend a strip of aluminum foil (5 cm. × 12 cm.) into triangular form and place it on edge in the beaker. Cover the beaker and boil the solution (being careful to avoid loss of liquid by spattering) for ten minutes, but do not evaporate to small volume.

Wash the cover glass and sides of the beaker. The copper should now be in the form of a precipitate at the bottom of the beaker or adhering loosely to the aluminum sheet. Remove the sheet, wash it carefully with hydrogen sulphide water and place it in a small beaker. Decant the solution through a filter, wash the precipitated copper twice by decantation with hydrogen sulphide water, and finally transfer the copper to the filter paper, where it is again washed thoroughly, being careful at all times to keep the precipitated copper covered with the wash water. Remove and discard the filtrate and place an Erlenmeyer flask under the funnel. Pour 15 cc. of dilute nitric acid (sp. gr. 1.20) over the aluminum foil in the beaker, thus dissolving any adhering copper. Wash the foil with hot water and remove it. Warm this nitric acid solution and pour it slowly through the filter paper, thereby dissolving the copper on the paper, receiving the acid solution in the Erlenmeyer flask. Before washing the paper, pour 5 cc. of saturated bromine water (Note 3) through it and finally wash the paper carefully with hot water and transfer any particles of copper which may be left on it to the Erlenmeyer flask. Boil to expel the bromine. Add concentrated ammonia drop by drop until the appearance of a deep blue coloration indicates an excess. Boil until the deep blue is displaced by a light bluish green coloration, or until brown stains form on the sides of the flask. Add 10 cc. of strong acetic acid (Note 4) and cool under the water tap. Add a solution containing about 3 grams of potassium iodide, as in the standardization, and titrate with thiosulphate solution until the yellow of the liberated iodine is nearly discharged. Add 5 cc. of freshly prepared starch solution and titrate to the disappearance of the blue color.

From the data obtained, calculate the percentage of copper (Cu) in the ore.

Notes. — 1. Nitric acid, because of its oxidizing power, is used as a solvent for the sulphide ores. As a strong acid it will also dissolve the copper from carbonate ores. The hydrochloric acid is added to dissolve oxides of iron and to precipitate silver and lead. The sulphuric acid displaces the other acids, leaving a solution containing sulphates only. It also, by its dehydrating action, renders silica from silicates insoluble.

2. Unless proper precautions are taken to insure the correct concentrations of acid the copper will not precipitate quantitatively on the

aluminum foil; hence care must be taken to follow directions carefully at this point. Lead and silver have been almost completely removed as sulphate and chloride respectively, or they too would be precipitated on the aluminum. Bismuth, though precipitated on aluminum, has no effect on the analysis. Arsenic and antimony precipitate on aluminum and would interfere with the titration if allowed to remain in the lower state of oxidation.

3. Bromine is added to oxidize arsenious and antimonous compounds from the original sample, and to oxidize nitrous acid formed by the action of nitric acid on copper and copper sulphide.

4. This reaction can be carried out in the presence of sulphuric and hydrochloric acids as well as acetic acid, but in the presence of these strong acids arsenic and antimonic acids may react with the hydriodic acid produced with the liberation of free iodine, thereby reversing the process and introducing an error.

STOICHIOMETRY

The final titration of copper in the analysis of copper ore is the same as that involved in the standardization of thiosulphate against pure copper (see above). Potassium iodide reduces copper ions to cuprous iodide which precipitates, and the liberated iodine is titrated with thiosulphate. The valence of copper changes by one and hence the equivalent weight of copper is $\frac{Cu}{1} = 63.57$.

Many other oxidizing agents can be determined by essentially the same method. That is, the oxidizing agent is allowed to oxidize an unmeasured excess of potassium iodide and liberate its own equivalent of free iodine which in turn is titrated with standard sodium thiosulphate. This is a direct determination and calculations are the same as if the original oxidizing agent were titrated with the thiosulphate, the latter being oxidized to tetrathionate ($Na_2S_4O_6$).

The analysis of pyrolusite, for example, can be made by an iodimetric process (Bunsen method). The ore is treated with hydrochloric acid which is oxidized by the manganese dioxide liberating free chlorine: $MnO_2 + 4 HCl \rightarrow MnCl_2 + Cl_2$. The latter is distilled over into a solution of potassium iodide and an equivalent amount of iodine is liberated: $Cl_2 + 2\ KI \rightarrow 2\ KCl + I_2$. The free iodine is then titrated with standard thiosulphate. This is a direct process although it involves three chemical changes.

Example I. — What weight of pyrolusite should be taken for analysis by the Bunsen method so that the volume of sodium thiosulphate (1 cc. $\backsimeq$ 0.006357 gram Cu) required shall be twice the percentage of manganese in the ore?

Solution. —

$$\text{Normality of thiosulphate} = \frac{0.006357}{1 \times \frac{Cu}{1000}} = 0.1000\ N$$

$$\frac{2 \times 0.1000 \times \frac{Mn}{2000}}{x} \times 100 = 1$$

$$x = 0.5493\ \text{gram.}\ \ Ans.$$

Among the oxidizing agents which can be determined by titration with thiosulphate after adding potassium iodide are:

(*a*) Lead peroxides, *e.g.* PbO_2, Pb_2O_3, and Pb_3O_4 (see analysis of pyrolusite by the permanganate process). The method is identical to the iodimetric method for pyrolusite.

(*b*) Hypochlorous acid ($OCl^- + 2\ I^- + 2\ H^+ \rightarrow Cl^- + I_2 + H_2O$). This can be applied to the analysis of bleaching powder for the determination of " available chlorine."

(*c*) Chlorate, iodates, periodates.

(*d*) Chromates, bichromates, and permanganates. Thus the analysis of chrome iron ore (see page 99) can be made by fusing with Na_2O_2 in the regular way, leaching with water, filtering, boiling to destroy excess peroxide, and acidifying. By adding excess potassium iodide, iodine is liberated by the bichromate and the free iodine can be titrated with standard thiosulphate.

(*e*) Ozone, hydrogen peroxide ($O_3 + 2\ KI + H_2O \rightarrow 2\ KOH + I_2 + O_2$; $H_2O_2 + 2\ KI + H_2SO_4 \rightarrow K_2SO_4 + I_2 + 2\ H_2O$).

(*f*) Iodides. By an indirect process. A measured excess of pure potassium iodate is added, the liberated iodine is boiled out and the excess iodate determined by adding an (unmeasured) excess of potassium iodide and titrating the liberated iodine with standard thiosulphate.

PROBLEMS

96. What is the value of 1 cc. of an iodine solution (1 cc. equivalent to 0.0300 gram $Na_2S_2O_3$) in terms of As_2O_3? *Answer:* 0.009385 gram.

97. 48 cc. of a solution of sodium thiosulphate are required to titrate the iodine liberated from an excess of potassium iodide solution by 0.3000 gram of pure KIO_3. ($KIO_3 + 5$ KI $+ 3$ $H_2SO_4 = 3$ $K_2SO_4 + 3$ $I_2 + 3$ H_2O.) What is the normal strength of the sodium thiosulphate and the value of 1 cc. of it in terms of iodine? *Answer:* 0.1753 N; 0.02224 gram.

98. One thousand cubic centimeters of 0.1079 N sodium thiosulphate solution is allowed to stand. Assume that one per cent by weight of the thiosulphate is decomposed by the carbonic acid present in the solution. To what volume must the solution be diluted to make it exactly 0.1 N as a reducing agent? ($Na_2S_2O_3 + 2$ $H_2CO_3 = H_2SO_3 + 2$ $NaHCO_3 + S$.)

Answer: 1090 cc.

99. An analyzed sample of stibnite containing 70.05% Sb is given for analysis. A student titrates it with a solution of iodine of which 1 cc. is equivalent to 0.004950 gram of As_2O_3. Due to an error on his part in standardization, the student's analysis shows the sample to contain 70.32% Sb. Calculate the true normal value of the iodine solution, and the percentage error in the analysis. *Answer:* 0.1000 N; 0.39%.

100. Weight of copper ore = 1.200 grams; volume of $Na_2S_2O_3$ used = 40.00 cc.; 1 cc. $Na_2S_2O_3 \backsimeq 0.004176$ gram $KBrO_3$. Calculate the percentage of copper in the ore in terms of Cu_2O. *Answer:* 35.78%.

101. What is the percentage of antimony (Sb) in a 0.2500-gram sample of stibnite if 20.83 cc. of iodine are used in the final titration? 1 cc. iodine $\backsimeq 0.004498$ gram As. *Answer:* 60.88%.

102. 40.48 cc. of a $KMnO_4$ solution will liberate from excess KI an amount of iodine which will be reduced by 20.24 cc. of a solution of $Na_2S_2O_3$ of which 1 cc. $\backsimeq 1$ cc. $I_2 \backsimeq 0.007496$ gram As. If 20.00 cc. of the thiosulphate were required to titrate a given sample of H_2O_2

($H_2O_2 + 2$ KI $+ H_2SO_4 \rightarrow K_2SO_4 + I_2 + 2$ H_2O)

what volume of oxygen gas (when measured under standard conditions) would be liberated if the same weight of H_2O_2 were titrated with the $KMnO_4$ solution? *Answer:* 44.8 cc.

DETERMINATION OF COPPER IN ORES

103. What volume of $Na_2S_2O_3$ solution (1 cc. ≎ 0.004873 gram $KIO_3 \cdot HIO_3$) will be required to titrate the iodine liberated by the chlorine evolved when a 0.450-gram sample of red lead containing 95.0% Pb_3O_4 (= $PbO_2 \cdot 2\ PbO$) is treated with hydrochloric acid? *Answer:* 8.31 cc.

104. Given an iodine solution (1 cc. ≎ 0.0198 gram As_2O_3) and a thiosulphate solution (1 cc. ≎ 0.00835 gram $KBrO_3$). Calculate (*a*) the weight of copper ore to be taken for analysis so that the percentage of copper may be found by dividing the burette reading by 2; (*b*) the burette reading in the titration of a 0.100-gram sample of pure Sb_2S_3.

Answer: 3.81 grams; 2.94 cc.

105. A 0.350-gram sample of impure potassium iodide is treated with 0.194 gram of pure K_2CrO_4 and the solution is boiled to expel all of the liberated iodine. The solution is then treated with excess potassium iodide and the liberated iodine is titrated with 10.0 cc. of $\frac{N}{10}$ sodium thiosulphate. Calculate the percentage purity of the sample of potassium iodide.

Answer: 94.8%.

106. If 20.0 cc. of thiosulphate (1 cc. ≎ 0.00490 gram $K_2Cr_2O_7$) are required for a certain sample of pyrolusite by the Bunsen method, what weight of $Na_2C_2O_4$ crystals should be added to a similar sample to require 20.0 cc. of $\frac{N}{10}$ permanganate solution by the indirect method?

Answer: 0.268 gram.

107. A sample of pyrolusite weighing 0.5000 gram is treated with an excess of hydrochloric acid, the liberated chlorine is passed into potassium iodide and the liberated iodine is titrated with sodium thiosulphate solution (49.66 grams of pure $Na_2S_2O_3 \cdot 5\ H_2O$ per liter). If 38.72 cc. are required, what volume of 0.25 normal permanganate solution will be required in an indirect determination in which a similar sample is reduced with 0.9012 gram $H_2C_2O_4 \cdot 2\ H_2O$ and the excess oxalic acid titrated?

Answer: 26.22 cc.

108. In the determination of sulphur in steel by evolving the sulphur as hydrogen sulphide, precipitating cadmium sulphide by passing the liberated hydrogen sulphide through ammoniacal cadmium chloride solution, and decomposing the CdS with acid in the presence of a measured amount of standard iodine, the following data are obtained: Sample, 5.027 grams; cc. $Na_2S_2O_3$ = 12.68; cc. Iodine = 15.59; 1 cc. Iodine ≎ 1.086 cc. $Na_2S_2O_3$; 1 cc. $Na_2S_2O_3$ ≎ 0.005044 gram Cu. Calculate the percentage of sulphur. ($H_2S + I_2 = 2\ HI + S$.) *Answer:* 0.107%.

109. Given the following data, calculate the percentage of iron in a sample of crude ferric chloride weighing 1.000 gram. The iodine liberated by the reaction $2\,FeCl_3 + 2\,HI = 2\,HCl + 2\,FeCl_2 + I_2$ is reduced by the addition of 50 cc. of sodium thiosulphate solution and the excess thiosulphate is titrated with standard iodine and requires 7.85 cc. 45 cc. I_2 solution $\Rightarrow$ 45.95 cc. $Na_2S_2O_3$ solution; 45 cc. As_2O_3 solution $\Rightarrow$ 45.27 cc. I_2 solution. 1 cc. arsenite solution $\Rightarrow$ 0.005160 gram As_2O_3. *Answer:* 23.77%.

110. Sulphide sulphur was determined in a sample of reduced barium sulphate by the evolution method, in which the sulphur was evolved as hydrogen sulphide and was passed into $CdCl_2$ solution, the acidified precipitate being titrated with iodine and thiosulphate. Sample, 5.076 grams; cc. $I_2 = 20.83$; cc. $Na_2S_2O_3 = 12.37$; 43.45 cc. $Na_2S_2O_3 \Rightarrow 43.42$ cc. I_2; 8.06 cc. $KMnO_4 \Rightarrow 44.66$ cc. $Na_2S_2O_3$; 28.87 cc. $KMnO_4 \Rightarrow 0.2004$ gram $Na_2C_2O_4$. Calculate the percentage of sulphide sulphur in the sample.

Answer: 0.050%.

111. What weight of pyrolusite containing 89.21% MnO_2 will oxidize the same amount of oxalic acid as 37.12 cc. of a permanganate solution, of which 1 cc. will liberate 0.0175 gram of I_2 from KI? *Answer:* 0.2493 gram.

112. A sample of pyrolusite weighs 0.2400 gram and is 92.50% pure MnO_2. The iodine liberated from KI by the manganese dioxide is sufficient to react with 46.24 cc. of $Na_2S_2O_3$ soln. What is the normal value of the thiosulphate? *Answer:* 0.1105 N.

113. A sample of chromite weighing 1.000 gram is fused with Na_2O_2, leached with water and acidified with H_2SO_4. The resulting solution is divided into two equal portions. One portion is treated with 50.00 cc. ferrous ammonium sulphate solution (containing 39.2 grams $FeSO_4 \cdot (NH_4)_2SO_4 \cdot 6\,H_2O$ per liter) and the excess requires 6.00 cc. $K_2Cr_2O_7$ solution (1 cc. $\Rightarrow$ 0.008376 gram Fe). How many cubic centimeters of sodium thiosulphate (1 cc. $\Rightarrow$ 0.01271 gram Cu) would be required to titrate the iodine liberated from excess potassium iodide by the other portion of the solution, and what is the percentage of Cr in the sample?

Answer: 20.50 cc.; 14.22%.

CHLORIMETRY

The processes included under the term *chlorimetry* comprise those employed to determine chlorine, hypochlorites, bromine, and hypobromites. The reagent employed is sodium arsenite in the presence of sodium bicarbonate. The reaction in the case of the hypochlorites is

$$NaClO + Na_3AsO_3 \rightarrow Na_3AsO_4 + NaCl.$$

The sodium arsenite may be prepared from pure arsenious oxide, as described below, and is stable for considerable periods; but commercial oxide requires resublimation to remove arsenic sulphide, which may be present in small quantity. To prepare the solution, dissolve about 5 grams of the powdered oxide, accurately weighed, in 10 cc. of a concentrated sodium hydroxide solution, dilute the solution to 300 cc., and make it faintly acid with dilute hydrochloric acid. Add 30 grams of sodium bicarbonate dissolved in a little water, and dilute the solution to exactly 1000 cc. in a measuring flask. Transfer the solution to a dry liter bottle and mix thoroughly.

It is possible to dissolve the arsenious oxide directly in a solution of sodium bicarbonate, with gentle warming, but solution in sodium hydroxide takes place much more rapidly, and the excess of the hydroxide is readily neutralized by hydrochloric acid, with subsequent addition of the bicarbonate to maintain neutrality during the titration.

The indicator required for this process is made by dipping strips of filter paper in a starch solution prepared as described on page 106, to which 1 gram of potassium iodide has been added. These strips are allowed to drain and spread upon a watch-glass until dry. When touched by a drop of the solution the paper turns blue until the hypochlorite has all been reduced and an excess of the arsenite has been added.

DETERMINATION OF THE AVAILABLE CHLORINE IN BLEACHING POWDER

Bleaching powder consists mainly of a calcium compound which is a derivative of both hydrochloric and hypochlorous acids. Its formula is CaClOCl. Its use as a bleaching or disinfecting agent, or as a source of chlorine, depends upon the amount of hypochlorous acid which it yields when treated with a stronger acid. It is customary to express the value of bleaching powder in terms of "available chlorine," by which is meant the chlorine present as hypochlorite, but not the chlorine present as chloride.

Procedure. — Weigh out from a stoppered test tube into a porcelain mortar about 3.5 grams of bleaching powder (Note 1). Triturate the powder in the mortar with successive portions of water until it is well ground and wash the contents into a 500 cc. measuring flask (Note 2). Fill the flask to the mark with water and shake thoroughly. Measure off 25 cc. of this semi-solution in a measuring flask, or pipette, observing the precaution that the liquid removed shall contain approximately its proportion of suspended matter.

Empty the flask or pipette into a beaker and wash it out. Run in the arsenite solution from a burette until no further reaction takes place on the starch-iodide paper when touched by a drop of the solution of bleaching powder. Repeat the titration, using a second 25 cc. portion.

From the volume of solution required to react with the bleaching powder, calculate the percentage of available chlorine in the latter, assuming the titration reaction to be that between chlorine and arsenious oxide:

$$As_4O_6 + 4\ Cl_2 + 4\ H_2O \rightarrow 2\ As_2O_5 + 8\ HCl.$$

Note that only one twentieth of the original weight of bleaching powder enters into the reaction.

Notes. — 1. The powder must be triturated until it is fine, otherwise the lumps will inclose calcium hypochlorite, which will fail to react with the arsenious acid. The clear supernatant liquid gives percentages which are below, and the sediment percentages which are above, the average. The liquid measured off should, therefore, carry with it its proper proportion of the sediment, so far as that can be brought about by shaking the solution just before removal of the aliquot part for titration.

2. Bleaching powder is easily acted upon by the carbonic acid in the air, which liberates the weak hypochlorous acid. This, of course, results in a loss of available chlorine. The original material for analysis should be kept in a closed container and protected from the air as far as possible. It is difficult to obtain analytical samples which are accurately representative of a large quantity of the bleaching powder. The procedure, as outlined, will yield results which are sufficiently exact for technical purposes.

III. PRECIPITATION METHODS

GENERAL DISCUSSION

The methods of analysis classified as precipitation or saturation methods are those in which a desired constituent is precipitated from solution by means of a standard solution of precipitating agent. As in the other methods thus far considered, an indicator must be used to show the exact completion of the reaction. Precipitation methods may be direct or indirect; that is, the precipitating agent may be added to a direct end-point, or an excess may be added and the excess determined by titration.

Computations are exactly the same in principle as those involved in acidimetry except that in the case of precipitation methods elements and radicals other than hydrogen enter into the metathesis, and to determine the equivalent weight it is usually only necessary to divide the molecular weight by the actual valence or total electrical charges on the reacting constituent. Thus the equivalent weight of di-sodium hydrogen phosphate as an acid is $\frac{Na_2HPO_4}{1} = 142.2$; as a sodium salt is $\frac{Na_2HPO_4}{2} = 71.01$; and as a phosphate is $\frac{Na_2HPO_4}{3} = 47.34$.

DETERMINATION OF SILVER AND HALIDE BY THE THIOCYANATE PROCESS

The addition of a solution of potassium or ammonium thiocyanate to one of silver in nitric acid causes a deposition of silver thiocyanate as a white, curdy precipitate. If ferric nitrate is also present, the slightest excess of the thiocyanate over that required to combine with the silver is indicated by the deep red which is characteristic of the thiocyanate test for iron.

The reactions involved are:

$$AgNO_3 + KSCN \rightarrow AgSCN + KNO_3,$$
$$3\ KSCN + Fe(NO_3)_3 \rightarrow Fe(SCN)_3 + 3\ KNO_3.$$

The ferric thiocyanate differs from the great majority of salts in that it is but very little dissociated in aqueous solutions, and the characteristic color appears to be occasioned by the formation of the un-ionized ferric salt.

The normal solution of potassium thiocyanate should contain a gram-molecular weight of the salt, or 97.17 grams per liter of solution. If ammonium thiocyanate is used, the amount is 76.11 grams.

PREPARATION OF THE SOLUTION

Procedure. — To prepare the solution for this determination, which should be approximately 0.05 N, dissolve about 5 grams of potassium thiocyanate, or 4 grams of ammonium thiocyanate, in a small amount of water; dilute this solution to 1000 cc. in a liter bottle and mix as usual.

Prepare 20 cc. of a saturated solution of ferric alum and add 5 cc. of dilute nitric acid (sp. gr. 1.20). About 5 cc. of this solution should be used as an indicator.

STANDARDIZATION

Method A

Procedure. — Crush a small quantity of silver nitrate crystals in a mortar (Note 1). Transfer them to a watch-glass and dry them for an hour at 110° C., protecting them from dust or other organic matter (Note 2). Weigh out two portions of about 0.5 gram each and dissolve them in 50 cc. of water. Add 10 cc. of dilute nitric acid which has been recently boiled to expel the lower oxides of nitrogen, if any, and then add 5 cc. of the indicator solution. Run in the thiocyanate solution from a burette, with constant stirring, allowing the precipitate to settle occasionally to obtain an exact recognition of the end-point, until a faint red tinge can be detected in the solution.

From the data obtained, calculate the normality of the thiocyanate solution.

Method B

Procedure. — Weigh out two portions of pure metallic silver (Note 3) of about 0.35 gram each. Dissolve in 15 cc. of dilute nitric acid (6 N) and boil until all the nitrous compounds are expelled. Add 5 cc. of the indicator solution and continue as in Method A.

Notes. — 1. The thiocyanate cannot be accurately weighed; its solutions must, therefore, be standardized against silver nitrate (or pure silver), either in the form of a standard solution or in small, weighed portions.

2. The crystals of silver nitrate sometimes inclose water which is expelled on drying. If the nitrate has come into contract with organic bodies, it suffers a reduction and blackens during the heating.

It is plain that a standard solution of silver nitrate (made by weighing out the crystals) is convenient or necessary if many titrations of this nature are to be made. In the absence of such a solution the liability of passing the end-point is lessened by setting aside a small fraction of the silver solution, to be added near the close of the titration.

3. Proof silver can be obtained from the U. S. Mint, Philadelphia, Pa. This standard has none of the disadvantages of silver nitrate mentioned in the preceding note.

DETERMINATION OF SILVER IN COIN

Procedure. — Weigh out two portions of the coin of about 0.5 gram each. Dissolve them in 15 cc. of dilute nitric acid (sp. gr. 1.2) and boil until all the nitrous compounds are expelled (Note 1). Cool the solution, dilute to 50 cc., and add 5 cc. of the indicator solution, and titrate with the thiocyanate to the appearance of the faint red coloration (Note 2).

From the corrected volume of the thiocyanate solution required, calculate the percentage of silver in the coin.

Notes. — 1. The reaction with silver may be carried out in nitric acid solutions and in the presence of copper, if the latter does not exceed 70 per cent. Above that percentage it is necessary to add silver in known quantity to the solution.

The liquid must be cold at the time of titration and entirely free from nitrous compounds, as these sometimes cause a reddening of the indicator solution. All utensils, distilled water, the nitric acid and the beakers must be free from chlorides, as the presence of these will cause precipitation of silver chloride, thereby introducing an error.

2. The solution containing the silver precipitate, as well as those from the standardization, should be placed in the receptacle for "silver residues" as a matter of economy.

DETERMINATION OF CHLORINE IN A CHLORIDE

Procedure. — Weigh out accurately two portions of the chloride of about 0.20 gram each. Dissolve in 200 cc. of hot water and add 5 cc. of dilute nitric acid which has been previously boiled to remove lower oxides of nitrogen. Calculate the weight of silver nitrate required theoretically to precipitate the chloride from the samples, assuming them to consist of pure sodium chloride unless more specific information as to their nature is available. Into separate small beakers weigh out accurately amounts of pure dry silver nitrate crystals about 10% in excess of the amounts calculated. Dissolve in a little water and add slowly to the corresponding solutions of chloride, rinsing out the beakers thoroughly with hot water to remove all of the silver nitrate (Note 1). Keep the solutions warm until the silver chloride has coagulated sufficiently to yield a clear filtrate. Filter off the precipitate (Note 2) and wash with hot water which has been slightly acidified with previously boiled nitric acid. Titrate the silver in the filtrate with standard thiocyanate solution using ferric alum as the indicator. Calculate the percentage of chlorine (Cl) in the chloride sample (Note 3).

Notes. — 1. It is also feasible to prepare a stock solution of silver nitrate and add it from a pipette of appropriate volume. The value of a pipetteful of the silver nitrate solution in terms of the thiocyanate solution is then established by separate titration. This method does away with the necessity of procuring pure silver nitrate crystals but tends to greater waste of silver.

2. Filtration is necessary since silver thiocyanate is more insoluble than silver chloride and the latter would be converted into the former during the titration.

It is possible to dilute the solution containing the suspended precipitate to exactly 500 cc. in a measuring flask, to filter the well-mixed solution through a dry filter, rejecting the first few cubic centimeters of filtrate, and to collect for titration exactly 250 cc. of the filtrate in a measuring flask. The final results must of course be multiplied by two. This method eliminates the washing of the precipitate and gives good results.

3. This method is equally applicable to the analysis of bromides,

DETERMINATION OF CHLORINE IN A CHLORIDE

iodides, cyanides, and thiocyanates, all of which yield quantitatively insoluble precipitates with silver ions from acid solution. Except in the case of the cyanide it is not necessary to filter the silver salt precipitate. Silver bromide and silver iodide are each more insoluble than silver thiocyanate.

STOICHIOMETRY

The following examples illustrate the computations involved in the above two types of analyses and in a few closely related determinations.

Example I. — What is the normality of a solution of potassium thiocyanate and how many grams of KSCN are contained in each liter if 19.80 cc. are required to titrate the silver in a 0.1000-gram sample of an alloy which contains 90.20% Ag and 9.80% Cu?

Solution. —

$$\frac{19.80 \times N \times \frac{Ag}{1000}}{0.1000} \times 100 = 90.20$$

$$N = 0.04223 = \text{normality KSCN.} \quad Ans.$$

$$0.04233 \times \frac{KSCN}{1} = 4.103 \text{ grams.} \quad Ans.$$

Example II. — To a half-gram sample of impure strontium chloride are added 1.784 grams of pure silver nitrate crystals. After dissolving, and filtering out the precipitated silver chloride, the filtrate requires 25.50 cc. of 0.2800 N KSCN. What is the percentage of $SrCl_2$ in the sample?

Solution. — Number of gram-milliequivalents $AgNO_3$ added =

$$\frac{1.784}{\frac{AgNO_3}{1000}} = 10.50$$

Number of gram-milliequivalents KSCN required =
$$25.50 \times 0.2800 = 7.14$$
Net gram-milliequivalents = $10.50 - 7.14 = 3.36$

$$\frac{3.36 \times \frac{SrCl_2}{2000}}{0.5000} \times 100 = 53.26\%. \quad Ans.$$

Example III. — A sample of feldspar weighs 2.000 grams. It is decomposed by heating with a mixture of calcium carbonate and ammonium chloride (J. L. Smith method) and after leaching with water, filtering and igniting, yields a mixture of sodium chloride and potassium chloride weighing 0.2558 gram. This mixture is dissolved in water and 35.00 cc. of $\frac{N}{10}$ AgNO$_3$ solution are added. The filtrate from the silver chloride precipitate then requires 0.92 cc. of $\frac{N}{50}$ KSCN solution to give a red color with ferric ions. Calculate the percentage of potassium (K) in the feldspar. Express also as % K$_2$O.

Solution. — Let x = grams KCl
Then 0.2558 − x = grams NaCl
Number of milliequivalents of chlorides

$$= \frac{x}{\frac{KCl}{1000}} + \frac{0.2558 - x}{\frac{NaCl}{1000}}.$$

Therefore, $\frac{x}{\frac{KCl}{1000}} + \frac{0.2558 - x}{\frac{NaCl}{1000}} = (35.00 \times 0.1000) - (0.92 \times 0.02000)$

whence $x = 0.243$ gram KCl

$$\frac{0.243 \times \frac{K}{KCl}}{2.000} \times 100 = 6.36\% \text{ K. } \textit{Ans.}$$

$$\frac{0.243 \times \frac{K_2O}{2\, KCl}}{2.000} \times 100 = 7.66\% \text{ K}_2\text{O. } \textit{Ans.}$$

(See page 145 for discussion of chemical factors.)

Example IV. — If a soluble cyanide is titrated with a solution of silver nitrate the silver ions first react to form a soluble complex salt: $2\, CN^- + Ag^+ \rightarrow Ag(CN)_2^-$. The next drop of silver solution then forms a precipitate of the normal silver cyanide: $Ag(CN)_2^- + Ag^+ \rightarrow Ag_2(CN)_2$. A study of the molal relationships in the above reactions shows that if a certain volume of silver solution is required to give the first

DETERMINATION OF CHLORINE IN A CHLORIDE

trace of permanent precipitate, an additional equal volume must be added to precipitate completely all of the cyanide as $Ag_2(CN)_2$. The Liebig method for determining cyanide makes use of this soluble complex formation. The sample is dissolved and titrated with standard silver nitrate solution to the first faint permanent turbidity.

A 0.2000-gram sample of impure sodium cyanide requires 24.95 cc. of $\frac{N}{20}$ $AgNO_3$ solution to form a faint permanent turbidity. What is the percentage purity of the sodium cyanide?

Solution. — $24.95 \times 2 = 49.90$ cc. = volume of $AgNO_3$ solution equivalent (as regards complete precipitation) to the NaCN.

$$\frac{49.90 \times \frac{1}{20} \times \frac{NaCN}{1000}}{0.2000} \times 100 = 61.13\%. \quad Ans.$$

Example V. — An alloy of nickel, free from interfering constituents, weighs 0.1000 gram and is dissolved in acid. The solution is made ammoniacal and is treated with 49.80 cc. of potassium cyanide solution: $Ni(NH_3)_6^{++} + 4\ CN^- + 6\ H_2O \rightarrow Ni(CN)_4^= + 6\ NH_4OH$. The excess cyanide is then titrated with 5.91 cc. of standard silver nitrate solution to a faint turbidity as in the Liebig method (see Example IV). The potassium cyanide solution contains 7.810 grams KCN per liter; the silver nitrate solution contains 0.01699 gram $AgNO_3$ per cubic centimeter. Calculate the percentage of nickel in the alloy.

Solution. — Normality of KCN = $\dfrac{7.810}{\frac{KCN}{1}} = 0.1200\ N$

Normality of $AgNO_3$ = $\dfrac{0.01699}{\frac{AgNO_3}{1000}} = 0.1000\ N$

5.91 cc. $AgNO_3 \backsimeq 5.91 \times \dfrac{0.1000}{0.1200} \times 2 = 9.85$ cc. KCN solution

$$\frac{(49.80 - 9.85) \times 0.1200 \times \dfrac{Ni}{4000}}{0.1000} \times 100 = 70.32\%. \quad Ans.$$

VOLUMETRIC ANALYSIS

PROBLEMS

114. In the volumetric analysis of silver coin (90% Ag), using a 0.5000 gram sample, what is the least normal value that a potassium thiocyanate solution may have and not require more than 50 cc. of solution in the analysis? *Answer:* 0.08339 N.

115. A mixture of pure lithium chloride and barium bromide weighing 0.6000 gram is treated with 45.15 cubic centimeters of 0.2017 N silver nitrate, and the excess titrated with 25.00 cc. of 0.1 N KSCN solution, using ferric alum as an indicator. Calculate the percentage of bromine as bromide in the sample. *Answer:* 40.11%.

116. A mixture of the chlorides of sodium and potassium from 0.5000 gram of a feldspar weighs 0.1500 gram, and after solution in water requires 22.71 cc. of 0.1012 N silver nitrate for the precipitation of the chloride ions. What are the percentages of Na_2O and K_2O in the feldspar?
Answer: 8.24% Na_2O; 9.14% K_2O.

117. A sample of alkali iodide containing inactive impurities weighs 0.5000 gram. It is dissolved in water, and 60.00 cc. of silver nitrate solution (containing the equivalent of 0.002122 gram of metallic silver per cubic centimeter) are added. This is in excess of the amount necessary to precipitate the iodide and the excess requires 1.03 cc. of potassium thiocyanate solution (of which 100 cc. will precipitate 0.1247 gram of silver from solution). Calculate the percentage of iodine present as iodide in the sample.
Answer: 29.64%.

118. A sample containing potassium cyanide weighs 0.400 gram and requires 16.00 cc. of $\frac{N}{8}$ silver nitrate solution to obtain a faint permanent turbidity. What is the percentage of KCN in the sample? If the sample also contained 10.0% of KCl, what volume of the silver nitrate solution would be required to precipitate the cyanide and chloride completely?
Answer: 65.1%; 36.3 cc.

119. In the analysis of a sample of silicate weighing 0.8000 gram, a mixture of NaCl and KCl weighing 0.2400 gram was obtained. The chlorides were dissolved in water, 50 cc. of $\frac{N}{10}$ $AgNO_3$ added, and the excess of silver titrated with KCNS solution using ferric alum as an indicator. In the last titration 14.46 cc. were used and the reagent was exactly 0.3% stronger in normality than the $AgNO_3$ solution. Find the percentage of K_2O and of Na_2O in the silicate. *Answer:* 12.6% K_2O; 5.3% Na_2O.

DETERMINATION OF CHLORINE IN A CHLORIDE

120. A mixture of KCN, KCNS, and K₂SO₄ (the last assumed to have no effect on the titration) weighing 0.6000 gram reacts with 18.4 cc. of AgNO₃ solution containing 5.35 grams AgNO₃ per liter, before a permanent precipitate is obtained. At this point 75.0 cc. more of the silver solution are added and the excess titrated with 12.0 cc. of $\frac{N}{15}$ KCNS. Find the percentage composition of the mixture.

Answer: 12.5% KCN; 15.8% KCNS; 71.7% K₂SO₄.

121. A mixture of LiCl and BaBr₂ weighing 0.5000 gram is treated with 37.60 cc. of $\frac{N}{5}$ silver nitrate and the excess of the latter titrated with 18.50 cc. of $\frac{N}{9}$ thiocyanate solution. Find the per cent Ba in the mixture.

Answer: 34.4%.

122. A nickel ore weighing 1.200 grams was analyzed by the volumetric method. The ammoniacal solution was treated with 48.00 cc. of cyanide solution (containing 0.0140 gram of KCN per cc.) and the excess cyanide requires 0.50 cc. of silver nitrate solution (containing 0.0125 gram of AgNO₃ per cc.). Calculate the percentage of nickel in the ore.

Answer: 12.5%.

123. What is the percentage of nickel in an ore if, when analyzed volumetrically by the cyanide method, 20.00 cc. of potassium cyanide solution (containing one tenth of a gram-millimole of KCN per cc.) and 1.50 cc. of silver nitrate (containing two tenths of a gram-millimole of AgNO₃ per cc.) were used? Weight of sample taken = 0.2500 gram.

Answer: 8.20%.

PART III
GRAVIMETRIC ANALYSIS
GENERAL DIRECTIONS

GRAVIMETRIC analysis involves the following principal steps: first, the weighing of the sample; second, the solution of the sample; third, the separation of some substance from solution containing, or bearing a definite relation to, the constituent to be measured, under conditions which render this separation as complete as possible; fourth, the segregation of that substance, commonly by filtration; and finally, the determination of its weight, or that of some derivative formed from it on ignition. For example, the gravimetric determination of aluminum is accomplished by solution of the sample, precipitation of the aluminum in the form of the hydroxide, collection of the hydroxide upon a filter, complete removal by washing of all foreign soluble matter, and the burning of the filter and ignition of the precipitate to aluminum oxide, in which condition it is weighed.

Among the operations which are common to nearly all gravimetric analyses are precipitation, filtration, washing of precipitates, ignition of precipitates, and the use of desiccators. In order to avoid burdensome repetitions in the descriptions of the various gravimetric procedures which follow, certain general instructions are introduced at this point. These instructions must, therefore, be considered to be as much a part of all subsequent procedures as the description of apparatus, reagents, or manipulations.

WEIGHING

The analytical balance, the fundamentally important instrument in gravimetric analysis, has already been described on pages 10 to 15.

PRECIPITATION

For successful gravimetric analyses those substances are precipitated which are least soluble under conditions which can be easily established, and which separate from solution in such a state that they can be filtered readily and washed free from impurities. In general, the substances are the same as those already familiar to the student of Qualitative Analysis.

When possible, substances are precipitated which separate in crystalline form, since such substances are less likely to clog the pores of filter paper and can be more completely washed. To increase the size of the crystals, which further promotes filtration and washing, it is often desirable to allow a precipitate to remain for some time in contact with the solution from which it has separated. The solution is usually kept warm during this period of "digestion." The small crystals gradually disappear and the larger crystals increase in size, probably as the result of the force known as surface tension, which tends to reduce the surface of a given mass of material to a minimum, combined with a slightly greater solubility of small crystals as compared with the larger ones.

Amorphous substances, such as ferric hydroxide, aluminum hydroxide, or silicic acid, separate in a gelatinous form and are relatively difficult to filter and wash. Substances of this class also exhibit a tendency to form colloidal solutions with pure water. To prevent this as far as possible, they are washed with solutions of volatile salts, as will be described in some of the following procedures.

In all precipitations the reagent should be added slowly, with constant stirring, and should be hot when circumstances permit. The slow addition is less likely to occasion contamination of the precipitate by the inclosure of other substances which may be in the solution, or of the reagent itself.

FUNNELS AND FILTERS

Filtration in analytical processes is most commonly effected through paper filters. In special cases these may be advantageously replaced by an asbestos filter in a perforated porcelain or platinum crucible, commonly known, from its originator, as a Gooch filter. The operation and use of a filter of this type is described on page 149. Porous crucibles of a material known as alundum may also be employed to advantage in special cases.

The glass funnels for use with paper filters should have an angle as near 60° as possible, and a narrow stem about six inches in length. The filters should be washed filters, *i.e.* those which have been treated with hydrochloric and hydrofluoric acids, and which on incineration leave a very small and definitely known weight of ash, generally about 0.00003 gram. Such filters are readily obtainable.

The filter should be carefully folded to fit the funnel according to either of the following two methods:

(*A*) Fold the filter paper along its diameter and again fold along the radius at right angles to the original fold. A cone is formed which, on opening, has an angle of 60°. Funnels for analytical use are supposed to have this same angle, but are rarely accurate. It is possible, however, with care, to fit a filter thus folded into a funnel in such a way as to prevent air from passing down between the paper and the funnel. An unbroken column of liquid in the stem, by its gentle suction, promotes the rate of filtration.

(*B*) (1) Fold the paper along one diameter; (2) open the paper and fold it at right angles to the first fold; (3) turn the paper over and mark on the edge the half-way point between two of the creases; (4) imagining the paper to be the face of a compass, hold it so that the mark corresponds to the "northeast" position; (5) fold the point of the crease corresponding to the "south" position upon this mark and crease the paper; (6) make a fold along the diameter at right angles to this last fold; (7) place the paper in the funnel with alternate segments folded over; (8) moisten the paper and with the finger, fit it snugly to the funnel. The filter paper will then have four short segments where there are three thicknesses and four where there is one thickness, alternately distributed around the funnel.

This paper can be more closely and uniformly fitted to the funnel and thereby prevents the entrance of air and the breaking of the column of liquid. In dissolving a precipitate from such a filter, the student should lift each of the four folds in order that the solvent may act upon any precipitate that may have worked its way underneath.

The paper should be of such size that the upper edge is about one fourth inch below the top of the funnel. Under no circumstances should the filter extend above the edge of the funnel, as it is then utterly impossible to effect complete washing.

To test the efficiency of the filter, fill it with distilled water. This water should soon fill the stem completely, forming a continuous column of liquid which, by its hydrostatic pressure, produces a gentle suction, thus materially promoting the rapidity of filtration. Unless the filter allows free passage of water under these conditions, it is likely to give much trouble when a precipitate is placed upon it.

The use of a suction pump to promote filtration is rarely advantageous in quantitative analysis, if paper filters are employed. The tendency of the filter to break, unless the point of the filter paper is supported by a perforated porcelain cone or a small "hardened filter" of parchment, and the tendency of the precipitates to pass through the pores of the filter, more than compensate for the possible gain in time. On the other hand, filtration by suction may be useful in the case of precipitates which do not require ignition before weighing, or in the case of precipitates which are to be discarded without weighing. This is best accomplished with the aid of the special apparatus called a Gooch filter referred to above.

FILTRATION AND WASHING OF PRECIPITATES

Solutions should be filtered while hot, as far as possible, since the passage of a liquid through the pores of a filter is retarded by friction, and this, for water at 100° C., is less than one sixth of the resistance at 0° C.

When the filtrate is received in a beaker, the stem of the funnel should touch the side of the receiving vessel to avoid loss by spattering. Neglect of this precaution is a frequent source of error.

The vessels which contain the initial filtrate should *always* be replaced by clean ones, properly labeled, before the washing of a precipitate begins. In many instances a finely divided precipitate which shows no tendency to pass through the filter at first, while the solution is relatively dense, appears at once in the washings. Under such conditions the advantages accruing from the removal of the first filtrate are obvious, both as regards the diminished volume requiring refiltration, and also the smaller number of washings subsequently required.

Much time may often be saved by washing precipitates by decantation, *i.e.* by pouring over them, while still in the original vessel, considerable volumes of wash-water and allowing them to settle. The supernatant, clear wash-water is then decanted through the filter, so far as practicable without disturbing the precipitate, and a new portion of wash-water is added. This procedure can be employed to special advantage with gelatinous precipitates, which fill up the pores of the filter paper. As the medium from which the precipitate is to settle becomes less dense it subsides less readily, and it ultimately becomes necessary to transfer it to the filter and complete the washing there.

A precipitate should never completely fill a filter. The wash-water should be applied at the top of the filter, above the precipitate. It may be shown mathematically that the washing is most *rapidly* accomplished by filling the filter well to the top with wash-water each time, and allowing it to drain completely after each addition; but that when a precipitate is to be washed with the *least possible volume* of liquid the latter should be applied in repeated *small* quantities.

Gelatinous precipitates should not be allowed to dry before complete removal of foreign matter is effected. They are likely to shrink and crack, and subsequent additions of wash-water pass through these channels only.

All filtrates and wash-waters without exception must be properly tested. *This lies at the foundation of accurate work*, and the student should clearly understand that it is only by the invariable application of this rule that assurance of ultimate reliability can be secured. Every original filtrate must be tested to prove complete precipitation of the compound to be separated, and the wash-waters must also be tested to assure complete removal of foreign material. In testing the latter, the amount first taken should be but a few drops if the filtrate contains material which is to be subsequently determined. When, however, the washing of the filter and precipitate is nearly completed the amount should be increased, and for the final test not less than 3 cc. should be used.

It is impossible to trust to one's judgment with regard to the washing of precipitates; the washings from *each precipitate* of a series simultaneously treated must be tested, since the rate of washing will often differ materially under apparently similar conditions. *No exception can ever be made to this rule.*

The habit of placing a clean common filter paper under the receiving beaker during filtration is one to be commended. On this paper a record of the number of washings can very well be made as the portions of wash-water are added.

It is an excellent practice, when possible, to retain filtrates and precipitates until the completion of an analysis, in order that, in case of question, they may be examined to discover sources of error.

For the complete removal of precipitates from containing vessels, it is often necessary to rub the sides of these vessels to loosen the adhering particles. This can best be done with a device made by slipping over the end of a stirring rod a strip of soft rubber sometimes called a " policeman."

DESICCATORS

Desiccators should be filled with fused, anhydrous calcium chloride, over which is placed a clay triangle, or an iron triangle covered with silica tubes, to support the crucible or other apparatus.

Pumice moistened with concentrated sulphuric acid may be used in place of the calcium chloride, and is essential in special cases; but for most purposes the calcium chloride, if renewed occasionally and not allowed to cake together, is efficient and does not slop about when the desiccator is moved.

Desiccators should never remain uncovered for any length of time as the dehydrating agents rapidly lose their efficiency on exposure to the air. The cover of the desiccator should be made air-tight by the use of a thin coating of vaseline.

CRUCIBLES

It is often necessary in quantitative analysis to employ fluxes to bring into solution substances which are not dissolved by acids. The fluxes in most common use are sodium carbonate and sodium or potassium acid sulphate. In gravimetric analysis it is usually necessary to ignite the separated substance after filtration and washing, in order to remove moisture, or to convert it through physical or chemical changes into some definite and stable form for weighing. Crucibles to be used in fusion processes must be made of materials which will withstand the action of the fluxes employed, and crucibles to be used for ignitions must be made of material which will not undergo any permanent change during the ignition, since the initial weight of the crucible must be deducted from the final weight of the crucible and product to obtain the weight of the ignited substance. The three materials which satisfy these conditions, in general, are platinum, porcelain, and silica.

Platinum crucibles have the advantage that they can be employed at high temperatures, but, on the other hand, these crucibles can never be used when there is a possibility of the reduction to the metallic state of metals like lead, copper, silver, or gold, which would alloy with and ruin the crucible. When platinum crucibles are used with compounds of arsenic or phosphorus, special precautions are necessary to prevent damage. This statement applies to both fusions and ignitions.

Fusions with sodium carbonate are usually made in platinum,

since porcelain or silica crucibles are attacked by this reagent. Acid sulphate fusions, which require comparatively low temperatures, can sometimes be made in platinum, although platinum is slightly attacked by the flux. Porcelain or silica crucibles may be used with acid fluxes.

Platinum crucibles should never be used for fusions with sodium hydroxide, potassium hydroxide, or sodium peroxide.

Silica crucibles are less likely to crack on heating than porcelain crucibles on account of their smaller coefficient of expansion. Ignition of substances not requiring too high a temperature may be made in porcelain or silica crucibles.

Iron, nickel, or silver crucibles are used in special cases.

In general, platinum crucibles should be used whenever such use is practicable, and this is the custom in private, research, or commercial laboratories. Platinum has, however, become so valuable that it is liable to theft unless constantly under the protection of the user. As constant protection is often difficult in instructional laboratories, it is advisable, in order to avoid serious monetary losses, to use porcelain or silica crucibles whenever these will give satisfactory service.

PREPARATION OF CRUCIBLES FOR USE

All crucibles, of whatever material, must always be cleaned, ignited, and allowed to cool in a desiccator before weighing, since all bodies exposed to the air condense on their surfaces a layer of moisture which increases their weight. The amount and weight of this moisture varies with the humidity of the atmosphere, and the latter may change from hour to hour. The air in the desiccator (see above) is kept at a constant and low humidity by the drying agent which it contains. Bodies which remain in a desiccator for a sufficient time (usually 20–30 minutes) retain, therefore, on their surfaces a constant weight of moisture which is the same day after day, thus insuring constant conditions.

Hot objects, such as ignited crucibles, should be allowed to cool in the air until, when held near the skin, but little heat is noticeable. If this precaution is not taken, the air within the desiccator is strongly heated and expands before the desiccator is covered. As the temperature falls, the air contracts, causing a reduction of air pressure within the covered vessel. When the cover is removed (which is often rendered difficult), the inrush of air from the outside may sweep light particles out of a crucible, thus ruining an entire analysis.

Constant heating of platinum causes a slight crystallization of the surface, which, if not removed, penetrates into the crucible. Gentle polishing of the surface destroys the crystalline structure and prevents further damage. If sea sand is used for this purpose, great care is necessary to keep it from the desk, since beakers are easily scratched by it, and subsequently crack on heating.

Platinum crucibles stained in use may often be cleaned by fusing in them potassium or sodium acid sulphate, or by heating with ammonium chloride. If the former is used, care should be taken not to heat so strongly as to expel all of the sulphuric acid, since the normal sulphates sometimes expand so rapidly on cooling as to split the crucible. The fused material should be poured out, while hot, on to a *dry* tile or iron surface.

IGNITION OF PRECIPITATES

Although the details of the ignition of a precipitate vary somewhat with the character of the precipitate, its moisture content, and the temperature to which it is to be heated, the general procedure may be considered to consist of three steps:

1. The precipitate is dried. This can be accomplished in several ways. A piece of wet filter paper can be folded over the top of the funnel containing the washed precipitate to protect it from dust, and the funnel placed in a hot closet for a few hours. The folded filter paper containing the precipitate can be placed in the crucible in which the ignition is to be made and dried in the hot closet.

A much more rapid method is to fold the edges of the paper over the precipitate and place in the crucible in which the ignition is to be made, preferably with the mouth of the paper cone toward the bottom of the crucible. The crucible is then supported at an incline on a wire triangle and a crucible cover is laid against the mouth of the crucible so as to give a chimney effect for the circulation of air as shown in Figure 2 B. A very small flame is then applied to *the cover*. The resulting circulation of warm air very quickly dries the paper and precipitate.

2. The filter paper is burned off. This is accomplished by applying a very small flame to the base of the inclined crucible containing the dried precipitate (see Figure 2 A). The paper should smoulder off and never be permitted to catch on fire. Otherwise there is danger of fine particles of precipitate being swept out and in the case of some precipitates, of reduction of the precipitate by the carbon of the paper.

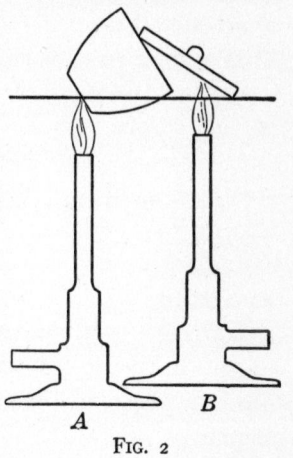

FIG. 2

3. The precipitate is ignited. After the paper has been burned off, the heat at the base of the crucible is gradually increased, usually to the full heat of the Tirrill or Bunsen burner. Often the final heating is made with the higher temperature of a Meker or Fischer burner or of a blast lamp. In any case, the final heating is made with the crucible in a vertical position.

Precipitates are always ignited to constant weight, that is, until the loss in weight between two heatings is negligible (usually less than 0.5 milligram).

STOICHIOMETRY

CHEMICAL FACTOR

In gravimetric analysis a constituent is isolated as a weighable compound of definite, known composition. From the weight of the latter the weight of the constituent can be calculated by multiplying by a factor. This factor is called a *chemical factor* and represents that weight of desired constituent equivalent to one unit weight of given substance. Thus, the chemical factor for converting a given weight of barium sulphate into an equivalent weight of sulphur is $\dfrac{S}{BaSO_4} = \dfrac{32.06}{233.4} = 0.1375$, since one atom of sulphur (atomic weight = 32.06) is present in one molecule of barium sulphate (molecular weight = 233.5). The chemical factor for converting a given weight of ferric oxide (Fe_2O_3) into the equivalent amount of ferrous oxide (FeO) is $\dfrac{2\,FeO}{Fe_2O_3} = \dfrac{143.6}{159.6}$, and for converting a given weight of Mn_3O_4 into an equivalent amount of manganese is $\dfrac{3\,Mn}{Mn_3O_4} = \dfrac{164.7}{228.7}$, since two molecules of ferrous oxide are equivalent to one molecule of ferric oxide, and three atoms of manganese are equivalent to one molecule of Mn_3O_4. A common error in expressing chemical factors is to omit the proper coefficient.

In reactions involving the formation of several intermediate compounds, it is in general unnecessary to calculate the weights of these compounds in order to find the amount of desired constituent. The knowledge of the mechanism of the reaction is desirable as a means of determining the proper coefficient in the chemical factor, and the chemical factor should represent *directly* the desired constituent equivalent to the substance weighed.

Example I. — A sample of magnetite ore (impure Fe_3O_4) weighing 0.5000 gram is fused with an oxidizing flux and the ferric compound so formed is eventually precipitated as ferric hydroxide ($Fe(OH)_3$) and ignited to ferric oxide (Fe_2O_3). The weight of the latter is found to be 0.4980 gram. What is the percentage of iron in the magnetite ore? Calculate also in terms of the oxide Fe_3O_4.

Solution. — $\dfrac{0.4980 \times \dfrac{2\,Fe}{Fe_2O_3}}{0.5000} \times 100 = 69.61\%$ Fe. *Ans.*

$\dfrac{0.4980 \times \dfrac{2\,Fe_3O_4}{3\,Fe_2O_3}}{0.5000} \times 100 = 96.27\%\ Fe_3O_4.$ *Ans.*

(In this problem it is not necessary to calculate the weight of the intermediate compound $Fe(OH)_3$.)

Example II. — What weight of pyrite ore (impure FeS_2) should be taken for analysis so that the number of centigrams of precipitated $BaSO_4$ shall be twice the percentage of FeS_2?

Solution. — $\dfrac{0.02 \times \dfrac{FeS_2}{2\,BaSO_4}}{x} \times 100 = 1$

$x = 0.5141$ gram. *Ans.*

PROBLEMS

124. Calculate the chemical factor for (*a*) Sn in SnO_2; (*b*) MgO in $Mg_2P_2O_7$; (*c*) P_2O_5 in $Mg_2P_2O_7$; (*d*) Fe in Fe_2O_3; (*e*) SO_4 in $BaSO_4$.
Answer: (*a*) 0.7879; (*b*) 0.3620; (*c*) 0.6378; (*d*) 0.6990; (*e*) 0.4115.

125. Calculate the log factor for (*a*) Pb in $PbCrO_4$; (*b*) Cr_2O_3 in $PbCrO_4$; (*c*) Pb in PbO_2 and (*d*) CaO in CaC_2O_4.
Answer: (*a*) 9.8069–10; (*b*) 9.3713–10; (*c*) 9.9376–10; (*d*) 9.6415–10.

126. How many grams of Mn_3O_4 can be obtained from 1 gram of MnO_2? How many ounces of Mn_3O_4 can be obtained from 1 pound of MnO_2?
Answer: 0.8774 gram; 14.04 oz.

127. How much As_2O_3 and how much CuO are equivalent to 1 gram of pure paris green, $Cu_3(AsO_3)_2 \cdot 2\,As_2O_3 \cdot Cu(C_2H_3O_2)_2$?
Answer: 0.5855 gram; 0.3139 gram.

128. Phosphate is sometimes determined by precipitating and weighing as $(NH_4)_3PO_4 \cdot 12\,MoO_3$. If the percentage of P_2O_5 were desired, what would be the chemical factor? *Answer:* 0.0378.

129. Bromide is sometimes determined by precipitation as silver bromide which when heated in a current of chlorine is converted to silver chloride. If the latter is weighed, what would be the chemical factor for finding the percentage of bromine? *Answer:* 0.5576.

130. Calculate (*a*) the grams of silver in one gram of silver chloride; (*b*) the grams of carbon dioxide liberated by the addition of an excess of acid to one gram of calcium carbonate; (*c*) the grams of $MgCl_2$ necessary to precipitate 1 gram of $MgNH_4PO_4$.
Answer: (*a*) 0.7526; (*b*) 0.4397; (*c*) 0.6940.

131. How many cubic centimeters of a solution of potassium bichromate containing 26.30 grams of $K_2Cr_2O_7$ per liter must be taken in order to yield 0.6033 gram of Cr_2O_3 after reduction and precipitation of the chromium?
$K_2Cr_2O_7 + 3\,SO_2 + H_2SO_4 = K_2SO_4 + Cr_2(SO_4)_3 + H_2O$.

Answer: 44.39 cc.

132. After oxidizing the arsenic in 0.5000 gram of pure As_2S_3 to arsenic acid, it is precipitated with "magnesia mixture" ($MgCl_2 + 2\,NH_4Cl$). If exactly 12.6 cc. of the mixture are required, how many grams of $MgCl_2$ per liter does the solution contain? $H_3AsO_4 + MgCl_2 + 3\,NH_4OH = MgNH_4AsO_4 + 2\,NH_4Cl + 3\,H_2O$.

Answer: 30.71 grams.

133. A mixture of barium oxide and calcium oxide weighing 2.2120 grams is transformed into mixed sulphates, weighing 5.023 grams. Calculate the grams of calcium oxide and barium oxide in the mixture.

Answer: 1.824 grams CaO; 0.3877 gram BaO.

DETERMINATION OF CHLORINE IN A SOLUBLE CHLORIDE

Method A
With the Use of a Gooch Filter

Procedure. — Weigh out to four significant figures duplicate samples of 0.25–0.30 gram of the chloride into 200–300 cc. beakers. Dissolve each portion of the chloride in 150 cc. of distilled water and add about ten drops of dilute nitric acid (sp. gr. 1.20) (Note 1). Calculate the volume of silver nitrate solution required to effect complete precipitation in each case, and add slowly about 5 cc. in excess of that amount, with constant stirring. Heat the solutions cautiously to boiling, stirring occasionally, and continue the heating and stirring until the precipitates settle promptly, leaving a nearly clear supernatant liquid (Note 2). This heating should not take place in direct sunlight (Note 3). The beaker should be covered with a watch-glass, and both boiling and stirring so regulated as to preclude any possibility of loss of material. Add to the clear liquid one or two drops of silver nitrate solution, to make sure that an excess of the reagent is present. If a precipitate, or cloudiness, appears as the drops fall into the solution, heat again, and stir until the whole precipitate has coagulated. The solution is then ready for filtration.

Prepare a Gooch filter as follows: Fold over the top of a Gooch funnel (Fig. 3) a piece of rubber-band tubing, such as is known as "bill-tie" tubing, and fit into the mouth of the funnel a perforated porcelain crucible (Gooch crucible), making sure that when the crucible is gently forced into the mouth of the funnel an airtight joint results. (A small 1 or 1¼-inch glass funnel may be used, in which case the rubber tubing is stretched over the top of the funnel and then drawn up over the side of the crucible until an airtight joint is secured.)

FIG. 3

Fit the funnel into the stopper of a filter bottle, and connect the filter bottle with the suction pump. Suspend some finely divided asbestos, which has been washed with acid, in 20 to 30 cc. of water (Note 4); allow this to settle, pour off the very fine particles, and then pour some of the mixture cautiously into the crucible until an even felt of asbestos, not over $\frac{1}{32}$ inch in thickness, is formed. A gentle suction must be applied while preparing this felt. Wash the felt thoroughly by passing through it distilled water until all fine or loose particles are removed, increasing the suction at the last until excess water is removed. Place on top of the felt the small, perforated porcelain disc and hold it in place by pouring a very thin layer of asbestos over it, washing the whole carefully; then place the crucible in a small beaker, and place both in a drying closet at 100–110° C. for thirty to forty minutes. Cool the crucible in a desiccator, and weigh. Heat again for twenty to thirty minutes, cool, and again weigh, repeating this until the weight is constant within 0.0003 gram. The filter is then ready for use.

Place the crucible in the funnel, and apply a gentle suction, *after which* the solution to be filtered may be poured in without disturbing the asbestos felt. When pouring liquid upon a Gooch filter hold the stirring-rod at first well down in the crucible, so that the liquid does not fall with any force upon the asbestos, and afterward keep the crucible well filled with the solution.

Decant the liquid above the silver chloride slowly upon the filter, leaving as much of the precipitate in the beaker as possible. Wash the precipitate twice by decantation with cold water; then transfer it to the filter with the aid of a stirring-rod with a rubber tip, and a stream from the wash-bottle.

Examine the first portions of the filtrate which pass through the filter with great care for asbestos fibers, which are most likely to be lost at this point. Refilter the liquid if any fibers are visible. Finally, wash the precipitate thoroughly with cold water until free from soluble silver salts (Note 5). To test the washings, disconnect the suction at the flask and remove the funnel or filter tube from the suction flask. Hold the end of

CHLORINE IN A SOLUBLE CHLORIDE

the tube over the mouth of a small test tube and add from a wash-bottle 2-3 cc. of water. Allow the water to drip through into the test tube and add a drop of dilute hydrochloric acid. No precipitate or cloud should form in the wash-water. Dry the filter and contents at 100-110° C. until the weight is constant within 0.0003 gram, as described for the preparation of the filter. Deduct the weight of the dry crucible from the final weight, and from the weight of silver chloride thus obtained calculate the percentage of chlorine in the sample of soluble chloride (Note 6).

Notes. — 1. The nitric acid is added before precipitation to lessen the tendency of the silver chloride to carry down with it other substances which might be precipitated from a neutral solution. A large excess of the acid would exert a slight solvent action upon the chloride.

2. The solution should not be boiled after the addition of the nitric acid before the presence of an excess of silver nitrate is assured, since a slight interaction between the nitric acid and the chloride ions is possible, by which a loss of chlorine, either as such or as hydrochloric acid, might ensue. The presence of an excess of the precipitant can usually be recognized at the time of its addition, by the increased readiness with which the precipitate coagulates and settles.

3. The precipitate should not be exposed to strong sunlight, since under those conditions a reduction of the silver chloride ensues which is accompanied by a loss of chlorine. The superficial alteration which the chloride undergoes in diffused daylight is not sufficient to materially affect the accuracy of the determination. It should be noted, however, that a slight error does result from the effect of light upon the silver chloride precipitate and in cases in which the greatest obtainable accuracy is required, the procedure described under "Method B" should be followed, in which this slight reduction of the silver chloride is corrected by subsequent treatment with nitric and hydrochloric acids.

4. The asbestos used in the Gooch filter should be of the finest quality and capable of division into minute fibrous particles. A coarse felt is not satisfactory.

The washed asbestos for this type of filter is prepared by digesting in concentrated hydrochloric acid, long-fibered asbestos which has been cut in pieces of about 0.5 cm. in length. After digestion, the asbestos is filtered off on a filter plate and washed with hot, distilled water until free from chlorides. A small portion of the asbestos is shaken with water, forming a thin suspension, which is bottled and kept for use.

5. The precipitate must be washed with warm water until it is absolutely free from silver and sodium nitrates. It may be assumed that the sodium salt is completely removed when the wash-water shows no evidence of silver. It must be borne in mind that silver chloride is somewhat soluble in hydrochloric acid, and only a single drop should be added. The washing should be continued until no cloudiness whatever can be detected in 3 cc. of the washings.

Silver chloride is but slightly soluble in water. The solubility varies with its physical condition within small limits, and is about 0.0018 gram per liter at 18° C. for the curdy variety usually precipitated. The chloride is also somewhat soluble in solutions of many chlorides, in solutions of silver nitrate, and in concentrated nitric acid.

As a matter of economy, the filtrate, which contains whatever silver nitrate was added in excess, may be set aside. The silver can be precipitated as chloride and later converted into silver nitrate.

6. The use of the Gooch filter commends itself strongly when a considerable number of halogen determinations are to be made, since successive portions of the silver halides may be filtered on the same filter, without the removal of the preceding portions, until the crucible is about two thirds filled. If the felt is properly prepared, filtration and washing are rapidly accomplished on this filter, and this, combined with the possibility of collecting several precipitates on the same filter, is a strong argument in favor of its use with any but gelatinous precipitates.

Method B
With the Use of a Paper Filter

Procedure. — Weigh out two portions of soluble chloride of about 0.25–0.3 gram each and proceed with the precipitation of the silver chloride as described under Method A above. When the chloride is ready for filtration prepare two 9 cm. washed paper filters. Decant the liquid through the filters, wash twice by decantation and transfer the precipitates to the filters, finally washing them until free from silver solution as described. The funnel should then be covered with a moistened filter paper by stretching it over the top and edges, to which it will adhere on drying. It should be properly labeled with the student's name and desk number, and then placed in a drying closet, at a temperature of about 100–110° C., until completely dry.

The perfectly dry filter is then opened over a circular piece of clean, smooth, glazed paper about six inches in diameter, placed upon a larger piece about twelve inches in diameter. The precipitate is removed from the filter as completely as possible by rubbing the sides gently together, or by scraping them cautiously with a feather which has been cut close to the quill and is slightly stiff (Note 1). In either case, care must be taken not to rub off any considerable quantity of the paper, nor to lose silver chloride in the form of dust. Cover the precipitate on the glazed paper with a watch-glass to prevent loss of fine particles and to protect it from dust from the air. Fold the filter paper carefully, roll it into a small cone, and wind loosely around *the top* a piece of small platinum wire (Note 2). Hold the filter by the wire over a small porcelain crucible (which has been cleaned, ignited, cooled in a desiccator, and weighed), ignite it, and allow the ash to fall into the crucible. Place the crucible upon a clean clay triangle, on its side, and ignite, with a low flame well at its base, until all the carbon of the filter has been consumed. Allow the crucible to cool, add two drops of concentrated nitric acid and one drop of concentrated hydrochloric acid, and heat *very cautiously*, to avoid spattering, until the acids have been expelled; then transfer the main portion of the precipitate from the glazed paper to the cooled crucible, placing the latter on the larger piece of glazed paper and brushing the precipitate from the smaller piece into it, sweeping off all particles belonging to the determination.

Moisten the precipitate with two drops of concentrated nitric acid and one drop of concentrated hydrochloric acid, and again heat with great caution until the acids are expelled and the precipitate is white, when the temperature is slowly raised until the silver chloride just begins to fuse at the edges (Note 3). The crucible is then cooled in a desiccator and weighed, after which the heating (without the addition of acids) is repeated, and it is again weighed. This must be continued until the weight is constant within 0.0003 gram in two consecutive weighings.

Deduct the weight of the crucible, and calculate the percentage of chlorine in the sample taken for analysis.

Notes. — 1. The separation of the silver chloride from the filter is essential, since the burning carbon of the paper would reduce a considerable quantity of the precipitate to metallic silver, and its complete reconversion to the chloride within the crucible, by means of acids, would be accompanied by some difficulty. The small amount of silver reduced from the chloride adhering to the filter paper after separating the bulk of the precipitate, and igniting the paper as prescribed, can be dissolved in nitric acid, and completely reconverted to chloride by hydrochloric acid. The subsequent addition of the two acids to the main portion of the precipitate restores the chlorine to any silver which may have been partially reduced by the sunlight. The excess of the acids is volatilized by heating.

2. The platinum wire is wrapped around the top of the filter during its incineration to avoid contact with any reduced silver from the reduction of the precipitate. If the wire were placed nearer the apex, such contact could hardly be avoided.

3. Silver chloride should not be heated to complete fusion, since a slight loss by volatilization is possible at high temperatures. The temperature of fusion is not always sufficient to destroy filter shreds; hence these should not be allowed to contaminate the precipitate.

STOICHIOMETRY

The method for the gravimetric determination of chloride is of course applicable to the determination of bromide or iodide. It is also possible to determine the percentage of each halide in samples containing mixtures of them. To do this, sufficient data must be obtained to furnish as many independent equations as there are unknown constituents to be determined.

Example I. — A sample containing NaCl, NaBr, and inert material weighs 1.000 gram, and with excess silver nitrate solution gives a precipitate consisting of AgCl and AgBr which weighs 0.5260 gram. By heating this precipitate in a current of chlorine gas the silver bromide is converted to silver chloride and the precipitate then weighs 0.4260 gram. What is the percentage of NaCl and of NaBr present in the original sample?

Solution. — Let x = weight of NaCl
and y = weight of NaBr,

Then $\left(x \times \dfrac{AgCl}{NaCl}\right) + \left(y \times \dfrac{AgBr}{NaBr}\right) = 0.5260$

and $\left(x \times \dfrac{AgCl}{NaCl}\right) + \left(y \times \dfrac{AgCl}{NaBr}\right) = 0.4260$

Solving, $x = 0.04225 = 4.23\%$ NaCl
$y = 0.2314 = 23.14\%$ NaBr. *Ans.*

An analogous gravimetric determination is that of the determination of sodium and potassium in a silicate ore or similar material. The sample is heated with a mixture of calcium carbonate and ammonium chloride, leached with water, the calcium removed, and the solution evaporated to dryness and ignited, leaving a mixture of sodium chloride and potassium chloride which is weighed and dissolved in water. Then the chloride is precipitated with silver nitrate and weighed. From these data, the percentage of Na_2O and of K_2O can be calculated. A method (*J. L. Smith Method*) which gives greater precision is to treat the weighed mixture of sodium chloride and potassium chloride with chlorplatinic acid (H_2PtCl_6) or perchloric acid ($HClO_4$) and alcohol and weigh the resulting precipitate of the potassium salt (K_2PtCl_6 or $KClO_4$). The amount of sodium can be calculated by difference.

Example II. — A silicate weighing 0.5000 gram is decomposed and a mixture of NaCl and KCl is subsequently obtained weighing 0.1180 gram. From this mixture a precipitate of AgCl is obtained weighing 0.2451 gram. What is the percentage of Na_2O and of K_2O in the silicate? If the alkali chlorides had been treated with chlorplatinic acid and alcohol, what weight of K_2PtCl_6 would have been obtained?

Let x = weight of KCl
Then $0.1180 - x$ = weight of NaCl

$\left(x \times \dfrac{AgCl}{KCl}\right) + \left((0.1180 - x) \times \dfrac{AgCl}{NaCl}\right) = 0.2451$

Solving, $\quad x = 0.0837$ gram KCl
$\quad\quad\quad 0.1180 - x = 0.0343$ gram NaCl

$$\left. \begin{array}{l} \dfrac{0.0837 \times \dfrac{K_2O}{2\ KCl} \times 100 = 10.6\%\ K_2O}{0.5000} \\[2ex] \dfrac{0.0343 \times \dfrac{Na_2O}{2\ NaCl} \times 100 = 3.64\%\ Na_2O}{0.5000} \end{array} \right\} Ans.$$

$$0.0837 \times \frac{K_2PtCl_6}{2\ KCl} = 0.2729 \text{ gram } K_2PtCl_6. \quad Ans.$$

PROBLEMS

134. If a sample of silver coin weighing 0.2500 gram gives a precipitate of AgCl weighing 0.2991 gram, what weight of AgI could have been obtained from the same weight of sample, and what is the percentage of silver in the coin? *Answer:* 0.4898 gr.; 90.05%.

135. One gram of a mixture of silver chloride and silver bromide is found to contain 0.6635 gram of silver. What is the percentage of bromine?
Answer: 21.30%.

136. A precipitate of silver chloride and silver bromide weighs 0.8132 gram. On heating in a current of chlorine, the silver bromide is converted to silver chloride, and the mixture loses 0.1450 gram in weight. Calculate the percentage of chlorine in the original precipitate. *Answer:* 6.13%.

137. A mixture of silver chloride and silver iodide on being heated in a current of chlorine is converted entirely into silver chloride and is found to have lost exactly 6 per cent of its weight. What is the percentage of chlorine in the original mixture? *Answer:* 20.92%.

138. In what proportion must NaCl and KI be mixed so that the mixture shall contain the same percentage of halogen as does pure KBr?
Answer: 1 : 1.4.

139. A sample of soluble salts weighs 1.200 grams and contains chloride, bromide, and iodide. With silver nitrate a precipitate of the silver salts of these halides is obtained which weighs 0.4500 gram. On heating this precipitate in a current of chlorine gas, the silver bromide and silver iodide are converted to silver chloride and the precipitate then weighs 0.3300 gram. A similar sample when treated with palladous chloride precipitates only the

iodide as PdI_2 and the latter precipitate weighs 0.0900 gram. Find the approximate percentages of chlorine, bromine, and iodine in the original sample.
Answer: 0.43% Cl; 11% Br; 5.3% I.

140. A half-gram sample of a silicate is decomposed by the J. L. Smith method and a mixture of NaCl and KCl is obtained which weighs 0.1803 gram. These halides are dissolved in water and treated with silver nitrate. The resulting precipitate weighs 0.3904 gram. Calculate the percentage of Na_2O and of K_2O in the silicate.
Answer: 8.78% Na_2O; 13.5% K_2O.

141. Analyzing a 0.5000-gram sample of a silicate ore by the J. L. Smith method gives 0.1500 gram of the mixed alkali salts (NaCl + KCl). From these are obtained 0.1200 gram of K_2PtCl_6. Find the percentage of Na_2O in the mineral.
Answer: 12.00%.

142. If 0.8000 gram of a mineral yields 0.2400 gram of NaCl + KCl and this mixture of chlorides contains exactly 58% of chlorine, find the percentage of Na_2O and of K_2O in the mineral.
Answer: 12.7% Na_2O; 3.83% K_2O.

143. In the analysis of a sample of feldspar weighing 1.060 grams, a mixture of the chlorides of sodium and potassium is obtained which weighs 0.2137 gram. Subsequent treatment converts the potassium into $KClO_4$ weighing 0.2800 gram. What is the percentage of Na_2O in the sample?
Answer: 3.19%.

144. In the J. L. Smith method for the determination of alkalies in feldspar, if the mixed alkali salts (KCl + NaCl) weigh 0.1506 gram and contain 55.00% chlorine, what weight of precipitate with perchloric acid would be subsequently obtained?
Answer: 0.121 gram.

DETERMINATION OF IRON AND OF SULPHUR IN FERROUS AMMONIUM SULPHATE, $FeSO_4 \cdot (NH_4)_2SO_4 \cdot 6\,H_2O$

DETERMINATION OF IRON

Procedure. — Weigh out into beakers (200–250 cc.) two portions of the sample of about 1 gram each (Note 1). Moisten with 5 cc. of dilute hydrochloric acid (Note 2) and dissolve in 50 cc. of water. Heat the solution to boiling, and while at the boiling point add concentrated nitric acid (sp. gr. 1.42), *drop by drop* (noting the volume used), until the brown coloration, which appears after the addition of a part of the nitric acid, gives place to a yellow or red (Note 3). Avoid a large excess of nitric acid, but be sure that the action is complete. Pour this solution cautiously into about 200 cc. of water, containing a slight excess of ammonia. Calculate for this purpose the amount of aqueous ammonia required to neutralize the hydrochloric and nitric acids added (see Appendix for data), and also to precipitate the iron as ferric hydroxide. Assume the ferrous ammonium sulphate taken for analysis to be pure (Note 4). The volume thus calculated will be in excess of that actually required for precipitation, since the acids are in part consumed in the oxidation process, or are volatilized. Heat the solution to boiling, and allow the precipitated ferric hydroxide to settle. Decant the clear liquid through a washed filter (11 cm.), keeping as much of the precipitate in the beaker as possible. Wash twice by decantation with 100 cc. of hot water. Reserve the filtrate. Dissolve the iron from the filter with hot, dilute hydrochloric acid (sp. gr. 1.12), adding it in small portions, using as little as possible and noting the volume used. Collect the solution in the beaker in which precipitation took place. Add 1 cc. of nitric acid (sp. gr. 1.42), boil for a few moments, and again pour into a calculated excess of ammonia.

Wash the precipitate twice by decantation, and finally transfer it to the original filter. Wash continuously with hot water until finally 3 cc. of the washings, acidified with nitric acid (Note 5), show no evidences of the presence of chlorides when tested with silver nitrate. The filtrate and washings are combined with those from the first precipitation and treated for the determination of sulphur, as prescribed on page 164.

Heat a platinum or porcelain crucible, cool it in a desiccator and weigh, repeating until a constant weight is obtained.

Fold the top of the filter paper over the moist precipitate of ferric hydroxide and transfer it cautiously to the crucible. Wipe the inside of the funnel with a small fragment of washed filter paper, if necessary, and place the paper in the crucible.

Dry the precipitate either in the hot closet or by means of a free flame exactly as prescribed on page 144. If the latter method is used, take great care to avoid loss by spattering. Smoke off the paper in the prescribed way, being careful not to raise the temperature sufficiently high to cause the paper to ignite.

When the paper is fully charred, move the burner to the base of the crucible and raise the temperature to the full heat of the burner for fifteen minutes, with the crucible still inclined on its side, but without the cover (Note 6). Finally set the crucible upright in the triangle, cover it, and heat at the full temperature of a blast lamp or other high temperature burner. Cool and weigh in the usual manner (Note 7). Repeat the strong heating until the weight is constant within 0.0003 gram.

From the weight of ferric oxide (Fe_2O_3) calculate the percentage of iron (Fe) in the sample (Note 8).

Notes. — 1. If a selection of pure material for analysis is to be made, crystals which are cloudy are to be avoided on account of loss of water of crystallization; and also those which are red, indicating the presence of ferric iron. If, on the other hand, the value of an average sample of material is desired, it is preferable to grind the whole together, mix thoroughly, and take a sample from the mixture for analysis.

2. When aqueous solutions of ferrous compounds are heated in the air, oxidation of the Fe^{++} ions to Fe^{+++} ions readily occurs in the absence of free acid. The H^+ and OH^- ions from water are involved in the oxidation process and the result is, in effect, the formation of some ferric hydroxide which tends to separate. Moreover, at the boiling temperature, the ferric sulphate produced by the oxidation hydro-

lyzes in part with the formation of a basic ferric sulphate, which also tends to separate from solution. The addition of the hydrochloric acid prevents the formation of ferric hydroxide and of ferric basic sulphate.

3. The nitric acid, after attaining a moderate strength, oxidizes the Fe^{++} ions to Fe^{+++} ions with the formation of an intermediate nitroso-compound similar in character to that formed in the "ring-test" for nitrates. The nitric oxide is driven out by heat, and the solution then shows by its color the presence of ferric compounds. A drop of the oxidized solution may be tested on a watch-glass with potassium ferricyanide, to insure a complete oxidation. This oxidation of the iron is necessary, since Fe^{++} ions are not completely precipitated by ammonia.

The ionic changes which are involved in this oxidation are expressed by the equation:

$$3\ Fe^{++} + NO_3^- + 4\ H^+ \rightarrow 3\ Fe^{+++} + NO + 2\ H_2O,$$

the H^+ ions coming from the acid in the solution, in this case either the nitric or the hydrochloric acid.

4. The ferric hydroxide precipitate tends to carry down some sulphuric acid in the form of basic ferric sulphate. This tendency is lessened if the solution of the iron is added to an excess of OH^- ions from the ammonium hydroxide, since under these conditions immediate and complete precipitation of the ferric hydroxide ensues. A gradual neutralization with ammonia would result in the local formation of a neutral solution within the liquid, and subsequent deposition of a basic sulphate as a consequence of a local deficiency of OH^- ions from the NH_4OH and a partial hydrolysis of the ferric salt. Even with this precaution the entire absence of sulphates from the first iron precipitate is not assured. It is, therefore, redissolved and again thrown down by ammonia. The organic matter of the filter paper may occasion a partial reduction of the iron during solution, with consequent possibility of incomplete subsequent precipitation with ammonia. The nitric acid is added to reoxidize this iron.

To avoid errors arising from the solvent action of ammoniacal liquids upon glass, the iron precipitate should be filtered without unnecessary delay.

5. The washings from the ferric hydroxide are acidified with nitric acid, before testing with silver nitrate, to destroy the ammonia which is a solvent for silver chloride.

The use of suction to promote filtration and washing is permissible, though not prescribed. The precipitate should not be allowed to dry during the washing.

6. These directions for the ignition of the precipitate must be closely followed. A ready access of atmospheric oxygen is of special importance to insure the reoxidation to ferric oxide of any iron which may be reduced to magnetic oxide (Fe_3O_4) during the combustion of the filter. The final heating over the blast lamp is essential for the complete expulsion of the last traces of water from the hydroxide.

7. Ignited ferric oxide is somewhat hygroscopic. On this account the weighings must be promptly completed after removal from the desiccator. In all weighings after the first, it is well to place the weights upon the balance-pan before removing the crucible from the desiccator. It is then only necessary to move the rider to obtain the weight.

8. The gravimetric determination of aluminum or chromium is comparable with that of iron just described, with the additional precaution that the solution must be boiled until it contains but a very slight excess of ammonia, since the hydroxides of aluminum and chromium are more soluble in it than ferric hydroxide.

The most important properties of these hydroxides, from a quantitative standpoint, other than those mentioned, are the following: All can be precipitated by the hydroxides of sodium and potassium, but always inclose some of the precipitant, and should be reprecipitated with ammonium hydroxide before ignition to oxides. Chromium and aluminum hydroxides dissolve in an excess of the caustic alkalies and form anions, probably of the formula AlO_2^- and CrO_2^-. Chromium hydroxide is reprecipitated from this solution on boiling. When first precipitated the hydroxides are all readily soluble in acids, but aluminum hydroxide dissolves with considerable difficulty after standing or boiling for some time. The precipitation of the hydroxides is promoted by the presence of ammonium chloride, but is partially or entirely prevented by the presence of tartaric or citric acids, glycerine, sugars, and some other forms of soluble organic matter. The hydroxides yield on ignition oxides suitable for weighing (Al_2O_3, Cr_2O_3, Fe_2O_3).

STOICHIOMETRY

It is sometimes necessary to calculate the volume of a reagent of known specific gravity and percentage composition in order to neutralize an acid or base or to precipitate a constituent. This calculation may be made by first computing the normality of the reagent and applying the stoichiometric principles of Volumetric Analysis, but it is usually easier to apply a chemical factor as illustrated in the following example.

Example. — How many cubic centimeters of ammonium hydroxide solution of density 0.950 (containing 12.72% NH$_3$ by weight) are required to neutralize 50.0 cc. of hydrochloric acid of density 1.100 (containing 20.0% HCl by weight)? How many cubic centimeters of the ammonium hydroxide solution are required to precipitate the iron from 0.800 gram of pure FeSO$_4 \cdot$(NH$_4$)$_2$SO$_4 \cdot$6 H$_2$O after oxidation of the iron to the ferric state?

Solution. — 50.0 cc. of the acid contain 50.0 × 1.100 × 0.200 grams of HCl. The weight of NH$_3$ required for neutralization would be $50.0 \times 1.100 \times 0.200 \times \dfrac{NH_3}{HCl} = 5.12$ grams. Since each cubic centimeter of ammonium hydroxide solution contains 1 × 0.950 × 0.1272 gram of NH$_3$, the volume of ammonium hydroxide required for neutralization would be

$$\frac{5.12}{1 \times 0.950 \times 0.1272} = 42.4 \text{ cc.} \quad Ans.$$

One molecule of ferrous ammonium sulphate furnishes one atom of ferrous iron which will be oxidized to one atom of ferric iron. The precipitation of one atom of ferric iron by ammonium hydroxide requires three molecules of the latter: Fe^{+++} + 3 NH$_4$OH → Fe(OH)$_3$ + 3 NH$_4^+$. Three molecules of ammonium hydroxide are equivalent to three molecules of NH$_3$: NH$_4$OH ⇌ NH$_3$ + H$_2$O. Hence three molecules of NH$_3$ are equivalent to one molecule of ferrous ammonium sulphate in the above reaction.

$$0.800 \times \frac{3 \text{ NH}_3}{\text{FeSO}_4 \cdot (\text{NH}_4)_2\text{SO}_4 \cdot 6 \text{ H}_2\text{O}} = 0.1043 \text{ gram NH}_3.$$

Since each cc. of the NH$_4$OH solution contains 1 × 0.950 × 0.1272 gram of NH$_3$: the volume of ammonium hydroxide solution required for precipitation is

$$\frac{0.1043}{1 \times 0.950 \times 0.1272} = 0.862 \text{ cc.} \quad Ans.$$

ANALYSIS OF FERROUS AMMONIUM SULPHATE

PROBLEMS

145. How many cubic centimeters of hydrochloric acid (sp. gr. 1.13 containing 25.75% HCl by weight) are required to exactly neutralize 25 cc. of ammonium hydroxide (sp. gr. 0.90 containing 28.33% NH_3 by weight)?
Answer: 47.03 cc.

146. How many cubic centimeters of ammonium hydroxide solution (sp. gr. 0.96 containing 9.91% NH_3 by weight) are required to precipitate the aluminum as aluminum hydroxide from a two-gram sample of alum $(KAl(SO_4)_2 \cdot 12\ H_2O)$? What will be the weight of the ignited precipitate?
Answer: 2.26 cc.; 0.2154 gram.

147. What volume of nitric acid (sp. gr. 1.05 containing 9.0% HNO_3 by weight) is required to oxidize the iron in one gram of $FeSO_4 \cdot 7\ H_2O$ in the presence of sulphuric acid? $6\ FeSO_4 + 2\ HNO_3 + 3\ H_2SO_4 = 3\ Fe_2(SO_4)_3 + 2\ NO + 4\ H_2O$.
Answer: 0.80 cc.

148. If 0.7530 gram of ferric nitrate $(Fe(NO_3)_3 \cdot 9\ H_2O)$ is dissolved in water and 1.37 cc. of HCl (sp. gr. 1.11 containing 21.92% HCl by weight) are added, how many cubic centimeters of ammonia (sp. gr. 0.96 containing 9.91% NH_3 by weight) are required to neutralize the acid and precipitate the iron as ferric hydroxide?
Answer: 2.63 cc.

149. To a suspension of 0.3100 gram of $Al(OH)_3$ in water are added 13.00 cc. of aqueous ammonia (sp. gr. 0.90 containing 28.4% NH_3 by weight). How many cubic centimeters of sulphuric acid (sp. gr. 1.18 containing 24.7% H_2SO_4 by weight) must theoretically be added to the mixture in order to bring the aluminum into solution?
Answer: 34.8 cc.

150. How many cubic centimeters of sulphurous acid (containing 75 grams SO_2 per liter) are required to reduce the iron in 1 gram of ferric alum $(KFe(SO_4)_2 \cdot 12\ H_2O)$? $Fe_2(SO_4)_3 + SO_2 + 2\ H_2O = 2\ FeSO_4 + 2\ H_2SO_4$.
Answer: 0.85 cc.

151. How many cubic centimeters of ammonium hydroxide (sp. gr. 0.946 containing 13.88% NH_3 by weight) are required to precipitate the iron as $Fe(OH)_3$ from a sample of pure $FeSO_4 \cdot (NH_4)_2SO_4 \cdot 6\ H_2O$, which requires 0.34 cc. of nitric acid (sp. gr. 1.350 containing 55.79% HNO_3 by weight) for oxidation of the iron? (See problem No. 147 for reaction.)
Answer: 4.74 cc.

152. In the analysis of an iron ore by solution, oxidation and precipitation of the iron as $Fe(OH)_3$, what weight of sample must be taken for analysis so that each one hundredth of a gram of the ignited precipitate of Fe_2O_3 shall represent one tenth of one per cent of iron?
Answer: 6.99 grams.

153. What weight of magnetite must be taken for analysis in order that, after precipitating and igniting all the iron to Fe_2O_3, the percentage of Fe_3O_4 in the sample may be found by multiplying the weight in grams of the ignited precipitate by 100? *Answer:* 0.9665 gram.

154. A 1-gram sample of limonite containing inactive impurities is dissolved in acid, and the solution is divided into two equal portions. One portion is reduced and titrated with $KMnO_4$ (of which 1 cc. ≎ 0.008193 gram $H_2C_2O_4 \cdot 2\,H_2O$). The other portion is just neutralized, and 40 cc. of 1.5 N ammonia are added to precipitate the iron. This is in excess of the necessary amount, and the number of cc. in excess is equal to the number of cc. of $KMnO_4$ required in the volumetric process. What is the per cent Fe in the sample? *Answer:* 46.13%.

DETERMINATION OF SULPHUR

Procedure. — Add to the combined filtrates from the ferric hydroxide about 0.6 gram of anhydrous sodium carbonate; cover the beaker, and then add dilute hydrochloric acid (sp. gr. 1.12) in moderate excess and evaporate to dryness on the water bath. Add 10 cc. of concentrated hydrochloric acid (sp. gr. 1.20) to the residue, and again evaporate to dryness on the bath. Dissolve the residue in water, filter if not clear, transfer to a 700 cc. beaker, dilute to about 400 cc., and cautiously add hydrochloric acid until the solution shows a distinctly acid reaction (Note 1). Heat the solution to boiling, and add *very slowly* and with constant stirring, 20 cc. in excess of the calculated amount of a hot 0.2 N barium chloride solution (Notes 2 and 3). Continue the boiling for about ten minutes, allow the precipitate to settle, and decant the liquid at the end of half an hour (Note 4). Replace the beaker containing the original filtrate by a clean beaker, wash the precipitated sulphate by decantation with hot water, and subsequently upon the filter until it is freed from chlorides, testing the washings as described in the determination of iron. Transfer the filter and precipitate to a weighed platinum or porcelain crucible, dry and smoke off the paper in the regular way, and ignite over a Tirrill burner until the weight is constant (Note 5). From the weight of $BaSO_4$ calculate the percentage of sulphur in the sample.

Notes. — 1. Barium sulphate is slightly soluble in hydrochloric acid, even dilute, probably as a result of the reduction in the degree of dissociation of sulphuric acid in the presence of the H^+ ions of the hydrochloric acid, and possibly because of the formation of a complex anion made up of barium and chlorine; hence only the smallest excess should be added over the amount required to acidify the solution.

2. The ionic changes involved in the precipitation of barium sulphate are very simple: $Ba^{++} + SO_4^{--} \rightarrow [BaSO_4]$.

This case affords one of the best illustrations of the effect of an excess of a precipitant in decreasing the solubility of a precipitate. If the conditions are considered which exist at the moment when just enough of the Ba^{++} ions have been added to correspond to the SO_4^{--} ions in the solution, it will be seen that nearly all of the barium sulphate has been precipitated, and that the small amount which then remains in the solution which is in contact with the precipitate must represent a saturated solution for the existing temperature, and that this solution is comparable with a solution of sugar to which more sugar has been added than will dissolve. It should be borne in mind that the quantity of barium sulphate in this *saturated solution is a constant quantity* for the existing conditions. The dissolved barium sulphate, like any electrolyte, is dissociated, and the equilibrium conditions may be expressed thus:

$$\frac{Conc'n\ Ba^{++} \times Conc'n\ SO_4^{--}}{Conc'n\ BaSO_4} = Constant,$$

and since *Conc'n BaSO₄* for the saturated solution has a constant value (which is very small), it may be eliminated, when the expression becomes *Conc'n* $Ba^{++} \times$ *Conc'n* $SO_4^{--} = Constant$, which is the "solubility product" of $BaSO_4$. If, now, an excess of the precipitant, a soluble barium salt, is added in the form of a relatively concentrated solution (the slight change of volume of a few cubic centimeters may be disregarded for the present discussion), the concentration of the Ba^{++} ions is much increased, and as a consequence the *Conc'n* SO_4 must decrease in proportion if the value of the expression is to remain constant, which is a requisite condition if the law of mass action upon which our discussion depends holds true. In other words, SO_4^{--} ions must combine with some of the added Ba^{++} ions to form $[BaSO_4]$; but it will be recalled that the solution is already saturated with $BaSO_4$, and this freshly formed quantity must, therefore, separate and add itself to the precipitate. This is exactly what is desired in order to insure more complete precipitation and greater accuracy, but a practical limit is placed upon the quantity of the precipitant which may be properly added by other conditions, as stated in the following note.

3. Barium sulphate, in a larger measure than most compounds, tends to carry down other substances which are present in the solution from which it separates, even when these other substances are relatively soluble, and including the barium chloride used as the precipitant. This is also notably true in the case of nitrates and chlorates of the alkalies, and of ferric compounds; and, since in this analysis ammonium nitrate has resulted from the neutralization of the excess of the nitric acid added to oxidize the iron, it is essential that this should be destroyed by repeated evaporation with a relatively large quantity of hydrochloric acid. During evaporation a mutual decomposition of the two acids takes place, and the nitric acid is finally decomposed and expelled by the excess of hydrochloric acid.

Iron is usually found in the precipitate of barium sulphate when thrown down from hot solutions in the presence of ferric salts. This, according to Kuster and Thiel (*Zeit. anorg. Chem.*, **22**, 424), is due to the formation of a complex ion $(Fe(SO_4)_2)$ which precipitates with the Ba^{++} ion, while Richards (*Zeit. anorg. Chem.*, **23**, 383) ascribes it to hydrolytic action, which causes the formation of a basic ferric complex which is occluded in the barium precipitate. Whatever the character of the compound may be, it has been shown that it loses sulphuric anhydride upon ignition, causing low results.

The contamination of the barium sulphate by iron is much less in the presence of ferrous than ferric salts. If, therefore, the sulphur alone were to be determined in the ferrous ammonium sulphate, the precipitation by barium might be made directly from an aqueous solution of the salt, which had been made slightly acid with hydrochloric acid. There is some occlusion, however, even with ferrous iron and it is best to precipitate and remove the iron completely before attempting to precipitate barium sulphate. Methods whereby ferric iron is held in solution as a complex ion with tartaric or citric acid likewise lessen the contamination of iron by barium sulphate but do not completely eliminate it.

4. The precipitation of the barium sulphate is probably complete at the end of a half-hour, and the solution may safely be filtered at the expiration of that time if it is desired to hasten the analysis.

As already noted, many precipitates of the general character of this sulphate tend to grow more coarsely granular if digested for some time with the liquid from which they have separated. It is therefore well to allow the precipitate to stand in a warm place for several hours, if practicable, to promote ease of filtration. The filtrate and washings should always be carefully examined for minute quantities of the sulphate which may pass through the pores of the filter. This is best accomplished by imparting to the filtrate a gentle rotary motion, when the sulphate, if present, will collect at the center of the bottom of the beaker.

5. A reduction of barium sulphate to the sulphide may very readily be caused by the reducing action of the burning carbon of the filter, and much care should be taken to prevent any considerable reduction from this cause. Subsequent ignition, with ready access of air, reconverts the sulphide to sulphate unless a considerable reduction has occurred. In the latter case it is expedient to add one or two drops of sulphuric acid and to heat cautiously until the excess of acid is expelled.

6. Barium sulphate requires about 400,000 parts of water for its solution. It is not decomposed at a red heat but suffers loss, probably of sulphur trioxide, at a temperature above 900° C

DETERMINATION OF SULPHUR IN PYRITE

The importance of pyrite in the manufacture of sulphuric acid makes the determination of sulphur in pyrite of great commercial importance. Many methods have been proposed for making this determination but only a few of these methods have withstood the test of time and experience. The methods in common use may be divided into two classes: (1) wet methods, in which the sulphur is oxidized by aqua regia (Lunge method) or by bromine (Allen and Bishop method); and (2) fusion methods, using such oxidizing fluxes as a sodium carbonate-potassium nitrate mixture (Fresenius method), or sodium peroxide. A wet process determines only that portion of the total sulphur which is available for the manufacture of sulphuric acid; a fusion method determines the total sulphur present in the pyrite. Both processes are here represented.

Method A
Lunge Method

Weigh out accurately into a 200 cc. casserole about 0.5 gram of the pyrite which has been ground to extreme fineness (Note 1). Tap the casserole so that the sample is spread out over the bottom and pour over it 20 cc. of aqua regia which has been freshly made by mixing three volumes of concentrated nitric acid (sp. gr. 1.42) and one volume of concentrated hydrochloric acid (sp. gr. 1.20). Cover immediately with a watch glass, and if the oxidizing action is vigorous allow to stand in the cold until such action slackens. Warm gently on the water bath but do not allow the oxidation to proceed too vigorously. If free sulphur separates it can be oxidized and brought into solution by adding a little powdered potassium chlorate, but it is best to start again with a new sample using this time three volumes of hydrochloric acid to one of nitric acid and allowing the acid to act more slowly upon the sample (Note 2).

When disintegration is complete, wash off the watch glass and evaporate on the *steam bath* to dryness. Moisten the residue with 5 cc. of concentrated hydrochloric acid and again evaporate to dryness (Note 3). Moisten the residue with 1 cc. of concentrated hydrochloric acid and add 100 cc. of hot water. Filter and wash with a hot 1% solution of hydrochloric acid and then thoroughly with hot water.

Pour the filtrate into a slight excess of ammonium hydroxide and allow the precipitate of $Fe(OH)_3$ to settle as much as possible from the hot solution. Decant the solution through a filter paper and wash the precipitate by decantation, finally transfering it to the paper and washing thoroughly with hot water.

Make the filtrate barely acid with hydrochloric acid and to the hot filtrate add very slowly with constant stirring a moderate excess of barium chloride solution. Allow to stand in a warm place for half an hour, filter, and wash with hot water until free from chlorides. Dry, and ignite as in the determination of sulphur in ferrous ammonium sulphate. Read again the notes pertaining to that analysis.

Method B
Sodium Peroxide Method

Thoroughly mix a 0.5 gram sample of the pyrite with 5 grams of sodium peroxide and 4 grams of anhydrous sodium carbonate in an iron or nickel crucible. Cut a circular opening in an asbestos board so that the crucible will fit snugly in the opening with the greater part of the crucible projecting below the asbestos (Note 4). Heat the mixture, gently at first, and finally nearly to the full heat of a Tirrill burner for 25 minutes. Allow the crucible to cool and place it in a 250 cc. beaker. Add 150 cc. of water and warm until the mass has completely disintegrated. Remove the crucible, washing it inside and outside with hot water and add to the solution 5 cc. of concentrated hydrochloric acid which has been saturated with liquid bromine (Note 5). Filter the still alkaline solution and wash the ferric hydroxide with hot water until free from sulphate. Acidify the filtrate with hydrochloric acid, evaporate to dryness to dehydrate any silicic acid, moisten the residue with 2 cc. of concentrated hydrochloric acid, add 100 cc. of hot water, filter, and wash the silica with hot water.

In the filtrate precipitate the sulphate and proceed as in Method A.

Notes. — 1. The grinding of a mineral should be carried out in an agate mortar with an agate pestle until all of the material will pass through a silk bolting cloth. Pyrite should not be ground too rapidly or with too great a pressure, otherwise appreciable amounts of sulphur are lost by volatilization due to oxidation to sulphur dioxide.

2. The use of potassium chlorate to oxidize any liberated sulphur has the objection that chlorate, like nitrate, contaminates the subsequent precipitate of barium sulphate, giving high results.

3. Repeated evaporation with hydrochloric acid accomplishes the destruction of nitrate and the dehydration of silicic acid to silica, which can be filtered off.

4. The gas flame should not be allowed to come near the top of the crucible, otherwise sulphur from the gas is absorbed into the melt. The use of an asbestos board helps to deflect the flame. A high temperature alcohol burner is sometimes used as a source of heat since it provides a flame which is free from sulphur compounds.

5. The strong alkaline solution is partially neutralized with acid in order that it may be filtered without disintegrating the filter paper. Bromine assures the complete oxidation of sulphur to sulphate.

STOICHIOMETRY

Calculations involved in the gravimetric determination of sulphur require no special consideration. The student should recall the volumetric method ("evolution method") for determining sulphur when present as sulphide in small quantities, such as in steel (see page 115). By this method, the sulphur is evolved by acid as hydrogen sulphide, and is eventually titrated with standard iodine solution ($H_2S + I_2 \rightarrow 2\,HI + S$).

PROBLEMS

155. What weight in grams of impure ferrous ammonium sulphate should be taken for analysis so that the number of centigrams of $BaSO_4$ obtained will represent five times the percentage of sulphur in the sample?

Answer: 0.6870 gram.

156. A sample of pure FeS$_2$ is analyzed by fusing a 2-gram sample and precipitating the sulphur as BaSO$_4$. How large an error in the weight of the precipitate must be made to produce an error amounting to 0.1 per cent of the apparent amount of S in the mineral?

Answer: 14.6 mg.

157. What weight of pyrite containing 36.40 per cent of sulphur must have been taken for analysis to give a precipitate of barium sulphate weighing 1.0206 grams?

Answer: 0.3850 gram.

158. What weight of pure sodium peroxide is theoretically required to oxidize 0.500 gram of pure FeS$_2$ according to the equation:

$$2\ \text{FeS}_2 + 15\ \text{Na}_2\text{O}_2 \rightarrow \text{Fe}_2\text{O}_3 + 4\ \text{Na}_2\text{SO}_4 + 11\ \text{Na}_2\text{O}?$$

What volume of $\frac{N}{5}$ barium chloride solution would be required to precipitate the resulting sulphate?

Answer: 2.44 grams; 83.4 cc.

159. A sample of pyrite ore weighs 0.2000 gram and gives 0.6230 gram of BaSO$_4$. How many cubic centimeters of oxygen gas (standard conditions) would be required to burn one gram of the ore according to the equation:

$$4\ \text{FeS}_2 + 11\ \text{O}_2 \rightarrow 2\ \text{Fe}_2\text{O}_3 + 8\ \text{SO}_2?$$

Answer: 412 cc.

160. Pure FeSO$_4 \cdot$(NH$_4$)$_2$SO$_4 \cdot$6 H$_2$O is mixed with inert matter and a sample of the mixture requires a number of cubic centimeters of barium chloride solution (25 grams BaCl$_2 \cdot$2 H$_2$O per liter) to precipitate the sulphur which is exactly twice the percentage of iron in the sample. What weight of sample was taken?

Answer: 0.574 gram.

161. A sample of pure FeSO$_4 \cdot$(NH$_4$)$_2$SO$_4 \cdot$6 H$_2$O gives a precipitate of BaSO$_4$ weighing 0.2334 gram. What volume of permanganate (1 cc. $\backsimeq$ 0.006300 gram H$_2$C$_2$O$_4 \cdot$2 H$_2$O) would be required to oxidize the iron in the same weight of sample?

Answer: 5.00 cc.

162. In a sample of steel weighing 5.00 grams a gravimetric determination of sulphur yields 23.3 milligrams of BaSO$_4$. If the same weight of sample were analyzed by the evolution method whereby the sulphur is evolved as H$_2$S and eventually titrated with standard iodine, what volume of the titrating solution would be required? The iodine has the same normality as a permanganate solution of which 20 cc. $\backsimeq$ 20 cc. of a solution of KHC$_2$O$_4 \cdot$H$_2$C$_2$O$_4 \cdot$2 H$_2$O of which 20 cc. $\backsimeq$ 20 cc. of 0.030 N NaOH solution. What is the percentage of sulphur in the steel?

Answer: 5.00 cc.; 0.064%.

163. In the determination of sulphur by the evolution method, a notebook contains the following data:

> Wt. sample   = 5.0275 grams.
> Iodine used   = 15.59 cc.
> $Na_2S_2O_3$ used = 12.68 cc.
> 1 cc. iodine ≏ 1.086 cc. $Na_2S_2O_3$.
> 1 cc. $Na_2S_2O_3$ ≏ 0.005044 gram Cu.

Find the percentage of sulphur and the weight of $BaSO_4$ obtainable from a 3-gram sample of the steel.   *Answer:* 0.107%; 0.0234 gram.

164. Using a 5-gram sample of steel, treatment with HCl evolves H_2S which is absorbed in an ammoniacal solution of $CdCl_2$. The precipitated CdS is dissolved in acid and the H_2S formed is immediately titrated with $\frac{N}{10}$ iodine solution, requiring 3.00 cc. Calculate the percentage of sulphur and the weight of $BaSO_4$ which could be obtained from the same weight of sample.   *Answer:* 0.096%; 0.0350 gram.

DETERMINATION OF PHOSPHORIC ANHYDRIDE IN APATITE

The mineral apatite is composed of calcium phosphate, associated with calcium chloride, or fluoride. Specimens are easily obtainable which are nearly pure and leave on treatment with acid only a slight siliceous residue.

For the purpose of a gravimetric determination, phosphoric acid is usually precipitated from ammoniacal solutions in the form of magnesium ammonium phosphate which, on ignition, is converted into magnesium pyrophosphate. Since the calcium phosphate of the apatite is also insoluble in ammoniacal solutions, this procedure cannot be applied directly. The separation of the phosphoric acid from the calcium must first be accomplished by precipitation in the form of ammonium phosphomolybdate in nitric acid solution, using ammonium molybdate as the precipitant. The " yellow precipitate," as it is often called, is not always of a definite composition, and therefore not suitable for direct weighing, but may be dissolved in ammonia, and the phosphate thrown out as magnesium ammonium phosphate.

Of the substances likely to occur in apatite, silicic acid alone interferes with the precipitation of the phosphoric acid in nitric acid solution.

PRECIPITATION OF AMMONIUM PHOSPHOMOLYBDATE

Procedure. — Grind the mineral in an agate mortar until no grit is perceptible. Transfer the substance to a weighing-tube, and weigh out two portions, not exceeding 0.20 gram each (Note 1) into two beakers of about 200 cc. capacity. Pour over them 20 cc. of dilute nitric acid (sp. gr. 1.20) and warm gently until solvent action has apparently ceased. Evaporate the solution cautiously to dryness, heat the residue in a hot closet for about an hour at 100–110° C., and treat it again with nitric acid as described above; separate the residue of silica by filtration on a small filter (7 cm.) and wash with warm water, using as little as possible (Note 2). Receive the filtrate in a beaker (200–500 cc.). Test the washings with ammonia for calcium phosphate, but add all such tests in which a precipitate appears to the original filtrate (Note 3). The filtrate and washings must be kept as small as possible and should not exceed 100 cc. in volume. Add aqueous ammonia (sp. gr. 0.96) until the precipitate of calcium phosphate first produced just fails to redissolve, and then add a few drops of nitric acid until this is again brought into solution (Note 4). Warm the solution until it cannot be comfortably held in the hand (about 60° C.) and, after removal of the burner, add 75 cc. of ammonium molybdate solution which has been *gently* warmed, but which must be perfectly clear. Allow the mixture to stand (preferably at a temperature of about 50 or 60° C.) for twelve hours (Notes 5 and 6). Filter off the yellow precipitate on a 9 cm. filter, and wash by decantation with a solution of ammonium nitrate made acid with nitric acid (Note 7). Allow the precipitate to remain in the beaker as far as possible. Test the washings for calcium with ammonia and ammonium oxalate (Note 3).

Add 10 cc. of molybdate solution to the filtrate, and leave it for a few hours. It should then be carefully examined for a *yellow* precipitate; a white precipitate may be neglected.

Notes. — 1. Magnesium ammonium phosphate, as noted below, is slightly soluble under the conditions of analysis. Consequently the unavoidable errors of analysis are greater in this determination than in those which have preceded it, and some divergence may be expected in duplicate analyses. It is obvious that the larger the amount of substance taken for analysis the less will be the relative loss or gain due to unavoidable experimental errors; but, in this instance, a check is placed upon the amount of material which may be taken both by the bulk of the resulting precipitate of ammonium phosphomolybdate and by the excessive amount of ammonium molybdate required to effect complete separation of the phosphoric acid, since a liberal excess above the theoretical quantity is demanded. Molybdic acid is one of the more expensive reagents.

2. Soluble silicic acid would, if present, partially separate with the phosphomolybdate, although not in combination with molybdenum. Its previous removal by dehydration is therefore necessary.

3. When washing the siliceous residue the filtrate may be tested for calcium by adding ammonia, since that reagent neutralizes the acid which holds the calcium phosphate in solution and causes precipitation; but after the removal of the phosphoric acid in combination with the molybdenum, the addition of an oxalate is required to show the presence of calcium.

4. An excess of nitric acid exerts a slight solvent action, while ammonium nitrate lessens the solubility; hence the neutralization of the former by ammonia.

5. The precipitation of the phosphomolybdate takes place more promptly in warm than in cold solutions, but the temperature should not exceed 60° C. during precipitation; a higher temperature tends to separate molybdic acid from the solution. This acid is nearly white, and its deposition in the filtrate on long standing should not be mistaken for a second precipitation of the yellow precipitate. The addition of 75 cc. of ammonium molybdate solution insures the presence of a liberal excess of the reagent, but the filtrate should be tested as in all quantitative procedures.

The precipitation is probably complete in many cases in less than twelve hours; but it is better, when practicable, to allow the solution to stand for this length of time. Vigorous shaking or stirring promotes the separation of the precipitate.

6. The composition of the "yellow precipitate" undoubtedly varies slightly with varying conditions at the time of its formation. When precipitated under the conditions prescribed in the above procedure its composition probably closely approximates that represented by the formula $(NH_4)_3PO_4 \cdot 12\ MoO_3$, and the equation for its precipitation may be written:

$$H_3PO_4 + 12(NH_4)_2MoO_4 + 21\ HNO_3$$
$$\rightarrow (NH_4)_3PO_4 \cdot 12\ MoO_3 + 21\ NH_4NO_3 + 12\ H_2O.$$

whatever other variations may occur in its composition, the ratio $12\ MoO_3 : 1\ P$ seems to hold fairly constant and this fact is utilized in certain volumetric processes for the determination of small amounts of phosphorous (see page 179).

7. A suitable wash solution can be prepared as follows: Mix 100 cc. of ammonia solution (sp. gr. 0.96) with 325 cc. of nitric acid (sp. gr. 1.2) and dilute with 100 cc. of water.

PRECIPITATION OF MAGNESIUM AMMONIUM PHOSPHATE

Procedure. — Dissolve the precipitate of phosphomolybdate upon the filter by pouring through it dilute aqueous ammonia (one volume of dilute ammonia (sp. gr. 0.96) and three volumes of water, which should be carefully measured), and receive the solution in the beaker containing the bulk of the precipitate. The total volume of filtrate and washings should not exceed 100 cc. Acidify the solution with dilute hydrochloric acid, and heat it nearly to boiling. Calculate the volume of magnesium ammonium chloride solution ("magnesia mixture") required to precipitate the phosphoric acid, assuming 40 per cent P_2O_5 in the apatite. Measure out about 5 cc. in excess of this amount, and pour it into the acid solution. Then add slowly dilute ammonium hydroxide (1 volume of strong ammonia (sp. gr. 0.90) and 9 volumes of water), stirring constantly until a precipitate forms. Then add a volume of filtered, concentrated ammonium hydroxide (sp. gr. 0.90) equal to approximately one ninth of the volume of liquid in the beaker (Note 1). Allow the whole to cool. The precipitated magnesium ammonium phosphate should then be definitely crystalline in appearance (Note 2). (If it is desired to hasten the precipitation, the solution may be cooled, first in cold tap water and then in ice-water, and stirred periodically for half an hour, when precipitation will usually be complete.)

Decant the clear liquid through a filter, and transfer the precipitate to the filter, using as wash-water a mixture of one volume of concentrated ammonia and nine volumes of water. It is not necessary to clean the beaker completely or to wash the precipitate thoroughly at this point, as it is necessary to purify it by reprecipitation.

Notes. — 1. Magnesium ammonium phosphate is not a wholly insoluble substance, even under the most favorable analytical conditions. It is least soluble in a liquid containing one tenth of its volume of concentrated aqueous ammonia (sp. gr. 0.90) and this proportion should be carefully maintained as prescribed in the procedure. On account of this slight solubility the volume of solutions should be kept as small as possible and the amount of wash-water limited to that absolutely required.

A large excess of the magnesium solution tends both to throw out magnesium hydroxide (shown by a persistently flocculent precipitate) and to cause the phosphate to carry down molybdic acid. The tendency of the magnesium precipitate to carry down molybdic acid is also increased if the solution is too concentrated. The volume should not be less than 90 cc., nor more than 125 cc., at the time of the first precipitation with the magnesia mixture.

2. The magnesium ammonium phosphate should be perfectly crystalline, and will be so if the directions are followed. The slow addition of the reagent is essential, and the stirring not less so. Stirring promotes the separation of the precipitate and the formation of larger crystals, and may therefore be substituted for digestion in the cold. The stirring-rod must not be allowed to scratch the glass, as the crystals adhere to such scratches and are removed with difficulty.

REPRECIPITATION AND IGNITION OF MAGNESIUM AMMONIUM PHOSPHATE

A single precipitation of the magnesium compound in the presence of molybdenum salts rarely yields a pure product. The molybdenum can be removed by solution of the precipitate in acid and precipitation of the molybdenum by hydrogen sulphide, after which the magnesium precipitate may be again thrown down. It is usually as satisfactory to dissolve the magnesium precipitate and reprecipitate the phosphate as magnesium ammonium phosphate as described below.

Procedure. — Dissolve the precipitate from the filter in a little dilute hydrochloric acid (sp. gr. 1.12), allowing the acid solution to run into the beaker in which the original precipitation was made (Note 1). Wash the filter with water until the wash-water shows no test for chlorides, but avoid an unnecessary amount of wash-water. Add to the solution 2 cc. (not more) of magnesia mixture, and then dilute ammonium hydroxide solution (sp. gr. 0.96), drop by drop, with constant stirring, until the liquid smells distinctly of ammonia. Stir for a few moments and then add a volume of strong ammonia (sp. gr. 0.90), equal to one ninth of the volume of the solution. Allow the solution to stand for some hours, and then filter off the magnesium ammonium phosphate, which should be distinctly crystalline in character. Wash the precipitate with dilute ammonia water as prescribed above, until finally 3 cc. of the washings, after acidifying with nitric acid, show no evidence of chlorides. Test both filtrates for complete precipitation by adding a few cubic centimeters of magnesia mixture and allowing them to stand for some time.

Transfer the moist precipitate to a weighed porcelain crucible and ignite, using great care to raise the temperature slowly while drying the filter in the crucible, and to insure the ready access of oxygen during the combustion of the filter paper, thus guarding against a possible reduction of the phosphate, which would result in disastrous consequences to the analysis (Note 2). Do not raise the temperature above moderate redness until the precipitate is white. (Keep this precaution well in mind.) Ignite finally at the highest temperature of the Tirrill burner, and repeat the heating until the weight is constant. If the ignited precipitate is persistently discolored by particles of unburned carbon, moisten the mass with a drop or two of concentrated nitric acid and heat cautiously, finally igniting strongly. The acid will dissolve magnesium pyrophosphate from the surface of the particles of carbon, which will then burn away. Nitric acid also aids as an oxidizing agent in supplying oxygen for the combustion of the carbon.

From the weight of magnesium pyrophosphate ($Mg_2P_2O_7$) obtained, calculate the percentage of phosphoric anhydride (P_2O_5) in the sample of apatite.

Notes. — 1. The ionic changes involved in the precipitation of the magnesium compound are

$$PO_4^{---} + NH_4^+ + Mg^{++} \rightarrow [MgNH_4PO_4].$$

The magnesium ammonium phosphate is readily dissolved by acids, even those which are no stronger than acetic acid. This is accounted for by the fact that two of the ions into which phosphoric acid may dissociate, the HPO_4^{--} or $H_2PO_4^-$ ions, exhibit the characteristics of very weak acids, in that they show almost no tendency to dissociate further into H^+ and PO_4^{---} ions. Consequently the ionic changes which occur when the magnesium ammonium phosphate is brought into contact with an acid may be typified by the reaction:

$$H^+ + Mg^{++} + NH_4^+ + PO_4^{---} \rightarrow Mg^{++} + NH_4^+ + HPO_4^{--};$$

that is, the PO₄⁻⁻⁻ ions and the H⁺ ions lose their identity in the formation of the new ion, HPO₄⁻⁻, and this continues until the magnesium ammonium phosphate is entirely dissolved.

2. During ignition the magnesium ammonium phosphate loses ammonia and water and is converted into magnesium pyrophosphate:

$$2\ MgNH_4PO_4 \rightarrow Mg_2P_2O_7 + 2\ NH_3 + H_2O.$$

The precautions mentioned in the procedure must be observed with great care during the ignition of this precipitate. The danger here lies in a possible reduction of the phosphate by the carbon of the filter paper, or by the ammonia evolved.

STOICHIOMETRY

The formula of the yellow precipitate of ammonium phosphomolybdate ($(NH_4)_3PO_4 \cdot 12\ MoO_3$) is of somewhat variable composition, but with small amounts of phosphate (such as would occur in the analysis of iron or steel) fairly good results can be obtained by filtering the yellow precipitate, drying at 110° C., and weighing as $(NH_4)_3PO_4 \cdot 12\ MoO_3$; or by igniting it gently to $P_2O_5 \cdot 24\ MoO_3$.

A more common method (*Ferric Alum Method*) makes use of the fact that the molybdenum in the precipitate can be reduced to the trivalent state and can then be titrated back to the valence of 6. The reduction is usually accomplished by means of a Jones reductor and the reduced solution passed directly into a solution of ferric alum. The reduced iron from the alum is then titrated with standard permanganate. In this method, in calculating the percentage of phosphorus, the milliequivalent is $\dfrac{P}{36000}$ since each molybdenum atom changes by 3 units of valence and each phosphorus atom is equivalent to 12 molybdenum atoms.

In the *Blair Method* the reduced molybdenum solution is allowed to drop from the Jones reductor into an empty flask and is then titrated directly with permanganate. In this case, there is a slight oxidation of the reduced molybdenum by the air before the titration is made and it has been found by experiment that the partially oxidized form corresponds in valence to the hypothetical oxide $Mo_{24}O_{37}$. That is, the permanganate oxidizes the molybdenum from an average valence of $\frac{37}{12}$ to a valence of 6. This corresponds to a change in valence of $\frac{35}{12}$. The net change in valence for 12 molybdenum atoms is 35 and since 12 molybdenum atoms are equivalent to one phosphorus atom, in calculating the percentage of phosphorus in the sample the milliequivalent is $\dfrac{P}{35000}$.

Still another volumetric method (*Handy Method*) for small percentages of phosphorus makes use of the acid character of the yellow precipitate. It is titrated with standard sodium hydroxide solution according to the following equation:

$2(NH_4)_3PO_4 \cdot 12\ MoO_3 + 46\ NaOH \rightarrow 2(NH_4)_2HPO_4$
$\qquad\qquad + (NH_4)_2MoO_4 + 23\ Na_2MoO_4 + 22\ H_2O.$

The milliequivalent weight of phosphorus by this process is obviously $\dfrac{P}{23000}$.

Example I. — If a 2-gram sample of steel is analyzed for phosphorus by the ferric alum method and 7.20 cc. of $\dfrac{N}{10}$ KMnO$_4$ are required, what net volume of $\dfrac{N}{20}$ NaOH would have been required by the Handy method and what weight of dried " yellow precipitate " and of ignited magnesium precipitate could have been obtained from the same weight of sample? What is the percentage of phosphorus in the steel?

Solution. — $7.20 \times \dfrac{1}{10} \times \dfrac{P}{36000} = 0.00062$ gram of P

$\qquad\qquad x \times \dfrac{1}{20} \times \dfrac{P}{23000} = 0.00062$

$\qquad\qquad\qquad\qquad x = 9.20$ cc. *Ans.*

$0.00062 \times \dfrac{(NH_4)_3PO_4 \cdot 12\ MoO_3}{P} = 0.038$ gram. *Ans.*

$\qquad 0.00062 \times \dfrac{Mg_2P_2O_7}{2\ P} = 0.0022$ gram. *Ans.*

$\qquad\qquad \dfrac{0.00062}{2} \times 100 = 0.031\%.$ *Ans.*

Example II. — If the molybdenum in a normal precipitate of ammonium phosphomolybdate obtained from a 2-gram sample of steel containing 0.050% P is reduced to such a valence that 9.30 cc. of $\frac{N}{10}$ KMnO₄ are required to reoxidize the molybdenum to the valence of 6, to what oxide was the molybdenum apparently reduced?

Solution. — Let x = valence of Mo in the reduced form. Then $6 - x$ = change in valence of Mo in the titration.

$$\frac{9.30 \times \frac{1}{10} \times \frac{P}{12(6-x)1000}}{2} \times 100 = 0.050$$

$x = 3.6$ = valence of Mo
Oxide = Mo₅O₉. *Ans.*

PROBLEMS

165. Given 0.350 gram of pure apatite with the formula Ca₃(PO₄)₂·CaFCl. What weight of (NH₄)₃PO₄·12 MoO₃ could be obtained from this weight of sample and what volume of magnesia mixture (1 N with respect to MgCl₂) would subsequently be required to precipitate the phosphate from an ammoniacal solution of the yellow precipitate?

Answer: 3.24 grams; 3.46 cc.

166. If the yellow precipitate from a 2.5-gram sample of steel is dissolved in 20.0 cc. of $\frac{N}{2}$ KOH solution and 27.0 cc. of $\frac{N}{3}$ HNO₃ solution are required to make the solution neutral to phenolphthalein (Handy method), what is the percentage of phosphorus in the steel? *Answer:* 0.054%.

167. Calculate the milliequivalent of P₂O₅, Mo₂₄O₃₇, and of MoO₃ in the Blair method for phosphorus. *Answer:* 0.00203; 0.0414; 0.0494.

168. What is the percentage of P in a steel if by the Ferric Alum method 14.0 cc. of $\frac{1}{12}$ N KMnO₄ are required for a 4.0-gram sample?

Answer: 0.025%.

169. A sample of apatite weighing 0.60 gram is analyzed for its phosphoric anhydride content. If the phosphate is precipitated as (NH₄)₃PO₄·12MoO₃, and the precipitate (after solution and reduction of the MoO₃ to Mo₂₄O₃₇), requires 100 cc. of normal KMnO₄ to oxidize it back to MoO₃, what is the percentage of P₂O₅? *Answer:* 33.81%.

GRAVIMETRIC ANALYSIS

170. In the analysis of a sample of steel weighing 1.881 grams the phosphorus was precipitated with ammonium molybdate and the yellow precipitate was dissolved, reduced, and titrated with $KMnO_4$. If the sample contained 0.025 per cent P and 6.01 cc. of $KMnO_4$ were used, to what oxide was the molybdenum reduced? 1 cc. $KMnO_4$ = 0.007188 gram $Na_2C_2O_4$.

Answer: Mo_4O_5.

171. 2.00 grams of steel furnish a yellow precipitate which when dissolved in 20.0 cc. of NaOH provides a solution which requires 27.0 cc. of HNO_3 for neutralization (Handy method). 2.00 cc. of the NaOH ⇌ 3.00 cc. of the HNO_3. 1.00 cc. of the NaOH ⇌ 1.00 cc. of $KHC_2O_4 \cdot H_2C_2O_4 \cdot 2\ H_2O$ solution ⇌ 1.00 cc. $KMnO_4$ solution ⇌ 0.0558 gram Fe. Calculate the percentage of P in the steel.

Answer: 0.0675%.

172. If a steel weighing 5 grams contains 0.0969% P and the normal yellow precipitate is reduced to a form which requires 50.0 cc. of $\frac{N}{10}$ $KMnO_4$ for reoxidation, to what oxide can the molybdenum be assumed to have been reduced?

Answer: Mo_3O_5.

173. What weight of dried yellow precipitate and what weight of ignited yellow precipitate can be obtained from 0.388 gram of pure $Ca_3(PO_4)_2 \cdot CaF_2$?

Answer: 3.75 grams; 3.60 grams.

174. What weight of steel should be taken for analysis such that the cc of $\frac{N}{9}$ caustic soda required to titrate a normal precipitate of ammonium phosphomolybdate will be 400 times as large as the per cent P in the steel?

Answer: 6.0 grams.

175. A mineral contains 60.0% of $Ca_3(PO_4)_2 \cdot CaClF$ and 40.0% inert material. Compute (a) the weight of magnesium pyrophosphate obtainable from 0.200 gram of the mineral; (b) the volume of $\frac{N}{7}$ NaOH solution necessary to dissolve the yellow precipitate from this weight of mineral and leave the solution neutral to phenolphthalein; (c) the volume of $\frac{N}{12}$ $KMnO_4$ required in the analysis of 0.0300 gram of the mineral assuming the yellow precipitate is reduced so that the average valence of the molybdenum is $3\frac{1}{6}$ in the reduced condition and is oxidized back to the valence of 6 by the permanganate.

Answer: 0.0660 gram; 95.5 cc.; 36.3 cc.

176. In the analysis of a sample of steel weighing 1.000 gram the phosphorus was precipitated with ammonium molybdate and the yellow precipitate was dissolved, reduced, and titrated with permanganate. If the sample contained 0.031 per cent P and 3.45 cc. of $KMnO_4$ were used, to what oxide was the molybdenum reduced? One cubic centimeter of $KMnO_4$ was equivalent to 0.02779 gram of $FeSO_4 \cdot 7\ H_2O$.

Answer: $Mo_{16}O_{25}$.

177. A solution containing phosphoric acid was treated with ammonium molybdate and an abnormal yellow precipitate was obtained, which after drying may be assumed to have consisted of $[(NH_4)_3PO_4]x\ [MoO_3]y$. This precipitate was dried, weighed, dissolved in ammonia water, and the solution was made up to 500 cc. Of this, 50 cc. were taken, made acid with H_2SO_4, reduced with amalgamated Zn, and passed directly into an excess of ferric alum which served to oxidize the trivalent molybdenum back to the hexavalent condition. To oxidize the reduced iron required a number of cc. of $\frac{N}{8}$ $KMnO_4$ equal to 15.39 times the weight in grams of the original yellow precipitate. What values of x and y may be taken in the formula of the yellow precipitate?

Answer: 2 and 25.

ANALYSIS OF LIMESTONE OR DOLOMITE

Limestones vary widely in composition from a nearly pure marble through the dolomitic limestones, containing varying amounts of magnesium, to the impure varieties, which contain also ferrous and manganous carbonates and siliceous compounds in variable proportions. Many other minerals may be inclosed in limestones in small quantities, and an exact qualitative analysis will often show the presence of sulphides or sulphates, phosphates, and titanates, the alkalies and even the heavy metals. No attempt is made in the following procedures to provide a complete quantitative scheme which would take into account all of these constituents. Such a scheme for a complete analysis of a limestone may be found in Bulletin No. 700 of the United States Geological Survey and in Hillebrand and Lundell's *Applied Inorganic Analysis*. It is assumed that, for these instructional determinations, a limestone is selected which contains only the more common constituents first enumerated above.

DETERMINATION OF MOISTURE

The determination of the amount of moisture in minerals or ores is often of great importance. Ores which have been exposed to the weather during shipment may have absorbed enough moisture to affect appreciably the results of analysis. Since it is essential that the seller and buyer should make their analyses upon comparable material, it is customary for each analyst to determine the moisture in the sample examined, and then to calculate the percentages of the various constituents with reference to a sample dried in the air, or at a temperature a little above 100° C., which, unless the ore has undergone chemical change because of the moisture, should be the same before and after shipment.

Procedure. — Spread 25 grams of the powdered sample on a weighed watch-glass; weigh to the nearest 10 milligrams only and heat at 105° C.; weigh at intervals of an hour, after cooling in a desiccator, until the loss of weight after an hour's heating does not exceed 10 milligrams. It should be noted that a variation in weight of 10 milligrams in a total weight of 25 grams is no greater relatively than a variation of 0.1 milligram when the sample taken weighs 0.25 gram.

DETERMINATION OF THE INSOLUBLE MATTER AND SILICA

Procedure. — Weigh out two portions of the original powdered sample (not the dried sample), of about 5 grams each, into 250 cc. casseroles, and cover each with a watch-glass (Note 1). Pour over the powder 25 cc. of water, and then add 50 cc. of dilute hydrochloric acid (sp. gr. 1.12) in small portions, warming gently, until nothing further appears to dissolve (Note 2). Evaporate to dryness on the water bath. Pour over the residue a mixture of 5 cc. of water and 5 cc. of concentrated hydrochloric acid (sp. gr. 1.20) and again evaporate to dryness, and finally heat for at least an hour at a temperature of 110° C. Pour over this residue 50 cc. of dilute hydrochloric acid (one volume acid (sp. gr. 1.12) to five volumes water), and boil for about five minutes; then filter and wash twice with the dilute hydrochloric acid, and then with hot water until free from chlorides. Transfer the filter and contents to a porcelain crucible, dry carefully over a low flame, and ignite to constant weight. The residue represents the insoluble matter and the silica from any soluble silicates (Note 3).

Calculate the total percentage of these in the limestone.

Notes. — 1. The relatively large weight (5 grams) taken for analysis insures greater accuracy in the determination of the ingredients which are present in small proportions, and is also more likely to be a representative sample of the material analyzed.

2. It is plain that the amount of the insoluble residue and also its character will often depend upon the strength of acid used for solution of the limestone. It cannot, therefore, be regarded as representing any well-defined constituent, and its determination is essentially empirical.

3. It is probable that some of the silicates present are wholly or partly decomposed by the acid, and the soluble silicic acid must be converted by evaporation to dryness and heating, into white, in-

soluble silica. This change is not complete after one evaporation. The heating at a temperature somewhat higher than that of the water bath for a short time tends to leave the silica in the form of a powder, which promotes subsequent filtration. The siliceous residue is washed first with dilute acid to prevent hydrolytic changes, which would result in the formation of appreciable quantities of insoluble basic iron or aluminum salts on the filter when washing with hot water.

If it is desired to determine the percentage of silica separately, the ignited residue should be mixed in a platinum crucible with about six times its weight of anhydrous sodium carbonate, and the procedure given on page 220 should be followed. The filtrate from the silica is then added to the main filtrate from the insoluble residue.

DETERMINATION OF FERRIC OXIDE AND ALUMINUM OXIDE (WITH MANGANESE)

Procedure. — To the filtrate from the insoluble residue add ammonium hydroxide until the solution just smells distinctly of ammonia, but do not add an excess. Then add 5 cc. of saturated bromine water (Note 1), and boil for five minutes. If the smell of ammonia has disappeared, again add ammonium hydroxide in slight excess, and 3 cc. of bromine water, and heat again for a few minutes. Finally add 10 cc. of ammonium chloride solution and keep the solution warm until it barely smells of ammonia; then filter promptly (Note 2). Wash the filter twice with hot water, then (after replacing the receiving beaker) pour through it 25 cc. of hot, dilute hydrochloric acid (one volume dilute HCl [sp. gr. 1.12] to five volumes water). A brown residue insoluble in the acid may be allowed to remain on the filter. Wash the filter five times with hot water, add to the filtrate ammonium hydroxide and bromine water as described above, and repeat the precipitation. Collect the precipitate on the filter already used, wash it free from chlorides with hot water, and ignite and weigh as described for ferric hydroxide on page 159. The residue after ignition consists of ferric oxide, alumina, and mangano-manganic oxide (Mn_3O_4), if manganese is present. These are commonly determined together (Note 3).

Calculate the percentage of the combined oxides in the limestone.

Notes. — 1. The addition of bromine water to the ammoniacal solutions serves to oxidize any ferrous hydroxide to ferric hydroxide and to precipitate manganese as $MnO(OH)_2$. The solution must contain not more than a bare excess of hydroxyl ions (ammonium hydroxide) when it is filtered, on account of the tendency of the aluminum hydroxide to redissolve.

The solution should not be strongly ammoniacal when the bromine is added, as strong ammonia reacts with the bromine, with the evolution of nitrogen.

2. The precipitate produced by ammonium hydroxide and bromine should be filtered off promptly, since the alkaline solution absorbs carbon dioxide from the air, with consequent partial precipitation of the calcium as carbonate. This is possible even under the most favorable conditions, and for this reason the iron precipitate is redissolved and again precipitated to free it from calcium. When the precipitate is small, this reprecipitation may be omitted.

3. In the absence of significant amounts of manganese the iron and aluminum may be separately determined by fusion of the mixed ignited precipitate, after weighing, with about ten times its weight of acid potassium sulphate, solution of the cold fused mass in water, and volumetric determination of the iron, as described on page 77. The aluminum is then determined by difference, after subtracting the weight of ferric oxide corresponding to the amount of iron found.

If a separate determination of the iron, aluminum, and manganese is desired, the mixed precipitate may be dissolved in acid before ignition, and the separation effected by special methods.

DETERMINATION OF CALCIUM

Procedure. — To the combined filtrates from the double precipitation of the hydroxides just described, add 5 cc. of dilute ammonium hydroxide (sp. gr. 0.96), and transfer the liquid to a 500 cc. graduated flask, washing out the beaker carefully. Cool to laboratory temperature, and fill the flask with distilled water until the lowest point of the meniscus is exactly level with the mark on the neck of the flask. Carefully remove any drops of water which are on the inside of the neck of the flask above the graduation by means of a strip of filter paper, make the solution uniform by pouring it out into a dry beaker and back into the flask several times. Measure off one fifth of this solution as follows (Note 1): Pour into a 100 cc. graduated flask about 10 cc. of the solution, shake the liquid thoroughly over the inner surface of the small flask, and pour it out. Repeat the same operation. Fill the 100 cc. flask until the lowest point of the meniscus is exactly level with the mark on its neck, remove any drops of solution from the upper part of the neck with filter paper, and pour the solution into a beaker (400-500 cc.). Wash out the flask with small quantities of water until it is clean, adding these to the 100 cc. of solution. When the duplicate portion of 100 cc. is measured out from the solution, remember that the flask must be rinsed out twice with that solution, as prescribed above, before the measurement is made. (A 100 cc. pipette may be used to measure out the aliquot portions, if preferred.)

Dilute each of the measured portions to 250 cc. with distilled water, heat the whole to boiling, and add ammonium oxalate solution slowly in moderate excess, stirring well. Boil for two minutes; allow the precipitated calcium oxalate to settle for a half-hour, and decant through a filter. Test the filtrate for complete precipitation by adding a few cubic centimeters of the precipitant, allowing it to stand for fifteen minutes. If no precipitate forms, make the solution slightly acid with hydrochloric acid (Note 2); see that it is properly labeled and reserve it to be combined with the filtrate from the second calcium oxalate precipitation (Notes 3 and 4).

Redissolve the calcium oxalate in the beaker with warm hydrochloric acid, pouring the acid through the filter. Wash the filter five times with water, and finally pour through it aqueous ammonia. Dilute the solution to 250 cc., bring to boiling, and add 1 cc. ammonium oxalate solution (Note 5) and ammonia in slight excess; boil for two minutes, and set aside for a half-hour. Filter off the calcium oxalate upon the filter first used, and wash free from chlorides. The filtrate should be made barely acid with hydrochloric acid and combined with the filtrate from the first precipitation. Begin at once the evaporation of the solutions for the determination of magnesium as described below.

The precipitate of calcium oxalate may be converted into calcium oxide by ignition without previous drying. After burning

ANALYSIS OF LIMESTONE OR DOLOMITE

the filter, it may be ignited for three quarters of an hour in a *platinum* crucible at the highest heat of the Bunsen or Tirrill burner, and finally for ten minutes at the blast lamp (Note 6). Repeat the heating over a blast lamp or a Meker burner until the weight is constant. As the calcium oxide absorbs moisture from the air, it must (after cooling) be weighed as rapidly as possible.

The precipitate may, if preferred, be placed in a weighed porcelain crucible. After burning off the filter and heating for ten minutes, the calcium precipitate may be converted into calcium sulphate by placing 2 cc. of dilute sulphuric acid in the crucible (cold), heating the covered crucible very cautiously over a low flame to drive off the excess of acid, and finally at redness to constant weight (Note 7).

From the weight of the oxide or sulphate, calculate the percentage of calcium oxide (CaO) in the limestone, remembering that only one fifth of the total solution is used for this determination.

Notes. — 1. If the calcium were precipitated from the entire solution, the quantity of the precipitate would be greater than could be properly treated. The solution is, therefore, diluted to a definite volume (500 cc.), and exactly one fifth (100 cc.) is measured off in a graduated flask or by means of a pipette.

2. The filtrate from the calcium oxalate should be made slightly acid immediately after filtration, in order to avoid the solvent action of the alkaline liquid upon the glass.

3. The accurate quantitative separation of calcium from magnesium as oxalate requires considerable care. The calcium precipitate usually carries down with it some magnesium, and this can best be removed by redissolving the precipitate after filtration, and reprecipitation in the presence of only the small amount of magnesium which was included in the first precipitate. When, however, the proportion of magnesium is not very large, the second precipitation of the calcium can usually be avoided by precipitating it from a rather dilute solution (800 cc. or so) and in the presence of a considerable excess of the precipitant, that is, rather more than enough to convert both the magnesium and calcium into oxalates.

4. The ionic changes involved in the precipitation of calcium as oxalate are exceedingly simple, and the principles discussed in connection with the barium sulphate precipitation on page 165 also apply here. The reaction is $C_2O_4^{--} + Ca^{++} \rightarrow [CaC_2O_4]$.

Calcium oxalate is nearly insoluble in water, and only very slightly soluble in acetic acid, but is readily dissolved by the strong mineral acids. This behavior with acids is explained by the fact that oxalic acid is a stronger acid than acetic acid; when, therefore, the oxalate is brought into contact with the latter there is almost no tendency to diminish the concentration of $C_2O_4^{--}$ ions by the formation of an acid less dissociated than the acetic acid itself, and practically no solvent action ensues. When a strong mineral acid is present, however, the ionization of the oxalic acid is much reduced by the high concentration of the H^+ ions from the strong acid, the formation of the undissociated acid lessens the concentration of the $C_2O_4^{--}$ ions in solution, more of the oxalate passes into solution to re-establish equilibrium, and this process repeats itself until all is dissolved.

The oxalate is immediately reprecipitated from such a solution on the addition of OH^- ions, which, by uniting with the H^+ ions of the acids (both the mineral acid and the oxalic acid) to form water, leave the Ca^{++} and $C_2O_4^{--}$ ions in the solution to recombine to form $[CaC_2O_4]$, which is precipitated in the absence of the H^+ ions. It is well at this point to add a small excess of $C_2O_4^{--}$ ions in the form of ammonium oxalate to decrease the solubility of the precipitate.

The oxalate precipitate consists mainly of $CaC_2O_4 \cdot H_2O$ when thrown down.

5. The small quantity of ammonium oxalate solution is added before the second precipitation of the calcium oxalate to insure the presence of a slight excess of the reagent, which promotes the separation of the calcium compound.

6. On ignition the calcium oxalate loses carbon dioxide and carbon monoxide, leaving calcium oxide:

$$CaC_2O_4 \cdot H_2O \rightarrow CaO + CO_2 + CO + H_2O.$$

For small weights of the oxalate (0.6 gram or less) this reaction may be brought about in a platinum crucible at the highest temperature of a Tirrill burner, but it is well to ignite larger quantities than this over the blast lamp until the weight is constant.

7. The heat required to burn the filter, and that subsequently applied as described, will convert most of the calcium oxalate to calcium carbonate, which is changed to sulphate by the sulphuric acid. The reactions involved are

$$CaC_2O_4 \rightarrow CaCO_3 + CO,$$
$$CaCO_3 + H_2SO_4 \rightarrow CaSO_4 + CO_2 + H_2O.$$

If a porcelain crucible is employed for ignition, this conversion to sulphate is to be preferred, as a complete conversion to oxide is difficult

ANALYSIS OF LIMESTONE OR DOLOMITE

to accomplish in such a crucible. The removal of the excess sulphuric acid requires extreme care to prevent spattering.

It is possible but difficult to ignite the calcium oxalate at such a temperature that it is converted only to calcium carbonate, in which form it can be weighed.

8. The determination of the calcium may be completed volumetrically by washing the calcium oxalate precipitate from the filter into dilute sulphuric acid, warming, and titrating the liberated oxalic acid with a standard solution of potassium permanganate as described on page 71. When a considerable number of analyses are to be made, this procedure will save much of the time otherwise required for ignition and weighing.

DETERMINATION OF MAGNESIUM

Procedure. — Evaporate the acidified filtrates from the calcium precipitates until the salts begin to crystallize, but do not evaporate to dryness (Note 1). Dilute the solution cautiously until the salts are brought into solution, adding a little acid if the solution has evaporated to very small volume. The solution should be carefully examined at this point and must be filtered if a precipitate has appeared. Heat the clear solution to boiling; remove the burner and add 25 cc. of a solution of di-sodium phosphate. Then add slowly dilute ammonia (1 volume strong ammonia (sp. gr. 0.90) and 9 volumes water) as long as a precipitate continues to form. Finally, add a volume of concentrated ammonia (sp. gr. 0.90) equal to one ninth of the volume of the solution, and allow the whole to stand for about twelve hours.

Decant the solution through a filter, wash it with dilute ammonia water, proceeding as prescribed for the determination of phosphoric anhydride on page 176, including the reprecipitation (Note 2), except that 3 cc. of di-sodium phosphate solution are added before the reprecipitation of the magnesium ammonium phosphate instead of the magnesia mixture.

From the weight of the pyrophosphate, calculate the percentage of magnesium oxide (MgO) in the sample of limestone. Remember that the pyrophosphate finally obtained is from one fifth of the original sample.

Notes. — 1. The precipitation of the magnesium should be made in as small a volume as possible, and the ratio of ammonia to the total volume of solution should be carefully provided for, on account of the relative solubility of the magnesium ammonium phosphate. This matter has been fully discussed in connection with the phosphoric anhydride determination.

2. The first magnesium ammonium phosphate precipitate is rarely wholly crystalline, as it should be, and is not always of the proper composition when precipitated in the presence of such large amounts of ammonium salts. The difficulty can best be remedied by filtering the precipitate and (without washing it) redissolving in a small quantity of hydrochloric acid, from which it may be again thrown down by ammonia after adding a little di-sodium phosphate solution. If the flocculent character was occasioned by the presence of magnesium hydroxide, the second precipitation, in a smaller volume containing fewer salts, will often result more favorably.

The removal of iron or alumina from a contaminated precipitate is a matter involving a long procedure, and a redetermination of the magnesium from a new sample, with additional precautions, is usually to be preferred.

DETERMINATION OF CARBON DIOXIDE

Absorption Apparatus

The apparatus required for the determination of the carbon dioxide should be arranged as shown in the cut (Fig. 4). The flask (A) is an ordinary wash-bottle, which should be nearly filled with dilute hydrochloric acid (100 cc. acid (sp. gr. 1.12) and 200 cc. of water). The flask is connected by rubber tubing (a) with the glass tube (b) leading nearly to the bottom of the evolution flask (B) and having its lower end bent upward and drawn out to small bore, so that the carbon dioxide evolved from the limestone cannot bubble back into (b). The evolution flask should preferably be a wide-mouthed Soxhlet extraction flask of about 150 cc. capacity because of the ease with which tubes and stoppers may be fitted into the neck of a flask of this type. The flask should be fitted with a two-hole rubber stopper. The condenser (C) may consist of a tube with two or three large bulbs blown in it, for use as an air-cooled condenser, or it may be a

FIG. 4

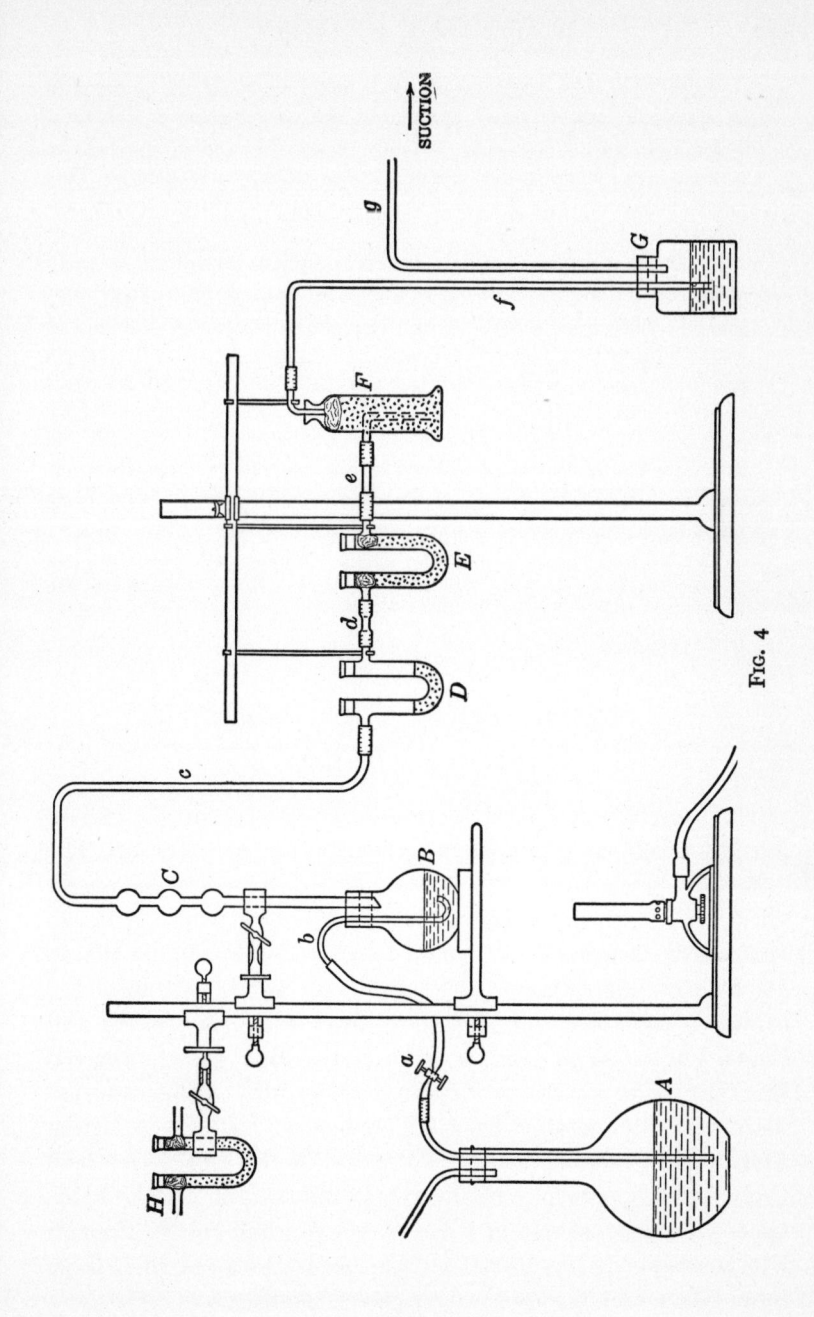

small water-jacketed condenser. The latter is to be preferred if a number of determinations are to be made in succession.

A glass delivery tube (*c*) leads from the condenser to the small U-tube (*D*) containing some glass beads or small pieces of broken glass moistened with a solution made by adding concentrated sulphuric acid to a saturated solution of silver sulphate. The short rubber tubing (*d*) connects the first U-tube to a second U-tube (*E*) which is filled with small dust-free lumps of dry calcium chloride previously saturated with carbon dioxide, with a small, loose plug of cotton at the top of each arm (Note 1). Both tubes should be closed by cork stoppers, the tops of which are cut off level with, or preferably forced a little below, the top of the U-tube, and then neatly sealed with sealing wax.

The carbon dioxide is absorbed in a Midvale tube (*F*) containing ascarite (Note 2). Loose plugs of cotton or glass wool are placed at the top and bottom of the tube to prevent loss of fine particles of the ascarite.

The small bottle (*G*) with concentrated sulphuric acid (sp. gr. 1.84) is so arranged that the tube (*f*) barely dips below the surface. This will prevent the absorption of water vapor by (*F*) and serves as an aid in regulating the flow of air through the apparatus. (*H*) is a U-tube filled with soda lime or ascarite.

All connections should be made glass to glass and all rubber tubing should be new, flexible, and tight fitting. Sealing wax should not be used except on cork stoppers as specified in the above directions.

Notes. — 1. The air current, which is subsequently drawn through the apparatus, to sweep all of the carbon dioxide into the absorption apparatus, is likely to carry with it some hydrochloric acid from the evolution flask. This acid is retained by the silver sulphate solution. The addition of concentrated sulphuric acid to this solution reduces its vapor pressure so far that very little water is carried on by the air current, and this slight amount is absorbed by the calcium chloride in (*E*). As the calcium chloride frequently contains a small amount of a basic material which would absorb carbon dioxide, it is necessary to pass carbon dioxide through (*E*) for a short time and then drive all the gas out with a dry air current for thirty minutes before use.

ANALYSIS OF LIMESTONE OR DOLOMITE

2. Ascarite is a commercial preparation and consists of asbestos which has been impregnated with sodium hydroxide. It is superior to soda lime as an absorbent for carbon dioxide. As carbon dioxide is absorbed the color of that part of the ascarite layer acted upon changes from gray to white. When nearly all of the ascarite has changed color it is discarded and the tube is filled with a fresh supply.

A concentrated solution of potassium hydroxide (1 : 2) can be used in a Geissler bulb as an absorbent for carbon dioxide but the apparatus is difficult to fill and clean, and the method is much less convenient.

The Analysis

Procedure. — Weigh out accurately into the flask (B) about 1 gram of limestone. Cover it with 15 cc. of water. Weigh the absorption apparatus (F) accurately after allowing it to stand for 30 minutes in the balance case, and wiping it carefully with a lintless cloth, taking care to handle it as little as possible after wiping (Note 1). Connect the absorption apparatus with (e) and (f).

To be sure that the whole apparatus is air-tight, disconnect the rubber tube from the flask (A), making sure that the tubes (a) and (b) do not contain any hydrochloric acid, close the pinchcock (a) and apply suction at (g). No bubbles should pass through (G) after a few seconds. When assured that the fittings are tight, shut off the suction and open (a) cautiously to admit air to restore atmospheric pressure. Reconnect the rubber tube with the flask (A). Open the pinchcocks (a), disconnect the suction, and blow over about 10 cc. of the hydrochloric acid from (A) into (B). When the action of the acid slackens, blow over (slowly) another 10 cc.

The rate of gas evolution should not exceed for more than a few seconds that at which about two bubbles per second pass through (G) (Note 2). Repeat the addition of acid in small portions until the action upon the limestone seems to be at an end, taking care to close (a) after each addition of acid (Note 3). Disconnect (A) and connect the rubber tubing with the soda-lime tube (H) and open (a). Then apply gentle suction at (g) in such a way that about two bubbles per second pass through (G). Place a small flame under (B) and *slowly* raise the contents to boiling and boil for three minutes. Then remove the burner from under

(B) and continue to draw air through the apparatus for 20–30 minutes (Note 4). Remove the absorption apparatus, stoppering the open ends of (F), leave the apparatus in the balance case for at least thirty minutes, wipe it carefully, remove the plugs, and weigh. The increase in weight is due to absorption of CO_2, from which its percentage in the sample may be calculated.

After cleaning (B) the apparatus is ready for the duplicate analysis.

Notes. — 1. The absorption tube has a large surface on which moisture may collect. By allowing it to remain in the balance case for some time before weighing, the amount of moisture absorbed on the surface is as nearly constant as practicable during two weighings, and a uniform temperature is also assured.

2. If the gas passes too rapidly into the absorption apparatus, some carbon dioxide may be carried through, not being completely retained by the absorbent.

3. The essential ionic changes involved in this procedure are the following: It is assumed that the limestone, which is typified by calcium carbonate, is very slightly soluble in water, and the ions resulting are Ca^{++} and CO_3^{--}. In the presence of H^+ ions of the mineral acid, the CO_3^{--} ions form [H_2CO_3]. This is not only a weak acid which, by its formation, diminishes the concentration of the CO_3^{--} ions, thus causing more of the carbonate to dissolve to re-establish equilibrium, but it is also an unstable compound and breaks down into carbon dioxide and water.

4. Carbon dioxide is dissolved by cold water, but the gas is expelled by boiling, and, together with that which is distributed through the apparatus, is swept out into the absorption bulb by the current of air. This air is purified by drawing it through the tube (H) containing soda lime, which removes any carbon dioxide which may be in it.

STOICHIOMETRY

It is occasionally necessary to eliminate from or introduce into a report of an analysis one or more constituents and to calculate the results to a new basis. Thus, a mineral may contain hygroscopic water which is not an integral part of the molecular structure. After complete analysis, it may be desirable to calculate the results to a dry basis as being more representative of the mineral under normal conditions. On the other hand, a

ANALYSIS OF LIMESTONE OR DOLOMITE

material may contain a very large amount of water, and because of the difficulty of proper sampling, a small sample may be taken for the determination of the water while the bulk of the material is dried, sampled, and analyzed. It may then be desirable to convert the results thus obtained to the basis of the original wet sample. This applies equally well to constituents other than water, and in any case, the method by which these calculations are made is based upon the fact that the constituents other than the ones eliminated or introduced are all changed in the same proportion, and the total percentage must remain the same.

Example I. — A sample of limestone gives the following analysis:

$$
\begin{aligned}
CaO &= 50.14\% \\
MgO &= 3.18\% \\
Fe_2O_3 + Al_2O_3 &= 2.20\% \\
SiO_2 &= 5.39\% \\
CO_2 &= \underline{39.10\%} \\
&\ 100.01\%
\end{aligned}
$$

On ignition, this limestone is converted to lime and the percentage of CO_2 in the lime is found to be reduced to 2.00%. What is the complete analysis of the lime?

Solution. — In the limestone the percentage of non-volatile constituents is $100.01 - 39.10 = 60.91\%$. In the lime the corresponding percentage of non-volatile constituents is $100.01 - 2.00 = 98.01\%$. The loss of the CO_2 has caused the percentages of the various non-volatile constituents to increase in the ratio of 98.01 to 60.91. The analysis of the lime is therefore:

$$
\begin{aligned}
CaO &= 50.14 \times \frac{98.01}{60.91} = 80.67\% \\
MgO &= 3.18 \times \frac{98.01}{60.91} = 5.12\% \\
Fe_2O_3 + Al_2O_3 &= 2.20 \times \frac{98.01}{60.91} = 3.54\%. \quad Ans. \\
SiO_2 &= 5.39 \times \frac{98.01}{60.91} = 8.68\% \\
CO_2 &= \underline{2.00\%} \\
&\ 100.01\%
\end{aligned}
$$

It is assumed that the student is already familiar with the simple applications of the three major gas laws, namely:

(1) (Boyle's Law) The volume of a fixed gas at constant temperature is inversely proportional to the pressure to which it is subjected.

(2) (Charles' Law) The volume of a fixed mass of a gas at constant pressure is directly proportional to the absolute temperature to which it is subjected. (Absolute temperature = 273 + temperature in Centigrade units.)

(3) (Dalton's Law) The pressure exerted by a mixture of gases is equal to the sum of the pressures of the individual components, and the pressure exerted by a single component is the same as the pressure that component would exert alone in the same volume.

Example II. — If a half-gram sample of the above limestone is treated with mineral acid, what volume of CO_2 gas would be evolved when measured over water at 21° C. and 755 mm. barometric pressure? (Vapor pressure of water at 21° = 18.50 mm.)

Solution. — $\dfrac{0.5000 \times 0.3910}{CO_2}$ = moles of CO_2 evolved

$\dfrac{0.5000 \times 0.3910}{CO_2} \times 22400$ = cc. of CO_2 (standard conditions)

$\dfrac{0.5000 \times 0.3910}{44.00} \times 22400 \times \dfrac{273 + 21}{273} \times \dfrac{760}{755 - 18.5}$ = 111 cc.

Ans.

PROBLEMS

178. A sample of magnesium carbonate, contaminated with SiO_2 as its only impurity, weighs 0.5000 gram and loses 0.1000 gram on ignition. What volume of disodium phosphate solution (containing 90 grams $Na_2HPO_4 \cdot 12\ H_2O$ per liter) will be required to precipitate the magnesium as magnesium ammonium phosphate?

Answer: 9.07 cc.

179. A sample of dolomite is analyzed for calcium by precipitating as the oxalate and igniting the precipitate. The ignited product is assumed to be CaO and the analyst reports 29.50% Ca in the sample. Owing to insufficient ignition, the product actually contained 8% of its weight of

ANALYSIS OF LIMESTONE OR DOLOMITE

$CaCO_3$. What is the correct percentage of calcium in the sample, and what is the percentage error?

Answer: 28.46%; 3.65% error.

180. What weight of impure calcite ($CaCO_3$) should be taken for analysis so that the volume in cubic centimeters of CO_2 obtained by treating with acid, measured dry at 18° C. and 763 mm., shall equal the percentage of CaO in the sample?

Answer: 0.2359 gram.

181. A sample of magnesia limestone has the following composition: Silica, 3.00%; ferric oxide and alumina, 0.20%; calcium oxide, 33.10%; magnesium oxide, 20.70%; carbon dioxide, 43.00%. In manufacturing lime from the above the carbon dioxide is reduced to 3.00%. How many cubic centimeters of normal $KMnO_4$ will be required to determine the calcium oxide volumetrically in a 1 gram sample of the lime?

Answer: 20.08 cc.

182. The calcium in a sample of dolomite weighing 0.9380 gram is precipitated as calcium oxalate and ignited to calcium oxide. What volume of gas, measured over water at 20° C. and 765 mm. pressure, is given off during ignition, if the resulting oxide weighs 0.2606 gram? (G. M. V. = 22.4 liters; V. P. water at 20° C. = 17.4 mm.)

Answer: 227 cc.

183. A limestone is found to contain 93.05% $CaCO_3$, and 5.16% $MgCO_3$. Calculate the weight of CaO obtainable from 3 tons of the limestone, assuming complete conversion to oxide. What weight of $Mg_2P_2O_7$ could be obtained from a 3-gram sample of the limestone?

Answer: 1.565 tons; 0.2044 gram.

184. A sample is prepared for student analysis by mixing pure apatite ($Ca_3(PO_4)_2 \cdot CaCl_2$) with an inert material. If 1 gram of the sample gives 0.4013 gram of $Mg_2P_2O_7$, how many cubic centimeters of ammonium oxalate solution (containing 40 grams of $(NH_4)_2C_2O_4 \cdot H_2O$ per liter) would be required to precipitate the calcium from the same weight of sample?

Answer: 25.60 cc.

185. If 0.6742 gram of a mixture of pure magnesium carbonate and pure calcium carbonate, when treated with an excess of hydrochloric acid, yields 0.3117 gram of carbon dioxide, calculate the percentage of magnesium oxide and of calcium oxide in the sample.

Answer: 13.22% MgO; 40.54% CaO.

186. A mixture of BaO and CaO weighing 1.792 grams, when treated with sulphuric acid and transformed to mixed sulphates, weighs twice the original amount. What is the percentage of CaO in the mixture?

Answer: 15.4%.

187. A certain dolomite contains 1.33% moisture, 1.20% SiO_2, 1.01% ferric and aluminum oxides combined, and the remainder is calcium carbonate and magnesium carbonate. The analysis shows 10.23% MgO. If this mineral is heated sufficiently to drive off all of the water and so that the percentage of CO_2 in the resulting product is 1.37%, what is the percentage of CaO in the ignited material?

Answer: 76.14%.

188. If a sample of a powder consisting of a mixture of equal weights of pure $CaCO_3$ and pure $MgCO_3$ yields a precipitate of calcium oxalate which requires 40.00 cc. of $KMnO_4$ (1 cc. $\backsimeq$ 0.008375 gram Fe), what weight of ignited magnesium precipitate could be obtained by precipitating the magnesium with alkali phosphate from the ammoniacal filtrate?

Answer: 0.3964 gram.

189. A certain chemical is subject to changes in composition due to the ease in which water is absorbed or lost. No other changes take place. If in a sample showing 12.00% H_2O the percentage of constituent a of the chemical is found to be 15.80%, what would be the percentage of a in a similar sample which shows only 3.90% H_2O?

Answer: 17.26%.

190. A sample of dolomite weighing 1.000 gram gives a precipitate of calcium oxalate requiring 55.00 cc. of $\dfrac{N}{5}$ $KMnO_4$ for titration. A similar weight of the dolomite weighs 0.9950 gram after complete drying and when treated with acid yields 150.0 cc. of CO_2 when measured over water at 26° C. and 768 mm. barometric pressure (V. P. of water at 26° = 25.0 mm.). Lime is made from this dolomite by strong ignition in which all of the moisture is lost and the percentage of CO_2 in the lime is only 0.70%. What weight of $CaSO_4$ is obtainable in the analysis of 0.5000 gram of the lime?

Answer: 0.507 gram.

ANALYSIS OF BRASS AND BRONZE

ELECTROLYTIC SEPARATIONS

General Discussion

When a direct current of electricity passes from one electrode to another through solutions of electrolytes, the individual ions present in these solutions tend to move toward the electrode of opposite electrical charge to that which each ion bears, and to be discharged by that electrode. Whether or not such discharge actually occurs in the case of any particular ion depends upon the potential (voltage) of the current which is passing through the solution, since for each ion there is, under definite conditions, a minimum potential below which the discharge of the ion cannot be effected. By taking advantage of differences in discharge-potentials, it is possible to effect separations of a number of the metallic ions by electrolysis, and at the same time to deposit the metals in forms which admit of direct weighing. In this way the slower procedures of precipitation and filtration may frequently be avoided. The following paragraphs present a brief statement of the fundamental principles and conditions underlying electro-analysis.

The total energy of an electric current as it passes through a solution is distributed among three factors, first, its potential, which is measured in volts, and corresponds to what is called " head " in a stream of water; second, current strength, which is measured in amperes, and corresponds to the volume of water passing a cross-section of a stream in a given time interval; and third, the resistance of the conducting medium, which is measured in ohms. The relation between these three factors is expressed by Ohm's law, namely, that $I = \dfrac{E}{R}$, when I is current strength, E potential, and R resistance. It is plain that, for a constant resistance, the strength of the current and its potential are mutually and directly interdependent.

As already stated, the applied electrical potential determines whether or not deposition of a metal upon an electrode actually occurs. The current strength determines the rate of deposition and the physical characteristics of the deposit. The resistance of the solution is generally so small as to fall out of practical consideration.

Approximate deposition-potentials have been determined for a number of the metallic elements, and also for hydrogen and some of the acid-forming radicals. The values given below are those required for deposition from normal solutions at ordinary temperatures with reference to a hydrogen electrode. They must be regarded as approximate, since several disturbing factors and some secondary reactions render difficult their exact application under the conditions of analysis. They are:

Zn	Fe	Cd	Ni	Pb	H	Cu	Ag	Hg	SO_4
+0.76	+0.43	+0.40	+0.22	+0.12	0	−0.34	−0.80	−0.86	+1.90

A more complete table is given in the Appendix.

In order to deposit copper from a normal solution of copper sulphate a minimum potential equal to the algebraic sum of the deposition-potentials of copper ions and sulphate ions must be applied, that is, + 1.56 volts. The deposition of zinc from a solution of zinc sulphate would require + 2.66 volts, but, since the deposition of hydrogen from sulphuric acid solution requires only + 1.90 volts, the quantitative deposition of zinc by electrolysis from a sulphuric acid solution of a zinc salt is not practicable. On the other hand, silver, if present in a solution of copper sulphate, would deposit with the copper.

The foregoing examples suffice to illustrate the application of the principle of deposition potentials, but it must further be noted that the values stated apply to normal solutions of the compounds in question, that is, to solutions of considerable concentrations. As the concentration of the ions diminishes, and hence fewer ions approach the electrodes, somewhat higher voltages are required to attract and discharge them. From this it follows that the concentrations should be kept as high as possible to effect complete deposition in the least practicable time, or else the potentials applied must be progressively increased as deposition proceeds. In practice, the desired result is obtained by starting with small volumes of solution, using as large an electrode surface as possible, and by stirring the solution to bring the ions in contact with the electrodes. This is, in general, a more convenient procedure than that of increasing the potential of the current during electrolysis, although that method is also used.

As already stated, those ions in a solution of electrolytes will first be discharged which have the lowest deposition potentials, and so long as these ions are present around the electrode in considerable concentration they, almost alone, are discharged, but, as their concentration diminishes, other ions whose deposition potentials are higher but still within that of the current applied, will also begin to separate. For example, from a nitric acid solution of copper nitrate, the copper ions will first be reduced and discharged at the cathode, but as they diminish in concentration, nitrate will also be reduced forming a variety of products, among them ammonia, and it may happen that if the current is passed through for a long time, such a solution will become alkaline. Oxygen is liberated at the anode and escapes as oxygen gas. It should be noted that the changes occurring at the cathode are reductions, while those at the anode are oxidations.

For analytical purposes, solutions of nitrates or sulphates of the metals are preferable to those of the chlorides, since liberated chlorine attacks the electrodes. In some cases, as, for example, that of silver, solution of salts forming complex ions, like that of the double cyanide of silver and potassium, yield better metallic deposits.

Most metals are deposited as such upon the cathode; a few, notably lead and manganese, separate in the form of dioxides upon the anode. It is evidently important that the deposited material should be so firmly adherent that it can be washed, dried, and weighed without loss in handling. To secure these conditions it is essential that the current density (that is, the amount of current per unit of area of the electrodes) shall not be too high.

In prescribing analytical conditions it is customary to state the current strength in " normal densities " expressed in amperes per 100 sq. cm. of electrode surface, as, for example, " $N.D_{100}$ = 2 amps."

If deposition occurs too rapidly, the deposit is likely to be spongy or loosely adherent and falls off on subsequent treatment. This places a practical limit to the current density to be employed, for a given electrode surface. The cause of the unsatisfactory character of the deposit is apparently sometimes to be found in the coincident liberation of considerable hydrogen and sometimes in the failure of the rapidly deposited material to form a continuous adherent surface. The effect of rotating electrodes upon the character of the deposit is referred to below.

The negative ions of an electrolyte are attracted to the anode and are discharged on contact with it. Anions such as the chloride ion yield chlorine atoms, from which gaseous chlorine molecules are formed and escape. The radicals which compose such ions as NO_3^- or SO_4^{--} are not capable of independent existence after discharge, and break down into oxygen and N_2O_5 and SO_3 respectively. The oxygen escapes and the anhydrides, reacting with water, re-form nitric and sulphuric acids.

The electrodes employed in electro-analysis are almost exclusively of platinum, since that metal alone satisfactorily resists chemical action of the electrolytes, and can be dried and weighed without change in composition. The platinum electrodes may be used in the form of dishes, foil, or gauze. The last, on account of the ease of circulation of the electrolyte, its relatively large surface in proportion to its weight and the readiness with which it can be washed and dried, is generally preferred.

Many devices have been described by the use of which the electrode upon which deposition occurs can be mechanically rotated. This has an effect parallel to that of greatly increasing the electrode surface and also provides a most efficient means of stirring the solution. With such an apparatus the amperage may be increased to 5 or even 10 amperes and depositions completed with great rapidity and accuracy. It is desirable, whenever practicable, to provide a rotating or stirring device, since, for example, the time consumed in the deposition of the amount of copper usually found in analysis may be reduced from the 20 to 24 hours required with stationary electrodes, and unstirred solutions, to about one half hour.

DETERMINATION OF TIN IN BRONZE

To a 0.5 gram sample of the bronze (Note 1) in a small beaker add 10–15 cc. of 6 N nitric acid and evaporate on a water bath nearly but not quite to dryness. Decant the residue of metastannic acid with three successive 20 cc. portions of hot 3 N nitric acid through a *hardened* filter paper, and then continue the washing by decantation with successive portions of hot water until the washings are free from copper. Metastannic acid has a tendency to run through even a hardened paper and the filtrate and washings must be examined carefully to make sure that they are perfectly clear. It is of course necessary to refilter if even a trace of the metastannic acid has passed through the paper. Save the combined filtrate and washings for the determination of copper and lead as in the analysis of brass below. Wash off thoroughly the metastannic acid from the filter paper into the original beaker using as small a volume of water as is practicable. Place the paper in a beaker, add 20 cc. of either ammonium sulphide or sodium sulphide solution, cover with a watch-glass, and warm gently for 10 minutes. Pour this solution into the beaker containing the metastannic acid and add 75 cc. more of the sulphide reagent. Save the filter paper. Digest the mixture containing the sulphide solution in a covered beaker on the steam bath for two hours. The tin should be dissolved, leaving a small residue of the sulphides of copper and lead. Filter and wash with a 10% solution of the alkali sulphide reagent, and finally wash with water.

Digest the filter paper containing the residue of the sulphides of copper and lead (together with the filter paper from which the metastannic acid was dissolved) with 15 cc. of hot 3 N nitric acid. Filter and wash with water. Neutralize this filtrate and washings with ammonium hydroxide and add to the main solution containing the copper and lead from the bronze. Ignite the filters in a porcelain crucible in the regular way and add the resulting weight of SnO_2 to that obtained below.

Dilute the sulphide solution to 500 cc., make slightly acid with acetic acid, cover the beaker, and allow to stand in a warm place over night. Decant through a filter, transfer the precipitate to the filter and wash with a 2% solution of ammonium nitrate which has been slightly acidified with acetic acid (Note 2). Dry and smoke off the paper in the regular way. Raise the temperature gradually until the sulphur has all burned off and then apply the full heat of the Tirrill burner. Finish the heating with a Meker burner or blast lamp and weigh as SnO_2. Report the percentage of tin (Sn).

Notes. — 1. Bronze is essentially an alloy of copper, tin, and lead; brass is essentially an alloy of copper, lead, and zinc; both may contain traces of iron and other elements. Brass dissolves completely in nitric acid; bronze leaves a residue of metastannic acid

$$(3\ Sn + 4\ HNO_3 + H_2O \rightarrow 3\ H_2SnO_3 + 4\ NO)$$

which can be filtered off and ignited to SnO_2. This is the basis of the determination of tin in bronze although for accurate results provision must be made for the fact that the metastannic acid invariably contains small amounts of copper and lead which must be recovered. By dissolving the metastannic acid in sodium sulphide or ammonium sulphide, a soluble thiostannate is formed (*e.g.* Na_2SnS_3) leaving insoluble CuS and PbS which can be dissolved in nitric acid and added to the main solution. By acidifying the thiostannate solution, SnS_2 is precipitated and can be ignited to and weighed as SnO_2.

2. The use of ammonium nitrate reagent as a washing solution for the SnS_2 has the advantage over water in that it hastens the complete combustion of the filter paper and prevents the formation of colloidal SnS_2 which would pass through the filter paper.

DETERMINATION OF COPPER AND LEAD IN BRONZE AND BRASS

Procedure. — In the analysis of bronze use the filtrate (which should not exceed 75 cc.) from the metastannic acid determination and proceed as described in the next paragraph. In the analysis of brass weigh out two portions of about 0.5 gram each

(Note 1) into tall, slender lipless beakers of about 100 cc. capacity. Dissolve the metal in a solution of 5 cc. of dilute nitric acid (sp. gr. 1.20) and 5 cc. of water, heating gently, and keeping the beaker covered. When the sample has all dissolved, wash down the sides of the beaker and the bottom of the watch-glass with water and dilute the solution to about 50 cc. Carefully heat to boiling and boil for a minute or two to expel nitrous fumes.

Meanwhile, four platinum electrodes, two anodes and two cathodes, should be cleaned by dipping in dilute nitric acid, washing with water and finally with 95 per cent alcohol (Note 2). The alcohol may be ignited and burned off. The electrodes are then cooled in a desiccator and weighed. Connect the electrodes with the binding posts (or other device for connection with the electric circuit) in such a way that the copper will be deposited upon the electrode with the larger surface, which is made the cathode. The beaker containing the solution should then be raised into place from below the electrodes until the latter reach nearly to the bottom of the beaker. The support for the beaker must be so arranged that it can be easily raised or lowered.

If the electrolytic apparatus is provided with a mechanism for the rotation of the electrode or stirring of the electrolyte, proceed as follows: Arrange the resistance in the circuit to provide a direct current of about one ampere. Pass this current through the solution to be electrolyzed, and start the rotating mechanism. Keep the beaker covered as completely as possible, using a split watch-glass (or other device) to avoid loss by spattering. When the solution is colorless, which is usually the case after about 35 minutes, rinse off the cover glass, wash down the sides of the beaker, add about 0.30 gram of urea and continue the electrolysis for another five minutes (Notes 3 and 4).

If stationary electrodes are employed, the current strength should be about 0.1 ampere, which may, after 12 to 15 hours, be increased to 0.2 ampere. The time required for complete deposition is usually from 20 to 24 hours. It is advisable to add 5 cc. of nitric acid (sp. gr. 1.2) if the electrolysis extends over this length of time. No urea is added in this case.

When the deposition of the copper appears to be complete, stop the rotating mechanism and slowly lower the beaker with the left hand, directing at the same time a stream of water from a wash bottle on both electrodes. Remove the beaker, shut off the current, and, if necessary, complete the washing of the electrodes (Note 5). Rinse the electrodes cautiously with alcohol and heat them in a hot closet until the alcohol has just evaporated, but no longer, since the copper is likely to oxidize at the higher temperature. (The alcohol may be removed by ignition if care is taken to keep the electrodes in motion in the air so that the copper deposit is not too strongly heated at any one point.)

Test the solution in the beaker for copper as follows, remembering that it is to be used for subsequent determinations of iron and zinc: Remove about 5 cc. and add a slight excess of ammonia. Compare the mixture with some distilled water, holding both above a white surface. The solution should not show any tinge of blue. If the presence of copper is indicated, add the test portion to the main solution, evaporate the whole to a volume of about 100 cc., and again electrolyze with clean electrodes (Note 6).

After cooling the electrodes in a desiccator, weigh them and from the weight of copper on the cathode and of lead dioxide (PbO_2) on the anode, calculate the percentage of copper (Cu) and of lead (Pb) in the brass.

Notes. — 1. It is obvious that the brass taken for analysis should be untarnished, which can be easily assured, when wire is used, by scouring with emery. If chips or borings are used, they should be well mixed, and the sample for analysis taken from different parts of the mixture.

2. The electrodes should be freed from all greasy matter before using, and those portions upon which the metal will deposit should not be touched with the fingers after cleaning.

3. Of the ions in solution, the H^+, Cu^{++}, Zn^{++}, and Fe^{+++} ions tend to move toward the cathode. The NO_3^- ions and the lead, probably in the form of PbO_2^{--} ions, move toward the anode. At the cathode the Cu^{++} ions are discharged and plate out as metallic copper. This alone occurs while the solution is relatively concentrated. Later on, H^+ ions are also discharged. In the presence of considerable quanti-

ties of H⁺ ions, as in this acid solution, no Zn^{++} or Fe^{+++} ions are discharged because of their greater deposition potentials. At the anode the lead is deposited as PbO_2 and oxygen is evolved.

For the reasons stated on page 203 care must be taken that the solution does not become alkaline if the electrolysis is long continued.

4. Urea reacts with nitrous acid, which may be formed in the solution as a result of the reducing action of the liberated hydrogen. Its removal promotes the complete precipitation of the copper. The reaction is $CO(NH_2)_2 + 2 HNO_2 \rightarrow CO_2 + 2 N_2 + 3 H_2O.$

5. The electrodes must be washed nearly or quite free from the nitric acid solution before the circuit is broken to prevent re-solution of the copper.

If several solutions are connected in the same circuit, it is obvious that some device must be used to close the circuit as soon as the beaker is removed.

6. The electrodes upon which the copper has been deposited may be cleaned by immersion in warm nitric acid. To remove the lead dioxide, add a few crystals of oxalic acid to the nitric acid.

DETERMINATION OF IRON

Most brasses and bronzes contain small percentages of iron (usually not over 0.1 per cent) which, unless removed, is precipitated as phosphate and weighed with the zinc.

Procedure. — To the solution from the precipitation of copper and lead by electrolysis, add dilute ammonia (sp. gr. 0.96) until the precipitate of zinc hydroxide which first forms re-dissolves, leaving only a slight red precipitate of ferric hydroxide. Filter off the iron precipitate, using a washed filter, and wash five times with hot water. Test a portion of the last washing with a dilute solution of ammonium sulphide to assure complete removal of the zinc.

The precipitate may then be ignited and weighed as ferric oxide, as described on page 159.

Calculate the percentage of iron (Fe) in the brass.

DETERMINATION OF ZINC

Procedure. — Acidify the filtrate from the iron determination with dilute nitric acid. Concentrate it to 150 cc. Add to the cold solution dilute ammonia (sp. gr. 0.96) cautiously until it barely smells of ammonia; then add *one drop* of a dilute solution of litmus (Note 1), and drop in, with the aid of a dropper, dilute nitric acid until the blue of the litmus just changes to red. It is important that this point should not be overstepped. Heat the solution nearly to boiling and pour into it slowly a filtered sodium of di-ammonium hydrogen phosphate [1] containing a weight of the phosphate about twelve times that of the zinc to be precipitated. (For this calculation the approximate percentage of zinc is that found by subtracting the sum of the percentages of the copper, lead, and iron from 100 per cent.) Keep the solution just below boiling for fifteen minutes, stirring frequently (Note 2). If at the end of this time the amorphous precipitate has become crystalline, allow the solution to cool for about four hours, although a longer time does no harm (Note 3), and filter upon an asbestos filter in a porcelain Gooch crucible. The filter is prepared as described on page 149, and should be dried to constant weight at 105° C.

Wash the precipitate thoroughly with a warm 1 per cent solution of the di-ammonium phosphate, and then five times with 50 per cent alcohol (Note 4). Dry the crucible and precipitate for an hour at 105° C., and finally to constant weight (Note 5). The filtrate should be made alkaline with ammonia and tested for zinc with a few drops of ammonium sulphide, allowing it to stand (Notes 6 and 7).

From the weight of the zinc ammonium phosphate ($ZnNH_4PO_4$) calculate the percentage of the zinc (Zn) in the brass.

Notes. — 1. The zinc ammonium phosphate is soluble both in acids and in ammonia. It is, therefore, necessary to precipitate the zinc in a nearly neutral solution, which is more accurately obtained by adding a drop of a litmus solution to the liquid than by the use of litmus paper.

2. The precipitate which first forms is amorphous, and may have a variable composition. On standing it becomes crystalline and then has

---

[1] The ammonium phosphate which is commonly obtainable contains some mono-ammonium salt, and this is not satisfactory as a precipitant. It is advisable, therefore, to weigh the amount of the salt required, dissolve it in a small volume of water, add a drop of phenolphthalein solution, and finally add dilute ammonium hydroxide solution cautiously until the solution just becomes pink, but do not add an excess.

the composition $ZnNH_4PO_4$. The precipitate then settles rapidly and is apt to occasion "bumping" if the solution is heated to boiling. Stirring promotes the crystallization.

3. In a carefully neutralized solution containing a considerable excess of the precipitant, and also ammonium salts, the separation of the zinc is complete after standing four hours. The ionic changes connected with the precipitation of the zinc as zinc ammonium phosphate are similar to those described for magnesium ammonium phosphate, except that the zinc precipitate is soluble in an excess of ammonium hydroxide, probably as a result of the formation of complex ions of the general character $Zn(NH_3)_4^{++}$.

4. The precipitate is washed first with a dilute solution of the phosphate to prevent a slight decomposition of the precipitate (as a result of hydrolysis) if hot water alone is used. The alcohol is added to the final wash-water to promote the subsequent drying.

5. The precipitate may be ignited and weighed as $Zn_2P_2O_7$, by cautiously heating the porcelain Gooch crucible within a nickel or iron crucible, used as a radiator. The heating must be very slow at first, as the escaping ammonia may reduce the precipitate if it is heated too quickly.

6. If the ammonium sulphide produced a distinct precipitate, this should be collected on a small filter, dissolved in a few cubic centimeters of dilute nitric acid, and the zinc reprecipitated as phosphate, filtered off, dried, and weighed, and the weight added to that of the main precipitate.

7. It has been found that some samples of asbestos are acted upon by the phosphate solution and lose weight. An error from this source may be avoided by determining the weight of the crucible and filter after weighing the precipitate. For this purpose the precipitate may be dissolved in dilute nitric acid, the asbestos washed thoroughly, and the crucible reweighed.

STOICHIOMETRY

Faraday's law expresses the relation between current strength and the quantities of the decomposition products which, under constant conditions, appear at the electrodes. It states that a given quantity of electricity acting for a given time causes the separation of chemically equivalent quantities of the various elements or radicals. It has been found by experiment that the passage of 96,500 coulombs (= 1 faraday) of electricity causes the separation of one gram-equivalent of substance at each electrode. A coulomb is an ampere-second (*i.e.* number of coulombs = number of amperes × number of seconds).

96,500 coulombs will therefore liberate

$\dfrac{Ag}{1}$ = 107.88 grams of silver from a solution of silver salt;

$\dfrac{Fe}{2}$ = 27.92 grams of iron from a solution of ferrous salt;

$\dfrac{Fe}{3}$ = 18.61 grams of iron from a solution of ferric salt.

The above reactions may be expressed by equations, as follows:

$$Ag^+ + \epsilon \rightarrow Ag$$
$$Fe^{++} + 2\,\epsilon \rightarrow Fe$$
$$Fe^{+++} + 3\,\epsilon \rightarrow Fe$$

where the symbol ϵ represents the electron, or unit of negative electricity. If the equations are considered as representing gram-atomic or gram-molecular ratios, then the symbol represents the faraday. That is, one, two, and three faradays are required to deposit a gram-atomic weight of metal from a solution of silver salt, ferrous salt, and ferric salt respectively.

Faraday's law applies to each electrode. A current of one ampere flowing for 96,500 seconds through a solution of copper sulphate is not only capable of depositing $\dfrac{Cu}{2}$ = 31.79 grams of copper at the cathode, but at the same time will liberate $\dfrac{O}{2}$, 8.000 grams of oxygen at the anode:

(cathode) $Cu^{++} + 2\,\epsilon \rightarrow Cu$
(anode) $H_2O - 2\,\epsilon \rightarrow 2\,H^+ + \tfrac{1}{2}\,O_2$.

Example I. — How many grams of copper will be deposited at the cathode and how many cubic centimeters of oxygen (measured under standard conditions) will be liberated at the anode by the passage of a current of 4 amperes for 30 minutes through a solution of copper sulphate, assuming no other reactions to take place at the cathode?

Solution. — Number of coulombs = 4 × 30 × 60 = 7200

Number of faradays = $\frac{7200}{96500}$

One faraday will liberate $\frac{Cu}{2}$ = 31.79 grams of copper at the cathode from a cupric solution.

One faraday will also liberate $\frac{O}{2}$ = 8.000 grams = ¼ mole = ¼ × 22,400 = 5600 cc. of oxygen at the anode.

$\frac{7200}{96500}$ × 31.79 = 2.372 grams Cu. *Ans.*

$\frac{7200}{96500}$ × 5600 = 417.8 cc. O_2. *Ans.*

In the above calculations it is assumed that all of the current is applied to the decomposition of the substance in question; that is, that the current efficiency is 100%. In an actual analysis this is not usually the case. The electrolysis of an acid solution of a copper salt will not only cause the deposition of copper at the cathode, but as the concentration of the copper diminishes, hydrogen is liberated in increasing amounts at the cathode. But in such cases the *sum* of the weights of the products discharged at each electrode exactly fulfills the requirements of Faraday's law. That is, in the copper electrolysis, for each faraday of electricity passed, the number of gram-equivalents of copper deposited added to the number of gram-equivalents of hydrogen liberated is unity.

Example II. — If it takes 18 minutes for a current of ½ ampere to deposit 0.5000 gram of metallic silver from a nitric acid solution of silver nitrate, what is the current efficiency for this deposition?

Solution. — Weight of Ag deposited under 100% current yield =

$$\frac{18 \times 60 \times \frac{1}{2}}{96500} \times \frac{Ag}{1} = 0.6039 \text{ gram}$$

Actual deposition = 0.5000 gram

$\frac{0.5000}{0.6039}$ × 100 = 82.79%. *Ans.*

In the electrolysis of a solution of brass, the solution contains the ions of copper, lead, and zinc, together with the ions of the acid used to dissolve the alloy. At the start of the electrolysis copper is deposited at the cathode and lead dioxide at the anode:

(cathode) $Cu^{++} + 2\epsilon \to Cu$
(anode) $Pb^{++} + 2 H_2O - 2\epsilon \to PbO_2 + 4 H^+$. (A)

From these equations it is evident that the passage of one faraday (assuming 100% current efficiency) results in (1) the deposition of $\frac{1}{2}$ mole (= 31.79 grams) of copper at the cathode; (2) the deposition of $\frac{1}{2}$ mole (= 119.6 grams) of lead dioxide at the anode; (3) the liberation of no gas; and (4) an increase in acidity of 2 gram-equivalents.

In brass the amount of lead is present in relatively small amounts. After it has been removed from solution the reactions at the electrodes are as follows:

(cathode) $Cu^{++} + 2\epsilon \to Cu$
(anode) $H_2O - 2\epsilon \to 2 H^+ + \frac{1}{2} O_2$. (B)

From these equations it is evident that the passage of one faraday now results in (1) the deposition of $\frac{1}{2}$ mole of copper at the cathode; (2) the liberation of $\frac{1}{4}$ mole (= 5600 cc. under standard conditions) of gas at the anode; and (3) an increase in acidity of 1 gram-equivalent.

After the copper has been removed from solution the reactions at the electrodes are:

(cathode) $2 H^+ + 2\epsilon \to H_2$
(anode) $H_2O - 2\epsilon \to 2 H^+ + \frac{1}{2} O_2$. (C)

From these equations it is evident that the passage of one faraday now results in (1) the liberation of $\frac{1}{2}$ mole of hydrogen at the cathode and $\frac{1}{4}$ mole of oxygen at the anode, or a total of $\frac{3}{4}$ mole of gas; and (2) no net change in acidity.

Under these conditions zinc cannot deposit from the solution even under continued electrolysis since the solution remains constantly acid, but if *nitric acid* is present there is invariably a reduction at the cathode of the nitrate radical to form various reduction products, notably ammonium ions:

(cathode) $NO_3^- + 8\epsilon + 10 H^+ \to NH_4^+ + 3 H_2O$
(anode) $4 H_2O - 8\epsilon \to 8 H^+ + 2 O_2$. (D)

ANALYSIS OF BRASS AND BRONZE

In this case the passage of one faraday results in (1) the liberation of $\frac{1}{4}$ mole of oxygen at the anode; and (2) a *net* decrease of $\frac{1}{4}$ gram-equivalent in acidity (*i.e.* 8 faradays cause a decrease of 10 H$^+$ at the cathode and an increase of 8 H$^+$ at the anode). Continued electrolysis in this case may result in complete neutralization of the acid, after which zinc will begin to deposit.

Example III. — Given a solution which is $\frac{1}{50}$ molal in cupric salt, $\frac{1}{200}$ molal in lead salt, and 0.500 normal in acid. It is electrolyzed with a current of 2 amperes and the volume of the solution is kept constant at 100 cc. Assuming 100% current efficiency, calculate (*a*) the acid normality of the solution when all of the lead has just been deposited; (*b*) the acid normality of the solution after all of the copper has just been deposited; (*c*) the acid normality of the solution after the current has been continued for 10 minutes longer; (*d*) the total volume of gas liberated during the entire electrolysis.

Solution. — Increase in acidity during the deposition of $\frac{1}{200}$ mole of PbO$_2$
      $= \frac{1}{200} \times 4 = 0.020$ gram-equivalent of H$^+$ (see A above)
      $= 0.020$ gram-equivalent per 100 cc. $= 0.200$ gram-equivalent per liter
Acid normality $= 0.500 + 0.200 = 0.700$ N. *Ans.*
Moles Cu deposited during the PbO$_2$ deposition $= \frac{1}{200}$
Moles Cu remaining $= \frac{3}{200}$
Increase in acidity during the deposition of $\frac{3}{200}$ moles of Cu
      $= \frac{3}{200} \times 2 = 0.030$ gram-equivalent (see B)
      $= 0.300$ gram-equivalent per liter
Acid normality $= 0.700 + 0.300 = 1.000$ N. *Ans.*
Change in acidity when the current is continued for 10 minutes $= 0$ (see C)
Acid normality $= 1.000$ N. *Ans.*
Gas evolved during PbO$_2$ deposition $= 0$ (see A)
Gas evolved during remaining Cu deposition $= \frac{3}{200} \times \frac{1}{2} = \frac{3}{400}$ mole (see B)
      $= \frac{3}{400} \times 22{,}400 = 168$ cc.

Gas evolved during the 10 minute continuation of the current

$$= \frac{10 \times 60 \times 2}{96500} \times \frac{3}{4} = 0.00933 \text{ mole (see C)}$$

0.00933 × 22,400 = 209 cc.

Total cc. = 168 + 209 = 377 cc.   *Ans.*

PROBLEMS

191. If in the analysis of a brass containing 28.00% zinc an error is made in weighing a 2.5 gram portion by which 0.001 gram too much is weighed out, what percentage error in the zinc determination would result? What volume of a solution of sodium hydrogen phosphate, containing 90 grams of $Na_2HPO_4 \cdot 12\ H_2O$ per liter, would be required to precipitate the zinc as $ZnNH_4PO_4$ and what weight of precipitate would be obtained?

Answer: (a) 0.04% error; (b) 39.97 cc.; (c) 1.909 grams.

192. 2.62 cubic centimeters of nitric acid (sp. gr. 1.42 containing 69.80% HNO_3 by weight) are required to just dissolve a sample of brass containing 69.27% Cu; 0.05% Pb; 0.07% Fe; and 30.61% Zn. Assuming the acid used as oxidizing agent was reduced to NO in every case, calculate the weight of the brass and the cubic centimeters of acid used as acid.

Answer: 0.992 gram; 1.97 cc.

193. How many cubic centimeters of HNO_3 (sp. gr. 1.13 containing 21.0% HNO_3 by weight) are required to dissolve 5 grams of brass, containing 0.61% Pb, 24.39% Zn, and 75% Cu, assuming reduction of the nitric acid to NO by each constituent? What fraction of this volume of acid is used for oxidation?

Answer: 55.06 cc.; 25%.

194. What weight of metallic copper will be deposited from a cupric salt solution by a current of 1.5 amperes during a period of 45 minutes, assuming 100% current efficiency? (1 Faraday = 96,500 coulombs.)

Answer: 1.335 grams.

195. In the electrolysis of a 0.8000 gram sample of brass, there is obtained 0.0030 gram of PbO_2, and a deposit of metallic copper exactly equal in weight to the ignited precipitate of $Zn_2P_2O_7$ subsequently obtained from the solution. What is the percentage composition of the brass?

Answer: 69.75% Cu; 29.92% Zn; 0.33% Pb.

196. A sample of brass (68.90% Cu, 1.10% Pb, and 30.00% Zn) weighing 0.9400 gram is dissolved in nitric acid. The lead is determined by weighing as $PbSO_4$, the copper by electrolysis and the zinc by precipitation with $(NH_4)_2HPO_4$ in a neutral solution.

ANALYSIS OF BRASS AND BRONZE

(a) Calculate the cubic centimeters of nitric acid (sp. gr. 1.42 containing 69.90% HNO_3 by weight) required to just dissolve the brass, assuming reduction to NO.

(b) Calculate the cubic centimeters of sulphuric acid (sp. gr. 1.84 containing 94% H_2SO_4 by weight) to displace the nitric acid.

(c) Calculate the weight of $PbSO_4$.

(d) The clean electrode weighs 10.9640 grams. Calculate the weight after the copper has been deposited.

(e) Calculate the grams of $(NH_4)_2HPO_4$ required to precipitate the zinc as $ZnNH_4PO_4$.

(f) Calculate the weight of ignited $Zn_2P_2O_7$.

Answer: (a) 2.48 cc; (b) 0.83 cc.; (c) 0.0152 gram; (d) 11.6116 grams; (e) 0.5705 gram; (f) 0.6573 gram.

197. How many milligrams of silver can be deposited from solution in 23 minutes by a current of 0.7 ampere at 100% current efficiency? How long would it take for the same current to deposit the same weight of nickel?

Answer: 1080 mgs.; 84.3 min.

198. What current efficiency was applied to the deposition of platinum from a solution of chlorplatinate if 0.200 gram of the metal was deposited in 5 minutes with a current of 17 amperes? *Answer:* 7.75%.

199. What weight of $CuSO_4 \cdot 5 H_2O$ must be dissolved in water so that after complete deposition of the copper by electrolysis, a solution will be obtained which is equivalent to 100 cc. of $\frac{N}{10}$ acid?

Answer: 1.249 grams.

200. Pure crystals of $CuSO_4 \cdot 5 H_2O$ are dissolved in water and the solution is electrolyzed with an average current of 0.60 ampere. The electrolysis is continued for 5 minutes after all the copper has been deposited and it is found that a total volume of 62.5 cc. of gas when measured dry at 18° C. and 745 mm. pressure has been evolved. What weight of crystals was taken for electrolysis? (Assume all the copper is deposited before hydrogen is evolved.) How many cubic centimeters of $\frac{N}{10}$ NaOH will the resulting solution neutralize?

Answer: 0.600 gram; 48.1 cc.

201. A sample of alloy (Cu-Pb-Zn) weighing 1.200 gram is dissolved in acid and electrolyzed with a current of 0.900 ampere. The cathode gains 0.6357 gram and the anode gains 0.240 gram. Compute the time theoretically required to deposit all of the copper, the volume of gas (measured under standard conditions) evolved during this time, and the gain in acidity in terms of milliequivalents of hydrogen ion. Compute also the percentage of zinc in the brass. *Answer:* 35.7 min.; 100.8 cc.; 22.0 me.; 29.8%.

202. A pure alloy of copper-zinc is dissolved in acid and electrolyzed with 0.500 ampere (100% current efficiency). It is found that just 40 minutes are required to deposit all of the copper. From the filtrate the zinc is precipitated as in the regulation method and the *ignited* precipitate weighs 0.245 gram. Calculate (a) the grams of copper deposited; (b) the percentage of copper in the alloy; (c) the volume of gas liberated (stand. conditions) during the 40 minute electrolysis; (d) the gain in acid normality of the solution assuming the volume to be kept constant at 500 cc.

Answer: 0.395 gram; 79.0%; 69.7 cc.; 0.0248.

203. A solution of brass in HNO_3 contains 1.10 grams of copper, 0.50 gram of Zn; 0.30 gram of Pb, and is 2 N in acid. The solution is electrolyzed under $1\frac{1}{2}$ amperes and the volume is kept at 100 cc. If the electrolysis is continued 20 minutes after the copper is all deposited, what is the normality of the solution as an acid? Assume that 40% of the current goes to the reduction of nitrate to ammonium ions. *Answer:* 2.355 N.

204. A solution containing $\frac{1}{100}$ mole Cu^{++}, $\frac{1}{500}$ mole Pb^{++}, and $\frac{1}{200}$ mole Zn^{++}, is also 2 normal in acid. It is electrolyzed with an average current of 2 amperes and the volume of the solution is kept at 100 cc. Assuming 100% efficiency, what is the acid normality of the solution when all of the lead is just out? What volume of gas (stand. conditions) has been liberated at this point? What is the acid normality of the solution when all of the copper is just out? What total volume of gas has been liberated at this point? What is the acid normality of the solution after the current is continued for 10 minutes longer? What is the total volume of gas which has been liberated during the entire electrolysis?

Answer: 2.08 N; 0 cc.; 2.24 N; 89.6 cc.; 2.24 N; 299 cc.

DETERMINATION OF SILICA IN SILICATES

Of the natural silicates, or artificial silicates such as slags and some of the cements, a comparatively few can be completely decomposed by treatment with acids, but by far the larger number require fusion with an alkaline flux to effect decomposition and solution for analysis. The procedure given below applies to silicates undecomposable by acids, of which the mineral feldspar is taken as a typical example. Modifications of the procedure, which are applicable to silicates which are completely or partially decomposable by acids, are given in the Notes on page 224.

PREPARATION OF THE SAMPLE

Grind about 3 grams of the mineral in an agate mortar (Note 1) until no grittiness is to be detected, or, better, until it will entirely pass through a sieve made of fine silk bolting cloth. The sieve may be made by placing a piece of the bolting cloth over the top of a small beaker in which the ground mineral is placed, holding the cloth in place by means of a rubber band below the lip of the beaker. By inverting the beaker over clean paper and gently tapping it, the fine particles pass through the sieve, leaving the coarser particles within the beaker. These must be returned to the mortar and ground, and the process of sifting and grinding repeated until the entire sample passes through the sieve.

Note. — 1. If the sample of feldspar for analysis is in the massive or crystalline form, it should be crushed in an iron mortar until the pieces are about half the size of a pea, and then transferred to a steel mortar, in which they are reduced to a coarse powder. A wooden mallet should always be used to strike the pestle of the steel mortar, and the blows should not be sharp.

It is plain that final grinding in an agate mortar must be continued until the whole of the portion of the mineral originally taken has been ground so that it will pass the bolting cloth, otherwise the sifted portion does not represent an average sample, the softer ingredients, if foreign matter is present, being first reduced to powder. For this reason it is best to start with not more than the quantity of the feldspar needed for analysis. The mineral must be thoroughly mixed after the grinding.

FUSION AND SOLUTION

Procedure. — Weigh into platinum crucibles two portions of the ground feldspar of about 0.8 gram each. Weigh on rough balances two portions of anhydrous sodium carbonate, each amounting to about six times the weight of the feldspar taken for analysis (Note 1). Pour about three fourths of the sodium carbonate into the crucible, place the latter on a piece of clean, glazed paper, and thoroughly mix the substance and the flux by carefully stirring for several minutes with a dry glass rod, the end of which has been recently heated and rounded in a flame and slowly cooled. The rod may be wiped off with a small fragment of filter paper, which may be placed in the crucible. Place the remaining fourth of the carbonate on the top of the mixture. Cover the crucible, heat it to dull redness for five minutes, and then gradually increase the heat to the full capacity of a Bunsen or Tirrill burner for twenty minutes, or until a quiet, liquid fusion is obtained (Note 2). Finally, heat the sides and cover strongly until any material which may have collected upon them is also brought to fusion.

Tilt the crucible and allow to cool in that position. This exposes more surface to the subsequent action of the solvent. Disintegrate the mass by placing the crucible in a previously prepared mixture of 100 cc. of water and 50 cc. of dilute hydrochloric acid (sp. gr. 1.12) in a covered casserole (Note 3). Remove the crucible as soon as disintegration is complete and clean the crucible and lid by means of a little hydrochloric acid, adding this acid to the main solution (Notes 4 and 5).

Notes. — 1. Quartz, and other minerals containing very high percentages of silica, may require eight or ten parts by weight of the flux to insure a satisfactory decomposition.

2. During the fusion the feldspar, which, when pure, is a silicate of aluminum and either sodium or potassium, but usually contains some iron, calcium, and magnesium, is decomposed by the alkaline flux. The sodium of the latter combines with the silicic acid of the silicate, with

the evolution of carbon dioxide, while about two thirds of the aluminum forms sodium aluminate and the remainder is converted into basic carbonate, or the oxide. The calcium and magnesium, if present, are changed to carbonates or oxides.

The heat is applied gently to prevent a too violent reaction when fusion first takes place.

3. The solution of a silicate by a strong acid is the result of the combination of the H^+ ions of the acid and the silicate ions of the silicate to form a slightly ionized silicic acid. As a consequence, the concentration of the silicate ions in the solution is reduced nearly to zero, and more silicate dissolves to re-establish the disturbed equilibrium. This process repeats itself until all of the silicate is brought into solution.

Whether the resulting solution of the silicate contains ortho-silicic acid (H_4SiO_4) or whether it is a colloidal solution of some other less hydrated acid, such as meta-silicic acid (H_2SiO_3), is a matter that is still debatable. It is certain, however, that the gelatinous material which readily separates from such solutions is of the nature of a hydrogel, that is, a colloid which is insoluble in water. This substance when heated to 100° C., or higher, is completely dehydrated, leaving only the anhydride, SiO_2. The changes may be represented by the equation:

$$SiO_3^{--} + 2\,H^+ \rightarrow [H_2SiO_3] \rightarrow H_2O + SiO_2.$$

4. A portion of the fused mass is usually projected upward by the escaping carbon dioxide during the fusion. The crucible must therefore be kept covered as much as possible and the lid carefully cleaned.

5. A gritty residue remaining after the disintegration of the fused mass by acid indicates that the substance has been but imperfectly decomposed. Such a residue should be filtered, washed, dried, ignited, and again fused with the alkaline flux; or, if the quantity of material at hand will permit, it is better to reject the analysis, and to use increased care in grinding the mineral and in mixing it with the flux.

DEHYDRATION AND FILTRATION

Procedure. — Evaporate the solution of the fusion to dryness, stirring frequently until the residue is a dry powder. Moisten the residue with 5 cc. of strong hydrochloric acid (sp. gr. 1.20) and evaporate again to dryness. Heat the residue for at least one hour at a temperature of 110° C. (Note 1). Again moisten the residue with concentrated hydrochloric acid, warm gently, making sure that the acid comes into contact with the whole of the residue, dilute to about 200 cc. and bring to boiling. Filter off the silica without much delay (Note 2), and wash five times with warm dilute hydrochloric acid (one part dilute acid (1.12 sp. gr.) to three parts of water). Allow the filter to drain for a few moments, then place a clean beaker below the funnel and wash with water until free from chlorides, discarding these washings. Evaporate the original filtrate to dryness, dehydrate at 110° C. for one hour (Note 3), and proceed as before, using a second filter to collect the silica after the second dehydration. Wash this filter with warm, dilute hydrochloric acid (Note 4), and finally with hot water until free from chlorides.

Notes. — 1. The silicic acid must be freed from its combination with a base (sodium, in this instance) before it can be dehydrated. The excess of hydrochloric acid accomplishes this liberation. By disintegrating the fused mass with a considerable volume of dilute acid the silicic acid is at first held in solution to a large extent. Immediate treatment of the fused mass with strong acid is likely to cause a semi-gelatinous silicic acid to separate at once and to inclose alkali salts or alumina.

A flocculent residue will often remain after the decomposition of the fused mass is effected. This is usually partially dehydrated silicic acid and does not require further treatment at this point. The progress of the dehydration is indicated by the behavior of the solution, which as evaporation proceeds usually gelatinizes. On this account it is necessary to allow the solution to evaporate on a steam bath, or to stir it vigorously, to avoid loss by spattering.

2. To obtain an approximately pure silica, the residue after evaporation must be thoroughly extracted by warming with hydrochloric acid, and the solution freely diluted to prevent, as far as possible, the inclosure of the residual salts in the particles of silica. The filtration should take place without delay, as the dehydrated silica slowly dissolves in hydrochloric acid on standing.

3. It has been shown by Hillebrand that silicic acid cannot be completely dehydrated by a single evaporation and heating, nor by several such treatments, unless an intermediate filtration of the silica occurs. If, however, the silica is removed and the filtrates are again evaporated and the residue heated, the amount of silica remaining in solution is usually negligible, although several evaporations and filtrations are required with some silicates to insure absolute accuracy.

It is probable that temperatures above 100° C. are not absolutely necessary to dehydrate the silica; but it is recommended, as tending to leave the silica in a better condition for filtration than when the lower temperature of the water bath is used.

The double evaporation and filtration spoken of above are essential because of the relatively large amount of alkali salts (sodium chloride) present after evaporation. For the highest accuracy in the determination of silica, or iron and alumina, it is also necessary to examine for silica the precipitate produced in the filtrate by ammonium hydroxide by fusing it with acid potassium sulphate and dissolving the fused mass in water. The insoluble silica is filtered, washed, and weighed, and the weight added to the weight of silica previously obtained.

Aluminum and iron are likely to be thrown down as basic salts from hot, very dilute solutions of their chlorides, as a result of hydrolysis. If the silica were washed only with hot water, the solution of these chlorides remaining in the filter after the passage of the original filtrate would gradually become so dilute as to throw down basic salts within the pores of the filter, which would remain with the silica. To avoid this, an acid wash-water is used until the aluminum and iron are practically removed. The acid is then removed by water.

IGNITION AND TESTING OF SILICA

Procedure. — Transfer the two washed filters belonging to each determination to a platinum crucible, which need not be previously weighed, and burn off the filter (Note 1). Ignite for thirty minutes over the blast lamp with the cover on the crucible, and then for periods of ten minutes, until the weight is constant.

When a constant weight has been obtained, pour into the crucible about 3 cc. of water, and then 3 cc. of hydrofluoric acid. *This must be done in a hood with a good draft and great care must be taken not to come into contact with the acid or to inhale its fumes (Note 2).*

If the precipitate has dissolved in this quantity of acid, add two drops of concentrated sulphuric acid, and heat very slowly (always under the hood) until all the liquid has evaporated, finally igniting to redness. Cool in a desiccator, and weigh the crucible and residue. Deduct this weight from the previous weight of crucible and impure silica, and from the difference calculate the percentage of silica in the sample (Note 3).

Notes. — 1. The silica undergoes no change during the ignition beyond the removal of all traces of water; but it has been shown that the silica holds moisture so tenaciously that prolonged ignition over the blast lamp is necessary to remove it entirely. This finely divided, ignited silica tends to absorb moisture, and should be weighed quickly.

2. Notwithstanding all precautions, the ignited precipitate of silica is rarely wholly pure. It is tested by volatilization of the silica as silicon fluoride after solution in hydrofluoric acid, and, if the analysis has been properly conducted, the residue, after treatment with the acids and ignition, should not exceed 1 mg.

The acid produces ulceration if brought into contact with the skin, and its fumes are excessively harmful if inhaled.

3. The impurities are probably weighed with the original precipitate in the form of oxides. The addition of the sulphuric acid displaces the hydrofluoric acid, and it may be assumed that the resulting sulphates (usually of iron or aluminum) are converted to oxides by the final ignition.

It is obvious that unless the sulphuric and hydrofluoric acids used are known to leave no residue on evaporation, a quantity equal to that employed in the analysis must be evaporated and a correction applied for any residue found.

4. If the silicate to be analyzed is shown by a previous qualitative examination to be completely decomposable, it may be directly treated with hydrochloric acid, the solution evaporated to dryness, and the silica dehydrated and further treated as described in the case of the feldspar after fusion.

A silicate which gelatinizes on treatment with acids should be mixed first with a little water, and the strong acid added in small portions with stirring, otherwise the gelatinous silicic acid incloses particles of the original silicate and prevents decomposition. The water, by separating the particles and slightly lessening the rapidity of action, prevents this difficulty. This procedure is one which applies in general to the solution of fine mineral powders in acids.

If a small residue remains undecomposed by the treatment of the silicate with acid, this may be filtered, washed, ignited and fused with sodium carbonate and a solution of the fused mass added to the original acid solution. This double procedure has an advantage, in that it avoids adding so large a quantity of sodium salts as is required for disintegration of the whole of the silicate by the fusion method.

STOICHIOMETRY

A careful, complete analysis of a silicate or other mineral of high degree of purity offers a means of establishing the empirical formula of the mineral. The percentages of the constituents of a mineral are usually expressed in terms of the oxides of the elements. If the percentage of each oxide constituent is divided by the molecular weight of that constituent, the number of moles (gram-molecular weights) of the constituent in 100 grams of the mineral is obtained. In any comparatively simple silicate, as with any other compound, these values must bear simple ratios to one another, since any molecule is always made up of whole numbers of atoms or molecular constituents. From these ratios of small whole numbers the empirical formula of the mineral can be determined. The actual formula of the mineral may of course be a multiple or sub-multiple of the empirical formula.

Since even apparently homogeneous specimens of mineral usually contain small amounts of impurities and since the percentages obtained by the average analyst using ordinary analytical methods are subject to slight errors, it can hardly be expected that the number of moles of the various constituents will stand to one another *exactly* in the ratio of small whole numbers although in the actual molecule (except in cases involving isomorphic replacement discussed below) they must do so. In many cases some judgment must be exercised in order to determine from the analysis the true molal ratios of the constituents in the molecule. A slide rule will be found to be almost indispensable for this purpose, since with one or two settings of the rule all possible ratios are visible.

Example I. — A sample of feldspar gives the following analysis:

$$K_2O = 16.90\%$$
$$Al_2O_3 = 18.31\%$$
$$SiO_2 = \underline{64.74\%}$$
$$99.95\%$$

What is the empirical formula of feldspar?

Solution. — In 100 grams of the mineral there are present:

$$\frac{16.90}{K_2O} = \frac{16.90}{94.20} = 0.180 \text{ mole of } K_2O$$

$$\frac{18.31}{Al_2O_3} = \frac{18.31}{102.1} = 0.179 \text{ mole of } Al_2O_3$$

$$\frac{64.74}{SiO_2} = \frac{64.74}{60.06} = 1.08 \text{ moles of } SiO_2$$

The number of moles of these constituents are nearly enough in the ratio of 1 : 1 : 6 to be within the limits of experimental error. The molecule is therefore made up of $K_2O \cdot Al_2O_3 \cdot 6\,SiO_2 = K_2Al_2Si_6O_{16}$. Dividing by 2 gives the simplest formula: $KAlSi_3O_8$. *Ans.*

It often happens that a certain constituent in a mineral is *partially* replaced by another constituent, usually of the same type and valence. Thus, Fe_2O_3 is often partially replaced by Al_2O_3 and vice versa. CaO may be partially replaced by MgO, MnO, FeO, etc. This phenomenon is called *isomorphic replacement* and since the replacement occurs in no definite proportion, the molal amounts of the constituents in such minerals do not necessarily bear any simple relation to one another. On the other hand, if constituent B partially replaces constituent A, the *sum* of the molal amounts of A and B would be the same as the molal amount of A if it had not been replaced. Consequently, when the molal quantities of the constituents of a mineral in themselves bear no simple ratio to one another, the quantities of constituents of the same type should be combined in an effort to obtain *sums* which do exist in ratios of simple whole numbers.

Example II. — A silicate gives the following analysis:

$$Al_2O_3 = 20.65\%$$
$$Fe_2O_3 = 7.03\%$$
$$CaO = 27.65\%$$
$$SiO_2 = \underline{44.55\%}$$
$$99.88\%$$

What is the empirical formula?

DETERMINATION OF SILICA IN SILICATES

Solution. — In 100 grams of the mineral there are

$$\left.\begin{array}{l}\dfrac{20.65}{Al_2O_3} = 0.202 \text{ mole of } Al_2O_3 \\ \dfrac{7.03}{Fe_2O_3} = 0.044 \text{ mole of } Fe_2O_3 \end{array}\right\} = 0.246 \text{ mole}$$

$$\dfrac{27.65}{CaO} = 0.493 \text{ mole of } CaO$$

$$\dfrac{44.55}{SiO_2} = 0.741 \text{ mole of } SiO_2$$

Only when the molal quantities of the first two constituents are combined are the above numerical results found to be in simple ratio to one another, these being approximately as 1 : 2 : 3. This shows isomorphic replacement between Fe_2O_3 and Al_2O_3, and the formula of the mineral may therefore be written:

$$(Al, Fe)_2O_3 \cdot 2\,CaO \cdot 3\,SiO_2$$

or $\quad Ca_2(Al, Fe)_2Si_3O_{11}$. *Ans.*

Isomorphic replacement is denoted by inclosing in parenthesis the symbols for the replacing elements and separating them by means of commas.

PROBLEMS

205. What volume of 6 N hydrofluoric acid is theoretically required to volatilize the silica from a half-gram sample of pure feldspar ($KAlSi_3O_8$)? What volume of SiF_4 measured dry at 29° C. and 765 mm. barometric pressure is produced? *Answer:* 3.58 cc.; 132.2 cc.

206. Willemite is a simple silicate of zinc containing 58.6% Zn. The percentages of ZnO and of SiO_2 total to 100%. What is the empirical formula of the mineral? *Answer:* Zn_2SiO_4.

207. A silicate gives the following analysis: FeO = 18.88%; Na_2O = 24.44%; MnO = 9.32%; SiO_2 = 47.36%. Write four possible different empirical formulas for the silicate. *Answer:* $Na_6MnFe_2Si_6O_{18}$
$Na_2(Mn, Fe)Si_2O_6$
$(Na_2, Fe, Mn)SiO_3$
$(Na_2Mn)_2FeSi_3O_9$.

208. Judging solely from the common valences of the constituents, which of the following silicates could not exist: $Na_2MgFe''Al_4Si_{16}O_{41}$; $Na_3(Ca, Mg)AlSi_5O_{14}$; $Na_2(Mg, Fe'')Al_4Si_{16}O_{41}$; $Na_2MgFe'''Al_4Si_{16}O_{41}$?

Answer: The last two.

209. What would be the empirical formula of a mineral of the following composition and what would be the percentage of Fe in a completely ignited sample? $CaO = 23.9\%$; $MgO = 3.10\%$; $Fe_2O_3 = 40.0\%$; $CO_2 = 33.0\%$. *Answer:* $2(Ca, Mg) \cdot Fe_2O_3 \cdot 3\ CO_2$; 41.76%.

210. What is the empirical formula of a mineral containing $3.37\%\ H_2O$; $19.10\%\ Al_2O_3$; $21.00\%\ CaO$; and $56.53\%\ SiO_2$?

Answer: $H_2Ca_2Al_2Si_5O_{16}$.

211. Two mineral samples from different localities gave the following analyses: (a) $CaO = 12.6\%$; $MgO = 19.0\%$; $FeO = 14.5\%$; $SiO_2 = 53.9\%$. (b) $CaO = 11.4\%$; $MgO = 5.8\%$; $FeO = 33.7\%$; $SiO_2 = 49.1\%$. Show that these minerals can be given the same empirical formula and give that formula. *Answer:* $Ca(Mg, Fe)_3(SiO_3)_4$.

212. Determine the empirical formula from the following analysis of a specimen of biotite: $H_2O = 1.09\%$; $K_2O = 14.0\%$; $MgO = 5.31\%$; $FeO = 20.6\%$; $Al_2O_3 = 21.4\%$; $SiO_2 = 37.6\%$.

Answer: $(H, K)_2(Mg, Fe)_2Al_2(SiO_4)_3$.

213. A sample of feldspar weighing 1.000 gram is fused and the silica determined. The weight of silica is 0.6460 gram. This is fused with 4 grams of sodium carbonate. How many grams of the carbonate actually combined with the silica in fusion, and what was the loss in weight due to carbon dioxide during the fusion? *Answer:* 1.135 grams; 0.4715 gram.

214. Heulandite is hydrous acid calcium metasilicate and yields on analysis 14.8 per cent water and 16.7 per cent alumina. If the calcium were precipitated as calcium oxalate from a 1-gram sample, 16.4 cc. of $\dfrac{N}{10}$ $KMnO_4$ would be required for oxidation. Three fifths of the water exists as water of crystallization. What is the empirical formula of heulandite?

Answer: $H_4CaAl_2(SiO_3)_6 \cdot 3\ H_2O$.

215. A one-gram sample of a certain silicate yields 0.4525 gram of silica, 0.3840 gram of alumina, 0.6070 gram of K_2PtCl_6, and 81.9 cc. of water vapor when measured at 120° C. and 750 mm. pressure. What is the empirical formula of the mineral? *Answer:* $H_2KAl_3(SiO_4)_3$.

APPENDIX

POTENTIOMETRIC TITRATIONS

Changes in Hydrogen Ion Concentration During Acidimetric Titrations

The principles underlying potentiometric titrations are best understood by first following the changes in hydrogen-ion concentration during an acidimetric or alkalimetric titration.

In any dilute solution at 25° C. the product of the hydrogen-ion concentration (expressed as moles per liter) and the hydroxide-ion concentration is 10^{-14}. In pure water these concentrations are each 10^{-7}; in an acid the hydrogen-ion concentration is greater than 10^{-7} and the hydroxide-ion concentration is correspondingly less; in an alkaline solution the hydrogen-ion concentration is less than 10^{-7} and the hydroxide-ion concentration is correspondingly greater.

When the concentration of the hydrogen ion in a solution is expressed in terms of a negative power of 10, that power (without the negative sign) is called the p_H *value* of the solution. Thus, pure water has a p_H value of 7 (since the concentration of the hydrogen ion is 10^{-7}). The p_H value of a solution in which the hydroxide-ion concentration is 10^{-3} (and hence the hydrogen-ion concentration is 10^{-11}) is 11.

$$p_H = \log \frac{1}{\text{concn. H}^+ \text{ ion}} = -\log \text{concn. H}^+ \text{ ion.}$$

Suppose 25 cc. of $\frac{N}{10}$ hydrochloric acid is diluted with 100 cc. of water and the solution is titrated with $\frac{N}{10}$ sodium hydroxide. At the beginning of the titration the hydrogen-ion concentration is high (about 10^{-2}; or $p_H = 2$). As the alkali is added, the hydrogen-ion concentration decreases (p_H value increases) and as 25 cc. is approached, the decrease becomes very rapid. At exactly 25 cc. the hydrogen-ion concentration is 10^{-7} ($p_H = 7$) and with a few drops more of the sodium hydroxide decreases rapidly to about 10^{-10} ($p_H = 10$) from which point the decrease is slower. Plotting the volume of sodium hydroxide added against the concentration of hydrogen ions gives the curve shown in Fig. 5A.

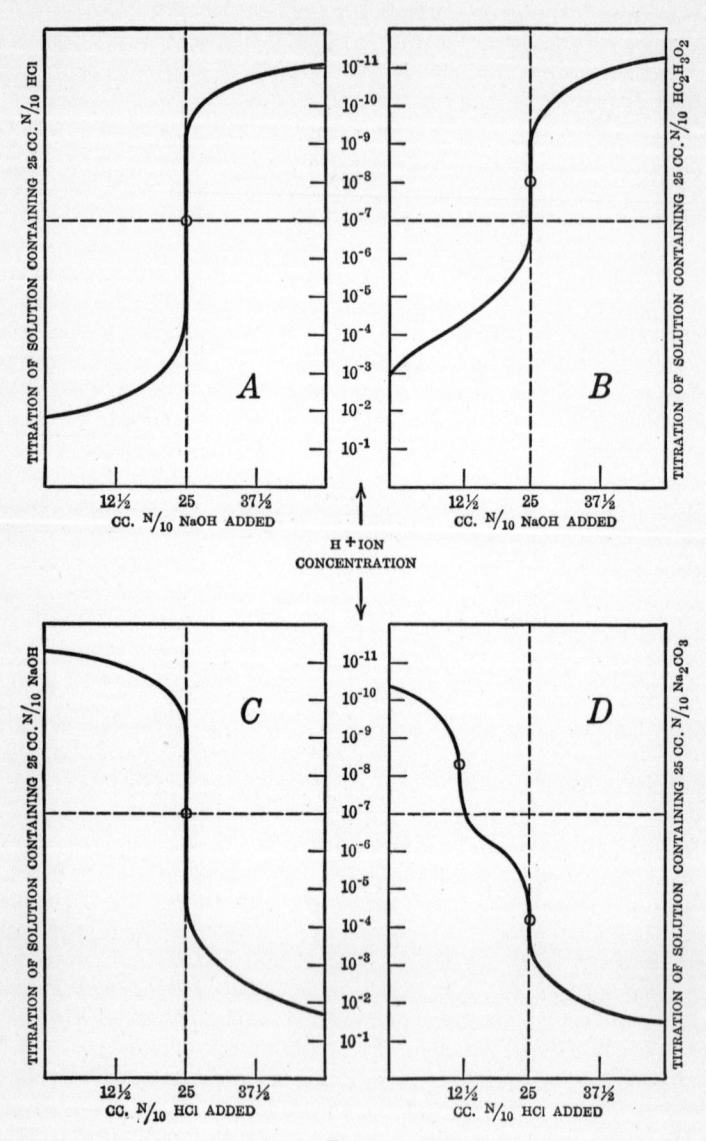

FIG. 5

As explained on page 33, theoretically the best indicator for the titration of a strong acid against a strong base is one that changes color at $p_H = 7$, but the change in the hydrogen-ion concentration is so rapid at the equivalence point that almost any common indicator gives satisfactory results.

Let us follow the hydrogen-ion concentration of a similar solution in which 25 cc. of $\frac{N}{10}$ acetic acid is used in place of 25 cc. of $\frac{N}{10}$ hydrochloric acid. In this case, the hydrogen-ion concentration at the start is less than before since acetic acid is less ionized than is hydrochloric acid, and if the hydrogen-ion concentrations are plotted (Fig. 5B) it will be seen that the inflection of the curve is much less abrupt. Furthermore, although the mid-point of the inflection is at 25 cc., the corresponding hydrogen-ion concentration is not 10^{-7} but about 10^{-8} ($p_H = 8$). This is to be expected (see page 33) for when a weak acid is titrated with a strong base, at the equivalence point (i.e. when acid and base have been added in chemically equivalent amounts) the solution is slightly basic due to the hydrolysis of the resulting salt (sodium acetate in this case). When an indicator is used to determine the equivalence point, one is therefore chosen which changes color on the alkaline side of the point of exact neutrality (e.g. phenolphthalein).

The titration of a base by an acid gives a curve which slopes in the opposite direction. Such a curve is given in the titration of 25 cc. of $\frac{N}{10}$ sodium hydroxide by $\frac{N}{10}$ hydrochloric acid (Fig. 5C). The titration of a weak base with a strong acid gives a curve which inflects at the equivalence point but at that point the hydrogen-ion concentration is greater than 10^{-7}. When an indicator is used in such a titration, one is chosen (e.g. methyl orange) which changes color on the acid side of the neutral point. The titration of sodium carbonate with hydrochloric acid (Fig. 5D) is an example of the last case and two inflections are obtained, one at the point where sodium carbonate has been completely converted into bicarbonate ($Na_2CO_3 + HCl \rightarrow NaHCO_3 + NaCl$) and the other at the point of complete reaction ($NaHCO_3 + HCl \rightarrow NaCl + CO_2 + H_2O$).

A potentiometric titration gives a means of determining and following the hydrogen-ion concentration of a solution during the process of an acidimetric or alkalimetric titration. By plotting the hydrogen-ion concentrations obtained at frequent intervals during the titration against the corresponding volumes of titrating solution added, curves similar to the ones given in Fig. 5 are obtained. From them the equivalence point (end-point) of the titration can be established without the use of an indicator. It is only necessary to find the volume of titrating solution corresponding to the mid-point of the inflection of the curve. Potentiometric methods are of especial

APPENDIX

importance in the titration of turbid or highly colored solutions where the use of an indicator is either unsatisfactory or impossible. Potentiometric methods also have the advantage of establishing the actual hydrogen-ion concentration of a solution as well as its total neutralizing power. They can also be used to advantage, as we shall see, in certain oxidation processes.

Specific Reduction Potentials and the Nernst Rule

Brief mention has already been made regarding specific reduction potentials (page 202). A table of these potentials is given in this Appendix and it should be noted that the numerical values are the relative potentials between the elements and a one molal solution of their ions. The potential between hydrogen gas and one molal hydrogen ion is arbitrarily taken as zero. For example, suppose a strip of zinc to be immersed in a solution which is one molal in zinc ions, and a strip of copper to be immersed in a solution which is one molal in cupric ions. If the metals are connected by means of a wire and the solutions are connected by means of a salt-bridge (an inverted capillary U-tube containing an electrolyte) or separated only by means of a porous wall, a current will flow in the wire from the copper to the zinc, and in the solution from the zinc to the copper. The metallic zinc is oxidized and dissolves; the copper ions are reduced and plate out. This is the principle of the Daniell cell. The voltage of the current under these conditions is the algebraic difference between the two separate specific reduction potentials; or $+0.76 - (-0.34) = 1.10$ volts.

The reduction potential becomes greater as the concentration of the metal ion becomes less; and less as the concentration of the ion becomes greater. A means of calculating the potential between a metal and a solution of its ions of a concentration other than one molal is available. This is the so-called Nernst Rule. In simplified form this states that at 25° C. the potential difference between a metal and a solution of its ions of concentration C_A, and the metal and a solution of its ions of concentration C_B, is given by the formula:

$$E = \frac{0.0591}{N} \log \frac{C_A}{C_B}$$

where N is the valence of the ion.

Example I. — The reduction potential between nickel and one molal nickel ions is $+0.22$ volt. What is the potential between nickel and a thousandth molal nickel solution?

Solution. —
$$E = \frac{0.0591}{2} \log \frac{1}{0.001} = 0.089$$

$0.22 + 0.089 = 0.31$ volt. *Ans.*

APPENDIX

If two electrodes of the same metal are placed in contact with solutions of its ions of two different concentrations and a circuit is made, the metal will plate out from the more concentrated solution and dissolve from the electrode in the more dilute solution. A current will therefore flow in the outer circuit from the electrode in contact with the less concentrated solution. Such a cell involving only one metal is called a *concentration cell* and its E. M. F. is found from the Nernst formula as in the preceding example.

Example II. — What is the E. M. F. of the concentration cell: Ag, Ag⁺(0.01 molal) — Ag, Ag⁺(0.0001 molal)?

Solution. —
$$E = \frac{0.0591}{1} \log \frac{0.01}{0.0001}$$
$$= 0.0591 \times 2$$
$$= 0.118 \text{ volt}. \quad Ans.$$

Consider now a concentration cell consisting of a hydrogen electrode (platinum black saturated with hydrogen gas) immersed in a solution of known hydrogen-ion concentration (for example, one molal) and of a hydrogen electrode immersed in a solution of hydrogen ions the concentration of which is desired. Connecting the electrodes with wire and the solutions with a salt-bridge, a current will flow through the wire and its voltage can be measured. Suppose in this case the E. M. F. is found to be 0.205 volt. Then from the Nernst formula:

$$0.205 = \frac{0.0591}{1} \log \frac{1}{x}$$

whence $x = 0.000339$

The solution is therefore 3.39×10^{-4} molal in hydrogen ions.

$$p_H = \log \frac{1}{3.39 \times 10^{-4}} = 3.47.$$

In actual practice it is not convenient to use as a standard half-cell a hydrogen electrode in one molal hydrogen ion solution. Instead, a calomel cell is used. This consists of metallic mercury in contact with a solution saturated with mercurous chloride and normal with respect to potassium chloride. (Sometimes $\frac{N}{10}$ KCl or saturated KCl solution is used.) The potential of this cell, using normal potassium chloride, differs from that of hydrogen against one molal hydrogen ion by 0.285 volt (= 0.338 volt using $\frac{N}{10}$ KCl; = 0.246 volt using saturated KCl). This calomel electrode is connected to the solution the hydrogen-ion concentration of which is desired through a salt-bridge consisting of a normal solution of potassium chloride. The E. M. F. of the current in this case is

$$E = 0.285 + \frac{0.0591}{1} \log \frac{1}{C}$$

Whence, $$\log C = -\frac{E - 0.285}{0.0591}$$

and, $$p_H = -\log C = \frac{E - 0.285}{0.0591}$$

Example III. — What is the hydrogen-ion concentration and the p_H value of a dilute solution of sulphuric acid at 25° C. if with a hydrogen electrode and a calomel electrode both dipping in the solution, a current is produced which has an E. M. F. of 485 millivolts?

Solution. —
$$\log C = -\frac{E - 0.285}{0.0591}$$

$$= -\frac{0.485 - 0.285}{0.0591}$$

$$= -3.384$$

$$C = 4.13 \times 10^{-4}. \quad Ans.$$

$$p_H = \frac{E - 0.285}{0.0591} = 3.384. \quad Ans.$$

An acidimetric or alkalimetric titration can be made by measuring in this way the hydrogen-ion concentration of the solution after the addition of each small increment of titrating solution. By plotting the hydrogen-ion concentrations against the volumes of titrating solution added, a curve is obtained which inflects suddenly as shown in Fig. 5. The volume corresponding to the mid-point of this inflection is the volume of titrating solution corresponding to the end-point of the titration. No indicator is used and the titration is independent of the color or turbidity of the solution or of the intensity of illumination. Incidentally, unless knowledge of the hydrogen-ion concentration of the solution at the beginning or during the progress of the titration is desired, the E. M. F. values can be plotted directly without converting them over to p_H values or hydrogen-ion concentrations. A curve is obtained which inflects in exactly the same manner as that made by plotting the hydrogen-ion concentrations and can be used to establish the end-point of the titration.

The Potentiometer Principle

The measurement of the electromotive force of a cell is usually made by means of a slide-wire arrangement as shown in Fig. 6. In this diagram, R represents a rheostat, G a sensitive galvanometer, K a key for closing the circuit, MO a wire of uniform cross-section, S a source of electricity of constant E. M. F., preferably from a storage battery, and E the cell to be measured. It is seen that the fall of potential MN is in opposition to the voltage of E, and when the two are equal, no current will flow through the galvanometer. Therefore, if the fall of potential MN is known, the voltage of E is measured without drawing any current from E.

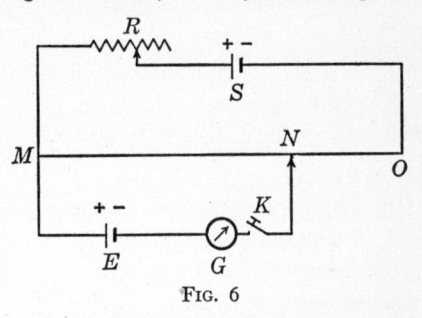

Fig. 6

Let us suppose now that a standard Weston cadmium cell with a voltage of 1.0183 volts is placed at E and the point N is so adjusted that MN spans 1018.3 scale divisions. The resistance R is then adjusted until the galvanometer shows no deflection. Hence every scale division now represents a fall of potential of one millivolt, and when the standard cell at E is replaced by the cell to be measured (Fig. 7) the new position N' which balances the cell shows directly the voltage in millivolts.

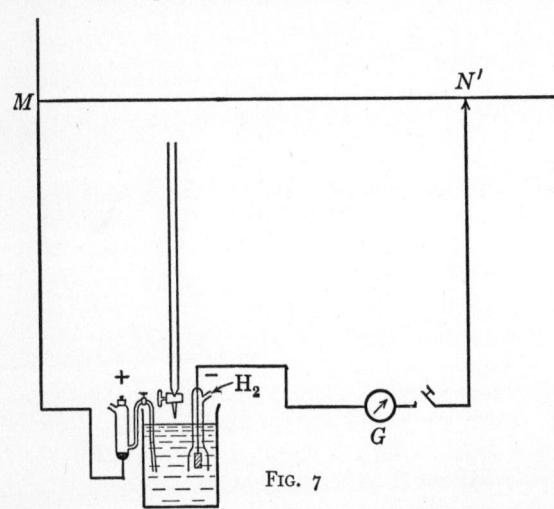

From the E. M. F. value of a cell consisting of a calomel electrode and a hydrogen electrode dipping in a solution (Fig. 7), the p_H value of the solution can be calculated from the formula given in the preceding section. In some forms of apparatus a constant resistance can be inserted in the circuit of such magnitude as to cause the slide-wire scale divisions to represent p_H values directly.

Fig. 7

Since in most potentiometric titrations the voltages are used merely to establish a titration graph from which the end-point can be determined, it is not necessary in such cases to use an apparatus which is as precise as is needed where exact p_H values are required. The Hildebrand apparatus is a simplified form of titration apparatus and the hook-up is illustrated in Fig. 8.

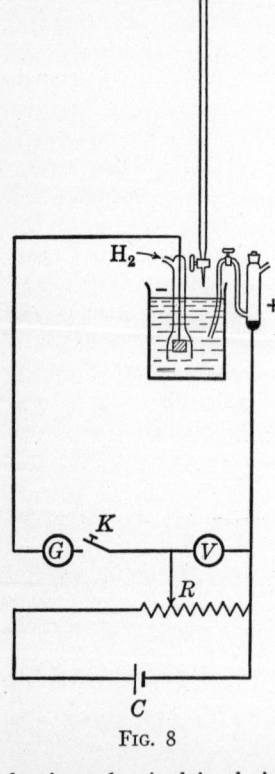

An outer circuit consists of a dry cell C, a rheostat R, and a voltmeter V. The resistance R is varied until no deflection of the galvanometer G is observed when the key K is momentarily closed. This indicates that the voltage of the outer (dry cell) circuit as read from the voltmeter is equal to that of the inner circuit as given by the solution. The titration is carried out by adding increments of titrating solution, with intermediate readings from the voltmeter which are plotted against the total volumes as explained above.

The Quinhydrone Electrode

In many potentiometric determinations of p_H values and electrometric titrations of acids, the use of the quinhydrone electrode is much more convenient than the use of the hydrogen electrode. The latter requires carefully prepared platinum sponge, a hydrogen generator, purifying trains, and is more or less troublesome to operate. The quinhydrone electrode on the other hand consists merely of a few crystals of an equimolecular mixture of quinone and hydroquinone (made by pouring a hot solution of ferric ammonium sulphate into a solution of hydroquinone and recrystallizing the precipitated crystals) added directly to the solution to be titrated. A plain platinum wire and the regular calomel cell are used as electrodes. The quinhydrone electrode has a certain hydrogen pressure which is very small and which is regulated by the equilibrium: $C_6H_4O_2 + 2H^+ + 2\epsilon$ (quinone)
$\rightleftarrows C_6H_4O_2H_2$. Its potential at 25° differs from the ordinary hydrogen elec-
(hydroquinone)
trode by 0.7000 volt. Using a calomel cell (in which the KCl is one normal) as the negative electrode and a temperature of 25° C.:

$$p_H = \frac{0.415 - E}{0.0591}.$$

Fig. 8

APPENDIX

At about $p_H = 7$ the value of E drops to zero and on the alkaline side of this point the calomel cell should be used as the positive electrode and the values of E given a negative sign.

The quinhydrone electrode does not give correct values in solutions which are more alkaline than about $p_H = 9$.

Oxidation-Reduction Titrations

Potentiometric titrations may be applied to oxidation and reduction reactions as well as to acidimetric reactions. In the latter case it was found that a difference of potential exists between hydrogen gas and a solution containing hydrogen ions. Similarly, a potential difference exists between ferrous and ferric ions. As in the case of the hydrogen concentration cell, if two solutions each containing ferrous and ferric ions but at different relative concentrations are connected internally by means of a salt-bridge and externally by means of a wire, a current will flow through the wire. In one solution the ferrous ions will have a relatively greater tendency to give a negative charge to the electrode (*i.e.* give up electrons to the wire) and in the other solution the ferric ions will have a relatively greater tendency to give a positive charge to the electrode (*i.e.* take up electrons from the wire). The current will flow through the wire from the solution of greater concentration of ferric ions to the solution of lesser concentration of ferric ions. As in the case of the hydrogen concentration cells the passage of electrons will tend to cause equalization of the relative concentrations of the two solutions.

The Nernst formula applied to the ferrous-ferric ion cell shows that its potential is

$$E = \frac{0.0591}{1} \log \frac{\frac{Fe^{++}}{Fe^{+++}}}{\frac{Fe_1^{++}}{Fe_1^{+++}}}.$$

If one of the solutions is taken as a standard and the relative concentration of ferrous ions to ferric ions, $\frac{Fe_1^{++}}{Fe_1^{+++}}$, is made unity, then the potential is

$$E = 0.0591 \log \frac{Fe^{++}}{Fe^{+++}}.$$

It is inconvenient to use as the standard a known ferrous-ferric ion equilibrium. Instead, the calomel cell is used as in acidimetric titrations. Its potential differs from that of the potential between ferrous and ferric ions of equal concentrations by 0.47 volt. The formula in this case therefore becomes:

$$E = 0.47 + 0.0591 \log \frac{Fe^{++}}{Fe^{+++}}.$$

If the E. M. F. is measured, the relative concentrations of ferrous and ferric ions may be calculated.

Inspection of this formula shows that in the titration of a ferrous salt with, for example, potassium bichromate, the ratio of concentration of ferrous ions to ferric ions will change during the process of the titration. The measured value of E will likewise slowly change. Only when the end-point is approximated and the concentration of ferrous ions becomes nearly zero will there be a very sudden change in E. This change is so abrupt that in oxidation titrations it is often unnecessary to tabulate the values for the E. M. F. in order to determine the volume of titrating solution corresponding to a sudden break in the curve. The titrating solution is added in small increments until the voltmeter shows a very sudden deflection and the volume is read directly from the burette.

Potentiometric titrations may of course be applied to oxidation reactions other than ferrous ions to ferric ions. The coefficient for the calomel electrode is different for different oxidation reactions, but the sudden change in voltage at the end-point is common to all. When the voltage is plotted graphically against volumes of titrating solution added, the end-point is found by bisecting the nearly vertical part of the curve, as in acidimetric titrations.

In potentiometric oxidation titrations potassium bichromate can often be used to greater advantage than potassium permanganate as the oxidizing medium because of its greater stability. Furthermore, in the determination of iron, the ferric iron can be reduced by means of stannous chloride and the solution can be titrated potentiometrically without destroying the excess stannous salt. A curve with two inflections is obtained, the first corresponding to the completion of the oxidation of the excess stannous salt, and the second corresponding to the completion of the oxidation of the ferrous salt. The difference between the volumes corresponding to the two inflections is the volume of standard solution equivalent to the iron in the sample.

PROBLEMS

216. Using a regular hydrogen electrode and calomel electrode, a dilute acid solution gives a potential measurement at 25° C. of 580 millivolts. What is the hydrogen-ion concentration and the p_H value of the solution? What color would be given to the solution by a drop of methyl orange?

Answer: 1.02×10^{-5}; 4.99; yellow.

217. What is the p_H value of a solution of which the hydrogen-ion concentration is 10^{-4} N? 8.5×10^{-11} N? Of which the hydroxide-ion concentration is 4.6×10^{-12} N? What would be the E. M. F. shown by each of these solutions using hydrogen-calomel electrodes?

Answer: 4; 10.07; 2.663; 521, 880, 442 millivolts.

218. The p_H value of a solution at 25° C. is 10.6. What is its hydrogen-ion concentration? Its hydroxide-ion concentration? What E. M. F.

would be given by this solution using regular hydrogen and calomel electrodes? *Answer:* 2.51 × 10⁻¹¹; 3.98 × 10⁻⁴; 0.911 volt.

219. A hydrogen electrode and a calomel electrode in contact with a solution at 25° C. show a potential difference of 740 millivolts. What is the p_H value of the solution? Is the solution acidic or basic as compared to pure water? What color would be given to the solution by a drop of phenolphthalein? Litmus? Methyl orange?

Answer: 7.7; basic; colorless; blue; yellow.

220. Plot the following values of millivolts against cubic centimeters of $\frac{N}{10}$ NaOH solution in the potentiometric titration of 2.50 grams of vinegar at 25 C. using the regular hydrogen-calomel electrodes. Calculate the percentage of acetic acid in the vinegar. At what volume of NaOH is the solution exactly neutral and at what volume does the titration (*stoichiometrical*) end-point occur? What is the p_H value at the end-point? 0.0 cc. = 420 millivolts; 4.0 cc. = 475; 8.0 cc. = 540; 12.0 cc. = 588; 16.0 cc. = 620; 18.0 cc. = 638; 19.0 cc. = 650; 19.4 cc. = 670; 19.8 cc. = 790; 20.0 cc. = 830; 20.2 cc. = 856; 20.5 cc. = 875; 21.0 cc. = 900; 22.0 cc. = 930; 24.0 cc. = 948; 28.0 cc. = 970; 32.0 cc. = 985.

Answer: 4.75%; 19.2 cc.; 19.8 cc.; 8.55.

221. A sample of pure $FeSO_4 \cdot (NH_4)_2SO_4 \cdot 6\,H_2O$ weighing 0.808 gram is dissolved in acidified water and titrated potentiometrically with bichromate solution. The following millivolts were obtained for the corresponding volumes of bichromate: 0.0 cc. = 355 millivolts; 2.50 cc. = 363; 5.00 cc. = 372; 7.50 cc. = 383; 10.0 cc. = 395; 15.0 cc. = 425; 17.5 cc. = 440; 19.0 cc. = 480; 20.0 cc. = 530; 21.0 cc. = 605; 22.0 cc. = 650; 23.0 cc. = 683; 24.0 cc. = 701; 25.0 cc. = 712; 30.0 cc. = 733; 35.0 cc. = 746.

A sample of limonite weighing 0.500 gram was then dissolved in HCl, the iron reduced with a slight excess of $SnCl_2$ and the solution titrated potentiometrically by means of the above bichromate solution (the excess stannous salts being oxidized first). The following millivolts were obtained for the corresponding volumes of bichromate: 0.0 cc. = 83 millivolts; 1.00 cc. = 92; 2.00 cc. = 105; 2.50 cc. = 125; 3.00 cc. = 152; 4.00 cc. = 209; 5.00 cc. = 262; 6.00 cc. = 303; 7.00 cc. = 334; 8.00 cc. = 348; 9.00 cc. = 356; 10.0 cc. = 361; 12.5 cc. = 380; 15.0 cc. = 391; 20.0 cc. = 409; 22.5 cc. = 419; 25.0 cc. = 430; 27.0 cc. = 452; 28.0 cc. = 475; 29.0 cc. = 512; 30.0 cc. = 561; 31.0 cc. = 588; 32.5 cc. = 612; 35.0 cc. = 627; 40.0 cc. = 641; 45.0 cc. = 648.

Calculate the percentage of iron (Fe) in the limonite. *Answer:* 27.5%.

APPENDIX

SAMPLE PAGES FOR LABORATORY RECORDS

Page A

Date....................

CALIBRATION OF BURETTE NO.

Temp. water = $25°$ (d. = 0.997)

Burette Readings	Difference Apparent Volume	Observed Weights	Difference	True Volumes	Calculated Correction	Total Correction
0.02		16.27				
10.12	10.10	26.35	10.08	10.11	+ .01	+ .01
20.09	9.97	36.26	9.91	9.94	− .03	− .02
30.16	10.07	46.34	10.08	10.11	+ .04	+ .02
40.19	10.03	56.31	9.97	10.00	− .03	− .01
50.00	9.81	66.17	9.86	9.89	+ .08	+ .07

These data to be obtained in duplicate for each burette.

Page B

Date....................

DETERMINATION OF COMPARATIVE STRENGTH HCl vs. NaOH

Determination	I		II	
		Corrected		Corrected
Final Reading HCl	48.02	48.08	43.12	43.14
Initial Reading HCl	0.12	.12	.17	.17
		47.96		42.97
		Corrected		Corrected
Final Reading NaOH	46.24	46.29	40.39	40.38
Initial Reading NaOH	1.75	1.75	.50	.50
		44.54		39.88
log cc. NaOH	1.6488		1.6008	
colog cc. HCl	8.3192 − 10		8.3668 − 10	
	9.9680 − 10		9.9676 − 10	
1 cc. HCl	.9290 cc. NaOH		.9282 cc. NaOH	
Mean		.9286		

Signed....................

APPENDIX

Page C
Date....................

STANDARDIZATION OF HYDROCHLORIC ACID

Weight sample and tube	9.1793		8.1731	
	8.1731		6.9187	
Weight sample	1.0062		1.2544	
Final Reading HCl	39.84	39.83	49.70	49.77
Initial Reading HCl	.00	.00	.04	.04
		39.83		49.73
Final Reading NaOH	.26	.26	.67	.67
Initial Reading NaOH	.12	.12	.36	.36
		.14		.31
Corrected cc. HCl	$39.83 - \dfrac{.14}{.93} = 39.68$		$49.73 - \dfrac{.31}{.93} = 49.40$	
log sample	0.0025		0.0983	
colog cc.	8.4014 − 10		8.3063 − 10	
colog milliequivalent Na₂CO₃ .	1.2757		1.2757	
	9.6796 − 10		9.6803 − 10	
Normal value HCl.....	.4782		.4789	
Mean		.4786		

Signed....................

Page D
Date....................

DETERMINATION OF CHLORINE IN CHLORIDE, SAMPLE NO.

Weight sample and tube	16.1721	15.9976
	15.9976	15.7117
Weight sample	.1745	.2859
Weight crucible + precipitate ..	14.4496	15.6915
Constant weights	14.4487	15.6915
	14.4485	
Weight crucible......	14.2216	15.3196
Constant weight	14.2216	15.3194
Weight AgCl	.2269	.3721
log Cl	1.5497	1.5497
log weight AgCl	9.3558 − 10	9.5706 − 10
log 100	2.0000	2.0000
colog AgCl	7.8438 − 10	7.8438 − 10
colog sample	0.7583	0.5438
	1.5076	1.5079
Cl in sample No.	32.18%	32.21%

Signed....................

STRENGTH OF REAGENTS

The concentrations given in this table are those suggested for use in the procedures described in the foregoing pages. It is obvious, however, that an exact adherence to these quantities is not essential.

	Grams per Liter	Approx. Relation to Normal Solution	Approx. Relation to Molal Solution
Ammonium oxalate, $(NH_4)_2C_2O_4 \cdot H_2O$	36	0.5 N	0.25
Barium chloride, $BaCl_2 \cdot 2 H_2O$	25	0.2 N	0.1
Magnesium ammonium chloride (of $MgCl_2$)	71	1.5 N	0.75
Mercuric chloride, $HgCl_2$	45	0.33 N	0.66
Potassium hydroxide, KOH (sp. gr. 1.27)	480		
Potassium thiocyanate, KSCN	5	0.05 N	0.05
Silver nitrate, $AgNO_3$	21	0.125 N	0.125
Sodium hydroxide, NaOH	100	2.5 N	2.5
Sodium carbonate, Na_2CO_3	159	3 N	1.5
Sodium phosphate, $Na_2HPO_4 \cdot 12 H_2O$	90	0.5 N or 0.75 N	0.25

Stannous chloride, $SnCl_2$, made by saturating hydrochloric acid (sp. gr. 1.20) with tin, diluting with an equal volume of water, and adding a slight excess of acid from time to time. A strip of metallic tin is kept in the bottle.

A solution of ammonium molybdate is best prepared as follows: Stir 100 grams of molybdic acid (MoO_3) into 400 cc. of cold, distilled water. Add 80 cc. of concentrated ammonium hydroxide (sp. gr. 0.90). Filter, and pour the filtrate slowly, with constant stirring, into a mixture of 400 cc. concentrated nitric acid (sp. gr. 1.42) and 600 cc. of water. Add to the mixture about 0.05 gram of microcosmic salt. Filter, after allowing the whole to stand for 24 hours.

Manganous sulphate titrating solution is prepared as follows: Dissolve 65 grams of $MnSO_4 \cdot 4 H_2O$ in 500 cc. of water and add 130 cc. of concentrated H_2SO_4 and 140 cc. of $H_3PO_4(85\%)$. Dilute to one liter.

The following data regarding the common acids and aqueous ammonia are based upon percentages given in the Standard Tables of the Manufacturing Chemists' Association of the United States [*J. S. C. I.*, 24 (1905), 787–790]. All gravities are taken at 15.5° C. and compared with water at the same temperature.

Aqueous ammonia (sp. gr. 0.96) contains 9.91 per cent NH_3 by weight, and corresponds to a 5.6 N and 5.6 molal solution.

APPENDIX

Aqueous ammonia (sp. gr. 0.90) contains 28.52 per cent NH₃ by weight, and corresponds to a 15.1 N and 15.1 molal solution.

Hydrochloric acid (sp. gr. 1.12) contains 23.81 per cent HCl by weight, and corresponds to a 7.3 N and 7.3 molal solution.

Hydrochloric acid (sp. gr. 1.20) contains 39.80 per cent HCl by weight, and corresponds to a 13.1 N and 13.1 molal solution.

Nitric acid (sp. gr. 1.20) contains 32.25 per cent HNO₃ by weight, and corresponds to a 6.1 N and 6.1 molal solution.

Nitric acid (sp. gr. 1.42) contains 69.96 per cent HNO₃ by weight, and corresponds to a 15.8 N and 15.8 molal solution.

Sulphuric acid (sp. gr. 1.84) contains 93.19 per cent H₂SO₄ by weight, and corresponds to a 34.8 N or 17.4 molal solution.

Sulphuric acid (sp. gr. 1.18) contains 24.74 per cent H₂SO₄ by weight, and corresponds to a 5.9 N or 2.95 molal solution.

The term *normal* (N), as used above, has the same significance as in volumetric analysis. The molal solution is assumed to contain one molecular weight in grams in a liter of solution.

DENSITIES AND VOLUMES OF WATER AT TEMPERATURES FROM 15–30° C.

Temperature Centigrade	Density	Volume
4°	1.000000	1.000000
15°	0.999126	1.000874
16°	0.998970	1.001031
17°	0.998801	1.001200
18°	0.998622	1.001380
19°	0.998432	1.001571
20°	0.998230	1.001773
21°	0.998019	1.001985
22°	0.997797	1.002208
23°	0.997565	1.002441
24°	0.997323	1.002685
25°	0.997071	1.002938
26°	0.996810	1.003201
27°	0.996539	1.003473
28°	0.996259	1.003755
29°	0.995971	1.004046
30°	0.995673	1.004346

Authority: Landolt, Börnstein, and Meyerhoffer's *Tabellen*, third edition.

APPENDIX

SENSITIVENESS OF INDICATORS

The table gives the approximate hydrogen-ion and hydroxide-ion concentrations required to produce the indicated change of color in dilute solutions (0.001 per cent) of the more common indicators.

Concentration of H^+	1×10^{-9}	1×10^{-8}	1×10^{-7}	1×10^{-6}	1×10^{-5}	1×10^{-4}	1×10^{-3}
Concentration of OH^-	1×10^{-5}	1×10^{-6}	1×10^{-7}	1×10^{-8}	1×10^{-9}	1×10^{-10}	1×10^{-11}
Phenolphthalein	Pink	Colorless					
Litmus		Violet-blue	Violet	Violet-pink			
Methyl red				Yellow	Pink		
Methyl orange					Yellow	Orange	Pink
Congo red					Red	Violet	Blue

ELECTROMOTIVE SERIES

Specific Reduction Potentials

The difference of potential between hydrogen gas and a one molal solution of hydrogen ions is arbitrarily taken as zero, and the tabulated values are the relative potentials between metals and one molal solutions of their ions.

Element	Volts	Element	Volts
$K° - K^+$	$+2.93$	$Cu^+ - Cu^{++}$	-0.17
$Na° - Na^+$	$+2.72$	$As° - As^{+++}$	-0.29
$Ca° - Ca^{++}$	$+2.60$	$Cu° - Cu^{++}$	-0.34
$Al° - Al^{+++}$	$+1.30$	$Co° - Co^{+++}$	-0.40
$Zn° - Zn^{++}$	$+0.76$	$Cu° - Cu^+$	-0.51
$Fe° - Fe^{++}$	$+0.43$	$2 I^- - I_2$	-0.53
$Cd° - Cd^{++}$	$+0.40$	$Fe^{++} - Fe^{+++}$	-0.75
$Ni° - Ni^{++}$	$+0.22$	$Ag° - Ag^+$	-0.80
$Pb° - Pb^{++}$	$+0.12$	$Hg° - Hg^{++}$	-0.86
$Sn° - Sn^{++}$	$+0.10$	$2 Br^- - Br_2$	-1.08
$Fe° - Fe^{+++}$	$+0.04$	$2 Cl^- - Cl_2$	-1.35
$H_2 - 2 H^+$	0.00	$Pb^{++} - PbO_2$	-1.44
$Sb° - Sb^{+++}$	-0.10	$Co^{++} - Co^{+++}$	-1.86
$Sn^{++} - Sn^{++++}$	-0.14	$2 F^- - F_2$	-1.96

APPENDIX

AMERICAN CHEMICAL SOCIETY
ATOMIC WEIGHTS
1930

	Symbol	Atomic Number	Atomic Weight		Symbol	Atomic Number	Atomic Weight
Aluminum	Al	13	26.97	Molybdenum	Mo	42	96.0
Antimony	Sb	51	121.77	Neodymium	Nd	60	144.27
Argon	A	18	39.94	Neon	Ne	10	20.183
Arsenic	As	33	74.93	Nickel	Ni	28	58.69
Barium	Ba	56	137.36	Nitrogen	N	7	14.008
Beryllium	Be	4	9.02	Osmium	Os	76	190.8
Bismuth	Bi	83	209.00	Oxygen	O	8	16.0000
Boron	B	5	10.82	Palladium	Pd	46	106.7
Bromine	Br	35	79.916	Phosphorus	P	15	31.02
Cadmium	Cd	48	112.41	Platinum	Pt	78	195.23
Calcium	Ca	20	40.07	Potassium	K	19	39.10
Carbon	C	6	12.00	Praseodymium	Pr	59	140.92
Cerium	Ce	58	140.13	Radium	Ra	88	225.97
Cesium	Cs	55	132.81	Radon	Rn	86	222
Chlorine	Cl	17	35.457	Rhenium	Re	75	188.7
Chromium	Cr	24	52.01	Rhodium	Rh	45	102.91
Cobalt	Co	27	58.94	Rubidium	Rb	37	85.44
Columbium	Cb	41	93.1	Ruthenium	Ru	44	101.7
Copper	Cu	29	63.57	Samarium	Sm	62	150.43
Dysprosium	Dy	66	162.46	Scandium	Sc	21	45.10
Erbium	Er	68	167.64	Selenium	Se	34	79.2
Europium	Eu	63	152.0	Silicon	Si	14	28.06
Fluorine	F	9	19.00	Silver	Ag	47	107.880
Gadolinium	Gd	64	157.26	Sodium	Na	11	22.997
Gallium	Ga	31	69.72	Strontium	Sr	38	87.63
Germanium	Ge	32	72.60	Sulphur	S	16	32.06
Gold	Au	79	197.2	Tantalum	Ta	73	181.5
Hafnium	Hf	72	178.6	Tellurium	Te	52	127.5
Helium	He	2	4.002	Terbium	Tb	65	159.2
Holmium	Ho	67	163.5	Thallium	Tl	81	204.39
Hydrogen	H	1	1.0078	Thorium	Th	90	232.12
Indium	In	49	114.8	Thulium	Tm	69	169.4
Iodine	I	53	126.932	Tin	Sn	50	118.70
Iridium	Ir	77	193.1	Titanium	Ti	22	47.90
Iron	Fe	26	55.84	Tungsten	W	74	184.0
Krypton	Kr	36	82.9	Uranium	U	92	238.14
Lanthanum	La	57	138.90	Vanadium	V	23	50.96
Lead	Pb	82	207.22	Xenon	Xe	54	130.2
Lithium	Li	3	6.940	Ytterbium	Yb	70	173.6
Lutecium	Lu	71	175.0	Yttrium	Y	39	88.92
Magnesium	Mg	12	24.32	Zinc	Zn	30	65.38
Manganese	Mn	25	54.93	Zirconium	Zr	40	91.22
Mercury	Hg	80	200.61				

LOGARITHMS OF NUMBERS

Natural numbers	0	1	2	3	4	5	6	7	8	9	1	2	3	4	5	6	7	8	9
											\multicolumn{9}{c	}{PROPORTIONAL PARTS.}
10	0000	0043	0086	0128	0170	0212	0253	0294	0334	0374	4	8	12	17	21	25	29	33	37
11	0414	0453	0492	0531	0569	0607	0645	0682	0719	0755	4	8	11	15	19	23	26	30	34
12	0792	0828	0864	0899	0934	0969	1004	1038	1072	1106	3	7	10	14	17	21	24	28	31
13	1139	1173	1206	1239	1271	1303	1335	1367	1399	1430	3	6	10	13	16	19	23	26	29
14	1461	1492	1523	1553	1584	1614	1644	1673	1703	1732	3	6	9	12	15	18	21	24	27
15	1761	1790	1818	1847	1875	1903	1931	1959	1987	2014	3	6	8	11	14	17	20	22	25
16	2041	2068	2095	2122	2148	2175	2201	2227	2253	2279	3	5	8	11	13	16	18	21	24
17	2304	2330	2355	2380	2405	2430	2455	2480	2504	2529	2	5	7	10	12	15	17	20	22
18	2553	2577	2601	2625	2648	2672	2695	2718	2742	2765	2	5	7	9	12	14	16	19	21
19	2788	2810	2833	2856	2878	2900	2923	2945	2967	2989	2	4	7	9	11	13	16	18	20
20	3010	3032	3054	3075	3096	3118	3139	3160	3181	3201	2	4	6	8	11	13	15	17	19
21	3222	3243	3263	3284	3304	3324	3345	3365	3385	3404	2	4	6	8	10	12	14	16	18
22	3424	3444	3464	3483	3502	3522	3541	3560	3579	3598	2	4	6	8	10	12	14	15	17
23	3617	3636	3655	3674	3692	3711	3729	3747	3766	3784	2	4	6	7	9	11	13	15	17
24	3802	3820	3838	3856	3874	3892	3909	3927	3945	3962	2	4	5	7	9	11	12	14	16
25	3979	3997	4014	4031	4048	4065	4082	4099	4116	4133	2	3	5	7	9	10	12	14	15
26	4150	4166	4183	4200	4216	4232	4249	4265	4281	4298	2	3	5	7	8	10	11	13	15
27	4314	4330	4346	4362	4378	4393	4409	4425	4440	4456	2	3	5	6	8	9	11	13	14
28	4472	4487	4502	4518	4533	4548	4564	4579	4594	4609	2	3	5	6	8	9	11	12	14
29	4624	4639	4654	4669	4683	4698	4713	4728	4742	4757	1	3	4	6	7	9	10	12	13
30	4771	4786	4800	4814	4829	4843	4857	4871	4886	4900	1	3	4	6	7	9	10	11	13
31	4914	4928	4942	4955	4969	4983	4997	5011	5024	5038	1	3	4	6	7	8	10	11	12
32	5051	5065	5079	5092	5105	5119	5132	5145	5159	5172	1	3	4	5	7	8	9	11	12
33	5185	5198	5211	5224	5237	5250	5263	5276	5289	5302	1	3	4	5	6	8	9	10	12
34	5315	5328	5340	5353	5366	5378	5391	5403	5416	5428	1	3	4	5	6	8	9	10	11
35	5441	5453	5465	5478	5490	5502	5514	5527	5539	5551	1	2	4	5	6	7	9	10	11
36	5563	5575	5587	5599	5611	5623	5635	5647	5658	5670	1	2	4	5	6	7	8	10	11
37	5682	5694	5705	5717	5729	5740	5752	5763	5775	5786	1	2	3	5	6	7	8	9	10
38	5798	5809	5821	5832	5843	5855	5866	5877	5888	5899	1	2	3	5	6	7	8	9	10
39	5911	5922	5933	5944	5955	5966	5977	5988	5999	6010	1	2	3	4	5	7	8	9	10
40	6021	6031	6042	6053	6064	6075	6085	6096	6107	6117	1	2	3	4	5	6	8	9	10
41	6128	6138	6149	6160	6170	6180	6191	6201	6212	6222	1	2	3	4	5	6	7	8	9
42	6232	6243	6253	6263	6274	6284	6294	6304	6314	6325	1	2	3	4	5	6	7	8	9
43	6335	6345	6355	6365	6375	6385	6395	6405	6415	6425	1	2	3	4	5	6	7	8	9
44	6435	6444	6454	6464	6474	6484	6493	6503	6513	6522	1	2	3	4	5	6	7	8	9
45	6532	6542	6551	6561	6571	6580	6590	6599	6609	6618	1	2	3	4	5	6	7	8	9
46	6628	6637	6646	6656	6665	6675	6684	6693	6702	6712	1	2	3	4	5	6	7	7	8
47	6721	6730	6739	6749	6758	6767	6776	6785	6794	6803	1	2	3	4	5	5	6	7	8
48	6812	6821	6830	6839	6848	6857	6866	6875	6884	6893	1	2	3	4	4	5	6	7	8
49	6902	6911	6920	6928	6937	6946	6955	6964	6972	6981	1	2	3	4	4	5	6	7	8
50	6990	6998	7007	7016	7024	7033	7042	7050	7059	7067	1	2	3	3	4	5	6	7	8
51	7076	7084	7093	7101	7110	7118	7126	7135	7143	7152	1	2	3	3	4	5	6	7	8
52	7160	7168	7177	7185	7193	7202	7210	7218	7226	7235	1	2	2	3	4	5	6	7	7
53	7243	7251	7259	7267	7275	7284	7292	7300	7308	7316	1	2	2	3	4	5	6	6	7
54	7324	7332	7340	7348	7356	7364	7372	7380	7388	7396	1	2	2	3	4	5	6	6	7

LOGARITHMS OF NUMBERS

Natural numbers.	0	1	2	3	4	5	6	7	8	9	1	2	3	4	5	6	7	8	9
											\multicolumn{9}{c	}{PROPORTIONAL PARTS}
55	7404	7412	7419	7427	7435	7443	7451	7459	7466	7474	1	2	2	3	4	5	5	6	7
56	7482	7490	7497	7505	7513	7520	7528	7536	7543	7551	1	2	2	3	4	5	5	6	7
57	7559	7566	7574	7582	7589	7597	7604	7612	7619	7627	1	2	2	3	4	5	5	6	7
58	7634	7642	7649	7657	7664	7672	7679	7686	7694	7701	1	1	2	3	4	4	5	6	7
59	7709	7716	7723	7731	7738	7745	7752	7760	7767	7774	1	1	2	3	4	4	5	6	7
60	7782	7789	7796	7803	7810	7818	7825	7832	7839	7846	1	1	2	3	4	4	5	6	6
61	7853	7860	7868	7875	7882	7889	7896	7903	7910	7917	1	1	2	3	4	4	5	6	6
62	7924	7931	7938	7945	7952	7959	7966	7973	7980	7987	1	1	2	3	3	4	5	6	6
63	7993	8000	8007	8014	8021	8028	8035	8041	8048	8055	1	1	2	3	3	4	5	5	6
64	8062	8069	8075	8082	8089	8096	8102	8109	8116	8122	1	1	2	3	3	4	5	5	6
65	8129	8136	8142	8149	8156	8162	8169	8176	8182	8189	1	1	2	3	3	4	5	5	6
66	8195	8202	8209	8215	8222	8228	8235	8241	8248	8254	1	1	2	3	3	4	5	5	6
67	8261	8267	8274	8280	8287	8293	8299	8306	8312	8319	1	1	2	3	3	4	5	5	6
68	8325	8331	8338	8344	8351	8357	8363	8370	8376	8382	1	1	2	3	3	4	4	5	6
69	8388	8395	8401	8407	8414	8420	8426	8432	8439	8445	1	1	2	2	3	4	4	5	6
70	8451	8457	8463	8470	8476	8482	8488	8494	8500	8506	1	1	2	2	3	4	4	5	6
71	8513	8519	8525	8531	8537	8543	8549	8555	8561	8567	1	1	2	2	3	4	4	5	5
72	8573	8579	8585	8591	8597	8603	8609	8615	8621	8627	1	1	2	2	3	4	4	5	5
73	8633	8639	8645	8651	8657	8663	8669	8675	8681	8686	1	1	2	2	3	4	4	5	5
74	8692	8698	8704	8710	8716	8722	8727	8733	8739	8745	1	1	2	2	3	4	4	5	5
75	8751	8756	8762	8768	8774	8779	8785	8791	8797	8802	1	1	2	2	3	3	4	5	5
76	8808	8814	8820	8825	8831	8837	8842	8848	8854	8859	1	1	2	2	3	3	4	5	5
77	8865	8871	8876	8882	8887	8893	8899	8904	8910	8915	1	1	2	2	3	3	4	4	5
78	8921	8927	8932	8938	8943	8949	8954	8960	8965	8971	1	1	2	2	3	3	4	4	5
79	8976	8982	8987	8993	8998	9004	9009	9015	9020	9026	1	1	2	2	3	3	4	4	5
80	9031	9036	9042	9047	9053	9058	9063	9069	9074	9079	1	1	2	2	3	3	4	4	5
81	9085	9090	9096	9101	9106	9112	9117	9122	9128	9133	1	1	2	2	3	3	4	4	5
82	9138	9143	9149	9154	9159	9165	9170	9175	9180	9186	1	1	2	2	3	3	4	4	5
83	9191	9196	9201	9206	9212	9217	9222	9227	9232	9238	1	1	2	2	3	3	4	4	5
84	9243	9248	9253	9258	9263	9269	9274	9279	9284	9289	1	1	2	2	3	3	4	4	5
85	9294	9299	9304	9309	9315	9320	9325	9330	9335	9340	1	1	2	2	3	3	4	4	5
86	9345	9350	9355	9360	9365	9370	9375	9380	9385	9390	1	1	2	2	3	3	4	4	4
87	9395	9400	9405	9410	9415	9420	9425	9430	9435	9440	0	1	1	2	2	3	3	4	4
88	9445	9450	9455	9460	9465	9469	9474	9479	9484	9489	0	1	1	2	2	3	3	4	4
89	9494	9499	9504	9509	9513	9518	9523	9528	9533	9538	0	1	1	2	2	3	3	4	4
90	9542	9547	9552	9557	9562	9566	9571	9576	9581	9586	0	1	1	2	2	3	3	4	4
91	9590	9595	9600	9605	9609	9614	9619	9624	9628	9633	0	1	1	2	2	3	3	4	4
92	9638	9643	9647	9652	9657	9661	9666	9671	9675	9680	0	1	1	2	2	3	3	4	4
93	9685	9689	9694	9699	9703	9708	9713	9717	9722	9727	0	1	1	2	2	3	3	4	4
94	9731	9736	9741	9745	9750	9754	9759	9763	9768	9773	0	1	1	2	2	3	3	4	4
95	9777	9782	9786	9791	9795	9800	9805	9809	9814	9818	0	1	1	2	2	3	3	4	4
96	9823	9827	9832	9836	9841	9845	9850	9854	9859	9863	0	1	1	2	2	3	3	4	4
97	9868	9872	9877	9881	9886	9890	9894	9899	9903	9908	0	1	1	2	2	3	3	4	4
98	9912	9917	9921	9926	9930	9934	9939	9943	9948	9952	0	1	1	2	2	3	3	4	4
99	9956	9961	9965	9969	9974	9978	9983	9987	9991	9996	0	1	1	2	2	3	3	3	4

ANTILOGARITHMS

Logarithms.	0	1	2	3	4	5	6	7	8	9	\multicolumn{9}{c	}{Proportional Parts.}
											1	2	3	4	5	6	7	8	9
.00	1000	1002	1005	1007	1009	1012	1014	1016	1019	1021	0	0	1	1	1	1	2	2	2
.01	1023	1026	1028	1030	1033	1035	1038	1040	1042	1045	0	0	1	1	1	1	2	2	2
.02	1047	1050	1052	1054	1057	1059	1062	1064	1067	1069	0	0	1	1	1	1	2	2	2
.03	1072	1074	1076	1079	1081	1084	1086	1089	1091	1094	0	0	1	1	1	1	2	2	2
.04	1096	1099	1102	1104	1107	1109	1112	1114	1117	1119	0	1	1	1	1	2	2	2	2
.05	1122	1125	1127	1130	1132	1135	1138	1140	1143	1146	0	1	1	1	1	2	2	2	2
.06	1148	1151	1153	1156	1159	1161	1164	1167	1169	1172	0	1	1	1	1	2	2	2	2
.07	1175	1178	1180	1183	1186	1189	1191	1194	1197	1199	0	1	1	1	1	2	2	2	2
.08	1202	1205	1208	1211	1213	1216	1219	1222	1225	1227	0	1	1	1	1	2	2	2	3
.09	1230	1233	1236	1239	1242	1245	1247	1250	1253	1256	0	1	1	1	1	2	2	2	3
.10	1259	1262	1265	1268	1271	1274	1276	1279	1282	1285	0	1	1	1	1	2	2	2	3
.11	1288	1291	1294	1297	1300	1303	1306	1309	1312	1315	0	1	1	1	2	2	2	2	3
.12	1318	1321	1324	1327	1330	1334	1337	1340	1343	1346	0	1	1	1	2	2	2	2	3
.13	1349	1352	1355	1358	1361	1365	1368	1371	1374	1377	0	1	1	1	2	2	2	3	3
.14	1380	1384	1387	1390	1393	1396	1400	1403	1406	1409	0	1	1	1	2	2	2	3	3
.15	1413	1416	1419	1422	1426	1429	1432	1435	1439	1442	0	1	1	1	2	2	2	3	3
.16	1445	1449	1452	1455	1459	1462	1466	1469	1472	1476	0	1	1	1	2	2	2	3	3
.17	1479	1483	1486	1489	1493	1496	1500	1503	1507	1510	0	1	1	1	2	2	2	3	3
.18	1514	1517	1521	1524	1528	1531	1535	1538	1542	1545	0	1	1	1	2	2	2	3	3
.19	1549	1552	1556	1560	1563	1567	1570	1574	1578	1581	0	1	1	1	2	2	3	3	3
.20	1585	1589	1592	1596	1600	1603	1607	1611	1614	1618	0	1	1	1	2	2	3	3	3
.21	1622	1626	1629	1633	1637	1641	1644	1648	1652	1656	0	1	1	2	2	2	3	3	3
.22	1660	1663	1667	1671	1675	1679	1683	1687	1690	1694	0	1	1	2	2	2	3	3	3
.23	1698	1702	1706	1710	1714	1718	1722	1726	1730	1734	0	1	1	2	2	2	3	3	4
.24	1738	1742	1746	1750	1754	1758	1762	1766	1770	1774	0	1	1	2	2	2	3	3	4
.25	1778	1782	1786	1791	1795	1799	1803	1807	1811	1816	0	1	1	2	2	2	3	3	4
.26	1820	1824	1828	1832	1837	1841	1845	1849	1854	1858	0	1	1	2	2	3	3	3	4
.27	1862	1866	1871	1875	1879	1884	1888	1892	1897	1901	0	1	1	2	2	3	3	3	4
.28	1905	1910	1914	1919	1923	1928	1932	1936	1941	1945	0	1	1	2	2	3	3	4	4
.29	1950	1954	1959	1963	1968	1972	1977	1982	1986	1991	0	1	1	2	2	3	3	4	4
.30	1995	2000	2004	2009	2014	2018	2023	2028	2032	2037	0	1	1	2	2	3	3	4	4
.31	2042	2046	2051	2056	2061	2065	2070	2075	2080	2084	0	1	1	2	2	3	3	4	4
.32	2089	2094	2099	2104	2109	2113	2118	2123	2128	2133	0	1	1	2	2	3	3	4	4
.33	2138	2143	2148	2153	2158	2163	2168	2173	2178	2183	0	1	1	2	2	3	3	4	4
.34	2188	2193	2198	2203	2208	2213	2218	2223	2228	2234	1	1	2	2	3	3	4	4	5
.35	2239	2244	2249	2254	2259	2265	2270	2275	2280	2286	1	1	2	2	3	3	4	4	5
.36	2291	2296	2301	2307	2312	2317	2323	2328	2333	2339	1	1	2	2	3	3	4	4	5
.37	2344	2350	2355	2360	2366	2371	2377	2382	2388	2393	1	1	2	2	3	3	4	4	5
.38	2399	2404	2410	2415	2421	2427	2432	2438	2443	2449	1	1	2	2	3	3	4	4	5
.39	2455	2460	2466	2472	2477	2483	2489	2495	2500	2506	1	1	2	2	3	3	4	5	5
.40	2512	2518	2523	2529	2535	2541	2547	2553	2559	2564	1	1	2	2	3	4	4	5	5
.41	2570	2576	2582	2588	2594	2600	2606	2612	2618	2624	1	1	2	2	3	4	4	5	5
.42	2630	2636	2642	2649	2655	2661	2667	2673	2679	2685	1	1	2	2	3	4	4	5	6
.43	2692	2698	2704	2710	2716	2723	2729	2735	2742	2748	1	1	2	3	3	4	4	5	6
.44	2754	2761	2767	2773	2780	2786	2793	2799	2805	2812	1	1	2	3	3	4	4	5	6
.45	2818	2825	2831	2838	2844	2851	2858	2864	2871	2877	1	1	2	3	3	4	5	5	6
.46	2884	2891	2897	2904	2911	2917	2924	2931	2938	2944	1	1	2	3	3	4	5	5	6
.47	2951	2958	2965	2972	2979	2985	2992	2999	3006	3013	1	1	2	3	3	4	5	5	6
.48	3020	3027	3034	3041	3048	3055	3062	3069	3076	3083	1	1	2	3	4	4	5	6	6
.49	3090	3097	3105	3112	3119	3126	3133	3141	3148	3155	1	1	2	3	4	4	5	6	6

ANTILOGARITHMS

Logarithms	0	1	2	3	4	5	6	7	8	9	1	2	3	4	5	6	7	8	9
.50	3162	3170	3177	3184	3192	3199	3206	3214	3221	3228	1	1	2	3	4	4	5	6	7
.51	3236	3243	3251	3258	3266	3273	3281	3289	3296	3304	1	2	2	3	4	5	5	6	7
.52	3311	3319	3327	3334	3342	3350	3357	3365	3373	3381	1	2	2	3	4	5	5	6	7
.53	3388	3396	3404	3412	3420	3428	3436	3443	3451	3459	1	2	2	3	4	5	6	6	7
.54	3467	3475	3483	3491	3499	3508	3516	3524	3532	3540	1	2	2	3	4	5	6	6	7
.55	3548	3556	3565	3573	3581	3589	3597	3606	3614	3622	1	2	2	3	4	5	6	7	7
.56	3631	3639	3648	3656	3664	3673	3681	3690	3698	3707	1	2	3	3	4	5	6	7	8
.57	3715	3724	3733	3741	3750	3758	3767	3776	3784	3793	1	2	3	3	4	5	6	7	8
.58	3802	3811	3819	3828	3837	3846	3855	3864	3873	3882	1	2	3	4	4	5	6	7	8
.59	3890	3899	3908	3917	3926	3936	3945	3954	3963	3972	1	2	3	4	5	5	6	7	8
.60	3981	3990	3999	4009	4018	4027	4036	4046	4055	4064	1	2	3	4	5	6	6	7	8
.61	4074	4083	4093	4102	4111	4121	4130	4140	4150	4159	1	2	3	4	5	6	7	8	9
.62	4169	4178	4188	4198	4207	4217	4227	4236	4246	4256	1	2	3	4	5	6	7	8	9
.63	4266	4276	4285	4295	4305	4315	4325	4335	4345	4355	1	2	3	4	5	6	7	8	9
.64	4365	4375	4385	4395	4406	4416	4426	4436	4446	4457	1	2	3	4	5	6	7	8	9
.65	4467	4477	4487	4498	4508	4519	4529	4539	4550	4560	1	2	3	4	5	6	7	8	9
.66	4571	4581	4592	4603	4613	4624	4634	4645	4656	4667	1	2	3	4	5	6	7	9	10
.67	4677	4688	4699	4710	4721	4732	4742	4753	4764	4775	1	2	3	4	5	7	8	9	10
.68	4786	4797	4808	4819	4831	4842	4853	4864	4875	4887	1	2	3	4	6	7	8	9	10
.69	4898	4909	4920	4932	4943	4955	4966	4977	4989	5000	1	2	3	5	6	7	8	9	10
.70	5012	5023	5035	5047	5058	5070	5082	5093	5105	5117	1	2	4	5	6	7	8	9	11
.71	5129	5140	5152	5164	5176	5188	5200	5212	5224	5236	1	2	4	5	6	7	8	10	11
.72	5248	5260	5272	5284	5297	5309	5321	5333	5346	5358	1	2	4	5	6	7	9	10	11
.73	5370	5383	5395	5408	5420	5433	5445	5458	5470	5483	1	3	4	5	6	8	9	10	11
.74	5495	5508	5521	5534	5546	5559	5572	5585	5598	5610	1	3	4	5	6	8	9	10	12
.75	5623	5636	5649	5662	5675	5689	5702	5715	5728	5741	1	3	4	5	7	8	9	10	12
.76	5754	5768	5781	5794	5808	5821	5834	5848	5861	5875	1	3	4	5	7	8	9	11	12
.77	5888	5902	5916	5929	5943	5957	5970	5984	5998	6012	1	3	4	5	7	8	10	11	12
.78	6026	6039	6053	6067	6081	6095	6109	6124	6138	6152	1	3	4	6	7	8	10	11	13
.79	6166	6180	6194	6209	6223	6237	6252	6266	6281	6295	1	3	4	6	7	9	10	11	13
.80	6310	6324	6339	6353	6368	6383	6397	6412	6427	6442	1	3	4	6	7	9	10	12	13
.81	6457	6471	6486	6501	6516	6531	6546	6561	6577	6592	2	3	5	6	8	9	11	12	14
.82	6607	6622	6637	6653	6668	6683	6699	6714	6730	6745	2	3	5	6	8	9	11	12	14
.83	6761	6776	6792	6808	6823	6839	6855	6871	6887	6902	2	3	5	6	8	9	11	13	14
.84	6918	6934	6950	6966	6982	6998	7015	7031	7047	7063	2	3	5	6	8	10	11	13	15
.85	7079	7096	7112	7129	7145	7161	7178	7194	7211	7228	2	3	5	7	8	10	12	13	15
.86	7244	7261	7278	7295	7311	7328	7345	7362	7379	7396	2	3	5	7	8	10	12	13	15
.87	7413	7430	7447	7464	7482	7499	7516	7534	7551	7568	2	3	5	7	9	10	12	14	16
.88	7586	7603	7621	7638	7656	7674	7691	7709	7727	7745	2	4	5	7	9	11	12	14	16
.89	7762	7780	7798	7816	7834	7852	7870	7889	7907	7925	2	4	5	7	9	11	13	14	16
.90	7943	7962	7980	7998	8017	8035	8054	8072	8091	8110	2	4	6	7	9	11	13	15	17
.91	8128	8147	8166	8185	8204	8222	8241	8260	8279	8299	2	4	6	8	9	11	13	15	17
.92	8318	8337	8356	8375	8395	8414	8433	8453	8472	8492	2	4	6	8	10	12	14	15	17
.93	8511	8531	8551	8570	8590	8610	8630	8650	8670	8690	2	4	6	8	10	12	14	16	18
.94	8710	8730	8750	8770	8790	8810	8831	8851	8872	8892	2	4	6	8	10	12	14	16	18
.95	8913	8933	8954	8974	8995	9016	9036	9057	9078	9099	2	4	6	8	10	12	15	17	19
.96	9120	9141	9162	9183	9204	9226	9247	9268	9290	9311	2	4	6	8	11	13	15	17	19
.97	9333	9354	9376	9397	9419	9441	9462	9484	9506	9528	2	4	7	9	11	13	15	17	20
.98	9550	9572	9594	9616	9638	9661	9683	9705	9727	9750	2	4	7	9	11	13	16	18	20
.99	9772	9795	9817	9840	9863	9886	9908	9931	9954	9977	2	5	7	9	11	14	16	18	20

INDEX

Acidimetry, general discussion of   31
Accuracy   3
Addition, retention of figures in .   28
Alkalimetry, general discussion of   31
Analytical balance, description of   10
Analytical chemistry, general
   directions for   3
   subdivisions of   1
Antimony, determination of, in
   stibnite   113
Apatite, analysis of   173
Atomic weights, table of . . .   245

Balance, description of   10
Bichromate, comparison with ferrous solution   93
   preparation of standard solution of   92
   standardization of   95
Bichromate process   91
Blair method   179
Bleaching powder, analysis of . .   124
Brass, analysis of   201
Bronze, analysis of   201
Burettes, calibration of   20
   description of   17
   preparation of for use   17
   reading of   18
   types of   17

Calcium, determination of, in
   dolomite   187
Calibration, definition of . . .   19
Calibration of burette   20
   of measuring flasks   23
   of pipettes   23
Carbon dioxide, determination of,
   in dolomite   192
Chemical factors   145
Chloride, analysis of . .   130, 149
Chlorimetry   123

Chlorine, determination of, in
   bleaching powder   124
   in chloride 130, 149
Chrome iron ore, analysis of . .   99
Chromite, analysis of   99
Chromium, determination of, in
   chromite   99
Coin, determination of silver in .   129
Combined oxides, determination
   of, in dolomite   186
Copper, determination of, in brass
   and bronze   206
   in ores   116
Crucibles   142
Cubic centimeter, definition of .   19
Cyanide, determination of . . .   132

Desiccators   141
Digit, definition of   27
Direct methods   9
Division, retention of figures in .   29
Dolomite, analysis of   184
Double chloride problems .   132, 154
Double indicator titrations . . .   55

Economy of time   3
Electrolysis problems   212
Electrolytic separations   201
Electrometric titrations   229
Electromotive series   244
Empirical formula, determination
   of   225
Equivalent weight, definition of   37
Equivalents, oxidation and reduction   63
Evaporation of liquids   7

Faraday's law   211
Ferric alum method   179
Ferricyanide indicator   92
Ferrous ammonium sulphate,
   analysis of   158

251

INDEX

Figure, definition of 27
Filter paper, method of folding . 138
Filtration 139
Formula, empirical 225
Funnels 137

Gas laws 198
Gram-equivalent weight, definition of 37
Gravimetric analysis, general directions for 136

Handy method 180
Hydrochloric acid, preparation of standard 35
  standardization of 44
Hydrogen-ion concentration, changes in during titration . 229

Ignition of precipitates 144
Indicators, general considerations of 31
  sensitiveness of, table of . . . 244
Indirect methods 9
Insoluble matter, determination of, in dolomite 185
Iodimetry 104
Iodine, preparation of standard solution of 105
  standardization of 107
Iron, determination of, in brass and bronze 209
  in ferrous ammonium sulphate . 158
  in limonite 76, 98

Jones reductor 77

Lead, determination of, in brass and bronze 206
Limestone, analysis of 184
Limonite, determination of iron in 76, 98
Liquids, evaporation of 7
  transfer of 6
Logarithms, proper use of . . . 30
  table of 246
Lunge method 168

Magnesium, determination of, in dolomite 191
Manganese dioxide, determination of, in pyrolusite . . . 84

Measuring flasks, calibration of 23
Measuring instruments 10
Measuring pipettes 23
Methyl orange, proper use of . . 32
Milliequivalent, definition of . . 37
Milliliter, definition of 20
Moisture, determination of, in dolomite 184
Multiplication, retention of figures in 29

Nernst rule 232
Neutralization, general considerations of 32
Neutralization methods 31
Nickel, determination of . . . 133
Normal solution, definition of . 25, 37
Normal temperature, definition of 19
Notebooks, method of keeping . 5
  sample pages of 240
Number, definition of 27

Oxalic acid, analysis of 52
Oxidation and reduction equivalents 63
Oxidation processes 62

Permanganate, comparison with ferrous solution 71
  preparation of standard solution of 69
  standardization of 71
Permanganate process 68
Phenolphthalein, proper use of . 32
Phosphoric anhydride, determination of, in apatite . . . 173
Phosphorus, determination of, in steel 179
Pipettes, calibration of 23
Potentiometer principle 235
Potentiometric titrations . . . 229
Precipitates, ignition of 144
  washing of 139
Precipitation 137
Precipitation methods 126
Pyrolusite, analysis of 84

Quantitative analysis, general directions for 3
  subdivisions of 1
Quinhydrone electrode 236

INDEX

Reagents, strengths of 242
   testing of 5
Reductor, Jones 77

Saturation methods 126
Significant figure, definition of . 27
   proper retention of 27
Silica, determination of, in dolomite 185
   in silicates 219
Silicates, analysis of 219
Silver, determination of, in coin . 129
Smith, J. L., method for alkalies . 155
Soda ash, composition of . . . 50
   analysis of 50
Sodium hydroxide, preparation of standard 31
   standardization of 45
Sodium peroxide method for sulphur 169
Specific reduction potentials 232, 244
Standardization, definition of . . 25
Standard solutions, definition of . 25
Starch, preparation of a solution of 106
Stibnite, analysis of 113
Subtraction, retention of figures in 28

Sulphur, determination of, in ferrous ammonium sulphate . . 164
   in pyrite 168
Superfluous figures, rejection of . 28

Thiocyanate process 127
Thiocyanate, standardization of . 127
Thiosulphate, preparation of standard solution of . . . 105
   standardization of 107
Tin, determination of, in bronze . 205
Transfer of liquids 6
Transfer pipettes 22
True liter, definition of 19

Volumetric analysis, definition of 8
   divisions of 8
   general directions for 24

Wash-bottles 6
Water, density of, table of . . . 243
Weighing, experiments in . . . 15
Weights, calibration of 15
   description of 14
   testing of 14

Zimmermann-Reinhardt method . 80
Zinc, determination of, in brass . 209

10962

Date Due